"Is there no way, said I, of escaping Charybdis, and at the same time keeping Scylla off when she is trying to harm my men?"

–Homer, *The Odyssey*, Book XII

"You will be hollow. We will squeeze you empty, and then we shall fill you with ourselves."

–George Orwell, *1984*

BMA

Food for Thought

Food for Thought

Perspectives on Eating Disorders

Nina Savelle-Rocklin

ROWMAN & LITTLEFIELD
Lanham • Boulder • New York • London

Published by Rowman & Littlefield
A wholly owned subsidary of The Rowman & Littlefield Publishing Group, Inc.
4501 Forbes Boulevard, Suite 200, Lanham, Maryland 20706
www.rowman.com

Unit A, Whitacre Mews, 26-34 Stannary Street, London SE11 4AB

British Library Cataloguing in Publication Information Available

Library of Congress Cataloging-in-Publication Data

Names: Savelle-Rocklin, Nina, author.
Title: Food for thought : perspectives on eating disorders /
  Nina Savelle-Rocklin.
Description: Lanham : Rowman & Littlefield, [2016] |
  Includes bibliographical references and index.
Identifiers: LCCN 2016039080 (print) | LCCN 2016042962 (ebook) |
ISBN 9781442246003 (cloth : alk. paper) | ISBN 9781442246027 (pbk. : alk. paper) |
  ISBN 9781442246010 (Electronic)
Subjects: LCSH: Eating disorders–Treatment. | Psychologist and patient.
Classification: LCC RC552.E18 S286 2016 (print) | LCC RC552.E18 (ebook) |
  DDC 616.85/26–dc23
LC record available at https://lccn.loc.gov/2016039080

Printed in the United States of America

Contents

Preface   ix

Acknowledgments   xiii

Introduction   xv

PART I: BACKGROUND   **1**

1   Prevalence and Common Misconceptions   3

2   Overview   17

PART II: ORIGINS   **47**

3   Object Hunger   49

4   Symbolic Representation   59

5   Body Language   69

6   The Wish–Fear Dilemma   83

7   An Unlaid Ghost   93

PART III: TREATMENT   **107**

8   On the Couch   109

9   Dreams   135

10 Common Impasses and Disruptions   145

11 A Consideration of Hate and Love   161

References   169

Index   183

About the Author   191

Preface

Several years ago I received an email from a new patient in treatment for binge eating. Jane was in her mid-twenties, strikingly attractive and stylish, with soft brown eyes and long blonde hair cascading down her back. Despite her pleasant appearance, my initial reaction was to feel guarded and slightly cautious in her presence. Jane was originally from the East Coast, and had recently moved to Los Angeles to pursue an acting career. She wrote:

> Just checking in. I wanted to write a list of what I ate at 4pm.
> A full size candy bar.
> a gallon of ice cream,
> a small chocolate cake, yuck
> a bowl of pasta and veggies with marinara and olive oil
> a box of chocolate chip cookies, approx 10 cookies about 135 cal each
> and about 11 hersheys bars, the small ones.
>
> didn't really feel like writing what I ate earlier. I snuck food.
> 4 regular bars of reeses peanut butter cups.
>
> 4 bagels
> bowl of pasta
> 3 glasses of oj
> a box of wheat thins
> 1 bag of pretzels,
> lemon iced tea.
> yes I feel ill.

A few weeks earlier, in the first moments of her initial consultation, Jane sat on the couch and pointed to her knee, which was scraped and red, the raw and bruised skin an open wound.

"Look what happened." She sounded like a little girl showing her mommy a boo-boo.

I looked at the scraped, bloodied knee. In that moment I became keenly aware of Jane's eyes on me, fastened intently on my face and awaiting my response.

I said, "That looks really painful."

She smiled and sighed deeply, relaxing back into the cushions. I later discovered that when Jane fell and hurt herself as a child, her mother responded by scolding, "You shouldn't have been running so fast," or, "You should be more careful." When Jane was bullied at school, her mother asked what she did to provoke the bullies. Jane's physical and emotional pain was usually met with dismissal, with the added insult of being perceived as responsible for her injuries or mistreatment.

By showing me her skinned knee, Jane was investigating whether I would respond the same way her mother had responded. Simultaneously she hoped for a new experience with me. She also exposed how raw and bruised she felt, and how emotionally battered she was inside.

Like many people who struggle with eating problems, Jane's primary relationship was to her body instead of to other people. As a child, she suffered ongoing verbal abuse from her mother. As she grew into adulthood, she began reenacting this abuse on her body, which functioned as her primary self. She identified with the hostility, indifference, and contempt with which she was treated as a child, relating to both her physical and emotional needs with equal hostility.

Jane binged on enormous quantities of food, notably all the types of food that she hated and her mother loved. She confided that she thought she would only stop bingeing after she gained 135 pounds—not coincidentally, the exact weight of her mother and the caloric count of the cookies she consumed.

I explained to Jane, as I do with all patients, that whatever was going on with food probably seemed to her as if it was "the" problem, but it was actually a "symptom" of deeper, hidden problems. Bingeing, restricting, purging all serve to express and also to hide a myriad of internal conflicts, most of which remain out of awareness but not out of operation. Our work in psychoanalysis is to identify that which is hidden and bring it to conscious awareness, and then work through those fears and hopes together.

THE ANALYTIC JOURNEY

In Homer's epic, *The Odyssey*, the hero Odysseus sails his ship through a narrow strait bordered on one side by a dangerous whirlpool called Charybdis, and a ravenous six-headed monster named Scylla on the other. By avoiding one danger, he risks the other, and therefore must decide between two terrible choices.

Many eating disorder patients face similar but equally painful choices, torn between staying true to themselves at the expense of their connections to other people and sacrificing their authentic selves in order to maintain some form of connection. Their unconscious solution is to use food to express inner turmoil. Some eschew all relationships and bonds, turning away from food as a way of expressing their indifference to their needs, whether those needs are in the form of human connection or food. Others eat out of loneliness, anger, or pain. They binge until they are filled up with food, instead of being fulfilled by relationships. They eat until they are stuffed to the point of pain, converting emotional pain to physical discomfort. Some purge, symbolically ridding themselves of disavowed emotions, conflicts, and ideas. Eating disorders serve the purpose of providing comfort, alleviating anxiety, expressing deprivation, distracting from painful or upsetting thoughts, soothing, symbolically filling a void, calming down, or more.

The psychoanalytic approach to eating disorders sheds light on the true nature of these internal conflicts, wishes, and emotions, and reformulates them into words. By deciphering the code and understanding the language of each person's eating disorder, these underlying conflicts can be identified and worked through, eliminating symptoms and freeing people from distress.

One patient who previously had psychotherapy, before being in analysis, distinguished between the two experiences by describing psychotherapy as analogous to snorkeling. He explained that for him, snorkeling was like dipping just below the surface, going only deep enough to see interesting things and make good observations. In contrast, he described analysis as akin to deep sea diving. As he put it, "Analysis takes you to the bottom of the ocean where it's pitch black and you can't see anything, so you have to shine a light to see what's going on down there."

I find this a poetic and resonant description of psychoanalysis. Analysts shine a light in the dark recesses of the mind, slowly bringing thoughts, wishes, ideas, and other hidden material up from the depths and allowing them to surface into conscious awareness. The analogy illustrates the importance of going far beyond insight in order to make a change. Our goal is not only to illuminate what lurks in the dark, but also to bring those hidden parts out of the darkness and into the light, so they can be processed and forever changed. In subsequent chapters I will show that the relationship between therapist and patient is one of the most powerful keys to change.

After all, one does not attempt deep sea diving alone.

The importance of the therapeutic relationship is one of the many features that set psychoanalysis apart from other forms of psychotherapy, along with the explication of the unconscious and the interpretation of dreams. When

I first began psychoanalytic training I felt as if I'd entered a mysterious world where the inhabitants spoke a strange and puzzling dialect. The doctoral candidates in my program were all licensed psychotherapists or medical professionals, many with decades of clinical experience, yet each of us initially struggled to make sense of the esoteric phrases and concepts central to analytic theories.

Concurrent with these challenges, my experience as a patient in analysis was deeply personal. I experienced epiphanies, discovered vulnerabilities, and shared moments of profound grief, as well as laughter, with my analyst. For me, the process of analysis is a psychological birth, bringing individuals truly, absolutely, and completely alive. When I tried to convey this experience to my nonanalytic colleagues, the arcane language of psychoanalysis created a roadblock. They could not get past the analytic vocabulary to understand its meaning.

This book was created out of my desire to close the gap between language and experience. By translating psychoanalytic jargon into user-friendly concepts, I hope to give readers a deeper understanding of the theory and treatment of eating disorders from a psychoanalytic perspective. Psychoanalysis is both a theory of the mind and a therapeutic technique that helps people understand why they do things they don't want to do, and why they don't do things they want to do. Through the exploration of a person's private and secret internal world and the curative experience of the therapeutic relationship, psychoanalysis provides a catalyst for lasting change and true healing. The experience may thus be understood as a psychological odyssey navigated by both patient and analyst, marked by unexpected shifts, detours, and surprises along the way. The process is intensive and mutual, not limited to symptom reduction, but instead is concerned with transforming the very structure of the way people relate to themselves and others.

Acknowledgments

Writing a book is a solitary process, but the outcome owes much to many other people. When I accepted an opportunity to present a case to renowned psychoanalyst Dr. Salman Akhtar, I had no idea what an enormous impact this decision would have on my life and professional career. That presentation led to a postgraduate supervision that continues to enrich me professionally and to a friendship for which I am deeply grateful. His mentorship led to others, such as that with Dr. Axel Hoffer, who also contributed greatly to my evolution as a writer (and who introduced me to opera). Drs. Akhtar and Hoffer both gave me opportunities to contribute to their publications and I'm tremendously thankful for their support and encouragement.

I've been fortunate to meet many other psychoanalysts who helped shape my analytic perspective. Dr. Vamik Volkan took the time to create a list of books to read as a postgraduate, and made himself available for questions and advice. When I was a candidate, Dr. William Bauer's intelligence and breadth of knowledge helped me navigate a few rocky challenges in my analytic work, while his humor kept me smiling during the toughest times. Dr. Diane Jacobs introduced me to classical analytic thought, providing a different perspective from which to consider subsequent cases. In her roles as supervisor, advisor, and instructor, she was always a source of encouragement and inspiration. Additional thanks goes to Dr. Susan Cofsky and Dr. Alan Karbelnig, both of whom also influenced my analytic thinking. In my training with Dr. Cofsky, first as an intern, and then as a candidate in pre-control case supervision, I found a resonant and respectful way to understand patients struggling with eating disorders. Dr. Karbelnig deepened my understanding of object relatedness, and expanded my ability to work relationally.

I am tremendously grateful to all of the men and women who walked into my office and sat or reclined on the couch, who put their faith in me and in the process of analysis, when there was little in their prior experiences to indicate that any modicum of trust was warranted. I stand in awe of their courage and their commitment to the truth, and I'm honored to have been a part of their journeys.

I am indebted to Dr. Sharzhad Siassi, for showing me understanding, compassion, attention, and kindness that not only helped me develop a new relationship to myself, but also contributed to my own work as an analyst. I am grateful for her patience, her insight, and for the gift of transformation I received as a result of our collaboration. She gave me a new perspective from which to experience myself, and also the world, and facilitated what can only be termed a psychological birth.

Special mention goes to my friends and colleagues, in particular Alli Spotts de Lazzer and Joan Lachkar, both of whom encouraged me and expressed their belief in me. I would also like to thank my parents, Dr. Arthur Asa Berger and Dr. Phyllis Berger, who provided a stellar example of intellectual curiosity and achievement, and have been extremely supportive of my writings.

This book could not have been written without the love and support of my immediate family. My daughters, Ariel and Kavanna, showed understanding beyond their years through this process, allowing me time to research and write when I could otherwise have been spending time with them. I feel honored and privileged to be the mother of these two remarkable girls.

Finally, I wish to thank my husband and *b'sherit*, David Rocklin. I am grateful for his willingness to sacrifice time together so that I could research, study, and write. His unwavering support, unconditional love, and belief in the importance of this work made it possible for me to complete this book. I dedicate this book to him.

Introduction

My clinical practice comprises adult women and men who struggle with various forms of disordered eating. They arrive at my door in the seemingly inexorable grip of anorexia, bulimia, or binge eating, reporting a preoccupation with food, weight, and/or body image, usually with corresponding deficits in their relationship to themselves and others. They often suffer with co-occurring problems such as depression, anxiety, obsessive-compulsive disorders, and self-harm. Due to the extremely specialized nature of my work, colleagues and new acquaintances often ask what it's like to treat eating disorders.

"I don't treat eating disorders," I say. "I treat people."

Each individual develops a pattern of symptoms due to his or her unique history and personality. I think of the psychoanalytic process as analogous to detective work; I collaborate with each patient to solve the mystery of why he or she developed a particular way of relating to self and others. Those reasons are as unique as each individual who develops an eating disorder.

A NOTE ABOUT SEMANTICS

In the last decades, it has become common for people in therapy to refer to themselves as "clients" and for therapists to talk about the therapist–client relationship. In psychoanalysis, those who undergo psychoanalysis are formally known as analysands but are more commonly referred to as "patients." Rarely is the term "clients" used. In part, this is because until recently psychoanalysts were almost all medical doctors, despite the fact that Sigmund Freud (1926) did not believe a medical degree was a mandatory requirement to become an analyst. Indeed, two of the leading pioneers in the field, his daughter Anna Freud and Melanie Klein, were not physicians. Until the late 1980s the majority of analysts were medical doctors, so the term "patient" is often believed to have derived from the medical model.

I prefer the explanation proposed by one of my colleagues (William Bauer, private communication 2011) who said the definition of a "patient" is that of a person who is suffering, and therefore most respectfully and fully captures the experience of the person on the couch. The term "client" connotes a more service-oriented relationship.

Similarly, Ronald Pies (2015) differentiates between providing treatment and being a healer, making the point that the terms "provider" and "client" do a disservice to the true nature of the doctor–patient relationship, which is concerned with the alleviation and elimination of suffering. The provider–client vernacular sanitizes the intensity of that suffering and minimizes the deep therapeutic bond that leads to the alleviation of pain.

For the purposes of this book, I use the terms "patient" and "analyst." From my perspective, this terminology most closely represents the true nature of the therapeutic dyad; psychoanalysis and psychoanalytic therapy involves a relationship between two human beings, both committed to the process of clarifying, understanding, working through, relating, proposing, thinking, disagreeing, and collaborating for the ultimate purpose of healing.

CHAPTER OVERVIEW

In the first section of the book, I cite information about the prevalence of binge eating, bulimia, and anorexia and explore common misconceptions about what causes eating disorders, including the concept of brain-based illness, the influence of the media, blaming the mother, and cognitive distortions. I contend that although eating disorders develop due to a range of factors, including genetic, environmental, social, and constitutional reasons, as well as a cultural zeitgeist that views the body as the primary self, privileging thinness and perfection as the means to inner happiness, disordered eating ultimately represents an unconscious solution to problems or conflicts. I present an overview of psychoanalysis and describe the various types of eating disorders, including those that are clinically diagnosable such as anorexia, bulimia, and binge eating disorder, using case examples of each type of eating disorder, and I also discuss subclinical symptoms, such as the relatively new phenomenon of orthorexia. Throughout the book I refer to specific examples from my practice and that of my colleagues. All names are fictitious and I have changed details to protect the identities and the confidentiality of those patients.

In the second section, I introduce the origins of disordered eating from a psychoanalytic lens, specifically from a primarily object-relations perspective. In the chapter on "object hunger" I draw attention to how early relationships with caregivers influence the development of eating disorders and explore the contribution of fathers to child and adolescent development, connecting deficits in those relationships with eating problems.

The chapter on symbolic representation examines problems in the areas of symbolism and development. I elucidate how fears about relationships with people are expressed through the relationship to food.

In the chapter on body language, I explain various intrapsychic and relational dilemmas involving the psyche–soma (mind–body) split. The term "intrapsychic" refers to the mental processes that take place within an individual, between different aspects of the mind, as opposed to relational conflicts that take place between two or more people.

The chapter on the wish–fear dilemma looks at eating disorders as an expression of conflicts about power, powerlessness, closeness, and loss of self. I explore issues surrounding dependence versus independence as well as merger and isolation.

In the following chapter I examine the compulsion to repeat and analyze how the past continues to impact the present. I discuss defense mechanisms such as identification with the aggressor, in which a person who was treated harshly, abusively, or neglectfully may take on the role of that abuser and be harsh, abusive, and neglectful to self and/or others.

The third section covers the specifics of treatment in the psychoanalytic approach to eating disorders, including the roles of transference, countertransference, and dreams. Transference refers to the unconscious phenomenon in which one person experiences another as similar to a significant person from the past, and attributes to this new person the feelings, attitudes, and perceptions of the past relationship. In effect, transference is the reexperiencing of childhood or past relationships in the present. Transference brings the past into the present and makes past conflicts available for understanding and working through. I delineate various types of transference (positive, erotic, eroticized, maternal, paternal) and show how they impact the treatment process.

Countertransference refers to the feelings an analyst experiences with and about a patient. Originally frowned upon as an impediment to treatment, the last several decades have seen a shift in the perspective on countertransference, which is now viewed as a means of deeply understanding patients, and can therefore be a tool for both insight and technique.

I discuss the use of dream work in the treatment of eating disorders, giving examples of how dreams are one means by which unconscious conflicts can be brought to conscious awareness and made available for working through. Sigmund Freud (1900) writes, "The interpretation of dreams is the royal road to a knowledge of the unconscious activities of the mind" (p. 608). Dreams help us access the otherwise hidden thoughts, conflicts, emotions, and wishes that, when not known, expressed or processed with words, may be enacted through a person's relationship to food, body, and others. I also elucidate the various types of disruptions and impasses that may arise in treatment, such as issues pertaining to the fee and suicidal ideation.

Last, I explore love and hate in the analytic setting. Analysis is an intense experience involving love and hate; both the patient's love and hatred toward the analyst and the analyst's feelings toward the patient have bearing on the analytic situation.

Far from being an intellectual experience based on insight, psychoanalysis is a journey undertaken between two people, patient and analyst, who mutually and collaboratively heal the wounds of the past in order to allow a new experience of present and future.

Part I

BACKGROUND

Chapter One

Prevalence and Common Misconceptions

In the United States, an estimated thirty million men and women suffer from anorexia, bulimia, and binge eating (Wade et al., 2011), a statistic that does not include subclinical presentations of disordered eating such as orthorexia. Unfortunately, only about 10 percent of the people who struggle with eating disorders seek treatment (Noordenbox, 2002).

Eating disorders pose a significant risk to the emotional and physical health of many people in Western society and are becoming increasingly common in Asia (Lee et al., 2010). Until recently, these disorders were commonly associated with affluent, Caucasian, teenage girls, but the reality is that they impact people of all ages, genders, and ethnicities. A plethora of studies have examined the prevalence of disordered eating in female adolescents, but little research addresses how these disorders impact adolescent boys, adult women, and men. The prevalence of eating disorders in adult populations, particularly men, is likely underreported and far higher than statistics suggest, due to factors such as shame or lack of access to health care. I currently treat several men whose ages range from the forties to the early seventies. They suffered in silence for decades, deeply ashamed of struggling with what they thought was "a girl's problem." Only when the media exposed the reality that males also get eating disorders, did they feel comfortable enough to seek help.

People with eating disorders have significantly elevated mortality rates, the highest rates occurring with anorexia (Arcelus et al., 2011). Eating disorders also have the highest mortality rate of any mental disorder (Sullivan, 1995). Severe anorexic and bulimic patients suffer electrolyte imbalances that may lead to heart failure, the leading cause of death in this population. Bulimia may cause esophageal and gastric ruptures, as well as major organ damage, particularly to the kidneys, liver, pancreas, and heart. Bingeing often leads to obesity and the associated risk of heart failure, fatty liver disease, Type 2

diabetes, kidney disease, and strokes. Other medical complications for anorexia and bulimia include bone loss and osteoporosis, dehydration, kidney
disease, anemia, and low white cell counts, which lowers the immune system
and creates vulnerability to disease and infection. Bulimic patients are at risk
of tooth decay, gum disease, and erosion of tooth enamel caused by acid from
vomiting. They may have bowel problems due to laxative overuse, as well
as dehydration. Individuals who are overweight as a result of bingeing have
increased rates of breast cancer, colon cancer, and endometrial cancer, as
well as high blood pressure and sleep apnea. According to the World Health
Organization (2015), a raised body mass index (BMI) is a major risk for car-
diovascular disease, a leading cause of death, and musculoskeletal disorders.

It is imperative to first ensure the physical safety and health of patients by
making sure they get medical care if needed. Over a century ago, Sigmund
Freud (1905a) cautioned, "Psychoanalysis should not be attempted when the
speedy removal of dangerous symptoms is required as, for example, in a case
of hysterical anorexia" (p. 264). When people's health is at risk, hospitalization may be necessary until they are medically stable, at which point they are
able to participate in outpatient treatment.

Some analytic therapists (Herzog et al., 1989) advocate an integrated pro-
tocol for the treatment of eating disorders, addressing both the psychological underpinnings and the potential medical complications of the disorders.
A team comprising a psychotherapist, a medical doctor, and in some cases a
psychiatrist and a dietitian is recommended as the standard of care for treatment of at-risk patients.

In addition to the physical dangers associated with eating disorders, there
is a high comorbidity of depression, anxiety, and substance abuse and an
increased risk of self-harm.

Eating disorders are therefore potentially lethal, impacting the physical and
mental/emotional health of many people, young and old, male and female, of
all cultures and socioeconomic levels.

COMMON MISCONCEPTIONS

Blame It on the Brain

In his play *The Tempest*, William Shakespeare (1623) introduces the theme
of nature and nurture when Prospero describes the antagonist Caliban as, "A
devil, a born devil on whose nature nurture can never stick." Shakespeare is
proposing that a person's basic nature cannot be influenced by his surround-
ings. In the ensuing nature vs. nurture debate, the pendulum has swung both
toward and away from nature as that which most influences human behavior.

Currently, much scientific research is focused on identifying the genetic determinants of diseases and behavior, including eating disorders. Our genes contain a genetic code, information that determines gender and physical characteristics such as hair and eye color. Changes in the genetic code are called mutations and, like all genetic information, can also be passed on from parents to children. Some gene mutations increase the risk of certain diseases such as cancer, cystic fibrosis, familial hypercholesterolemia (high cholesterol), sickle cell anemia, and more.

The language of genetics can sometimes be misleading. For example, the term "heritability" is often misunderstood. Renowned geneticist Richard Lewontin (2011a) explains, "When a biological characteristic is said to be 'heritable,' it means that it is capable of being transmitted from parents to offspring, just as money may be inherited, although neither is inevitable. In contrast, 'heritability' is a statistical concept." Heritability does not apply to individuals, nor does it measure the importance of genes. Heritability only reflects variation in traits; it says nothing about what causes those traits. The presence of a gene for certain trait does not mean a person is destined to develop that trait. For example, two of the best-known genes that lead to breast and ovarian cancers are the *BRCA1* and *BRCA2* genes. Even though someone with a mutated *BRCA1* or *BRCA2* gene has a high probability of developing breast cancer, only 5 to 10 percent of women with breast cancer (Campaeu et al., 2008) and 15 percent of women with ovarian cancer (P. Pal et. al., 2005) have a mutation in one of these genes. Clearly, there are other causes for these cancers besides genetic markers.

When it comes to personality traits and psychiatric disorders, the genetic connection is murky. Researchers have sought for decades to identify genes for behavioral characteristics such as intelligence and personality, as well as for major psychiatric disorders, yet they have failed to do so. One explanation for this failure is referred to (Slatkin, 2009; Zuk et al., 2012) as "the missing heritability problem," which means that single genetic variations have not been found to account for the heritability of diseases and behaviors. Researchers point to "missing heritability" as an explanation for their failure to discover genetic variants, which they believe to exist, but have not been located (and are thus "missing"). Another explanation is that these genes do not actually exist. Despite a new whole-genome scanning technique (Genome-Wide Association studies, or GWAs), the variation that geneticists expected to uncover has not been found. Latham and Wilson (2010) conclude that if GWAs are taken at face value, it refutes the belief that genetic predispositions are significant factors in the prevalence of most common diseases. They deem this, "a discovery of truly enormous significance."

The complex relationship between genes and behavior is a point of controversy in eating disorders. Over a decade ago, eating disorder researcher

Cynthia Bulik (*Newsweek*, 2005) stated that genetics loads the proverbial gun and the environment "pulls the trigger." This is consistent with the growing field of epigenetics, which suggests that the environment can turn "on" or "off" a specific gene. For example, able-bodied people walk upright on two feet, so we assume that walking is genetically hardwired. That is not true. Though the capacity to walk upright is genetic, the parents have to evoke the ability to walk by saying, "Come on, stand up," and encouraging babies to stand up and walk. However, if a child is raised in circumstances in which he or she never sees anyone walking, or is not encouraged to walk, then the child never learns to walk. Many feral children, who were lost or abandoned to fend for themselves, are often raised by animals, and discovered walking on all fours (D. Candland, 1993; M. Newton, 2002). Only when they are brought into contact with other humans do they learn to walk upright. Thus the presence of a genetic disposition is not enough to create behavior.

Researchers have long searched for that genetic bullet that "loads the gun," to which Bulik referred. Recent studies (H. Cui et al., 2013; Davis et al., 2013; Scott-van Zeeland et al., 2013) purport to have identified an eating disorder gene, yet these results have not been replicated. One proposed reason is there may be many genes which impact behavior. Mazzeo and Bulik (2009) write that eating disorders "are influenced by multiple genetic and environmental factors of small to moderate effect. There is not one gene for anorexia nervosa or one gene for bulimia nervosa. More likely there are a number of genes that code for proteins that influence traits that index vulnerability to these disorders" (p. 3).

Again, where are these elusive genes? In a detailed examination of decades of research, Jay Joseph (2006) reports, "despite over two decades of sustained work, genes for the major psychiatric disorders have not been discovered. Virtually all previous claims in favor of gene findings have failed replication attempts" (p. 13). No genes associated with intelligence have been replicated in follow-up studies (C. F. Chabris et al., 2012). Furthermore, no single gene has been identified as reliably associated with any psychiatric disorders or any aspect of human behavior within the "normal" range (Charney, 2013).

Much research on genetic markers for eating disorders relies on twin or adoption studies. In particular, studies of twins (both reared together and reared apart) are often cited as providing conclusive evidence supporting the importance of genetic influences on psychological trait differences. Such studies confirm that when one twin has an eating disorder, the other is more likely to have the condition. This appears to make a convincing case for a genetic component to eating disorders, yet upon closer examination, the original studies do not hold up. In a comprehensive and scholarly dissection of twin studies, Joseph (2015) exposes the conceptual and methodological flaws of these studies, challenging four decades of research that contends that genes alone or in large part determine human behavior or traits, independent of the environment. Joseph (2015; Joseph & Ratner, 2010) also argues that emphasis on scientifically unsupported genetic theories (which he details in his books) has caused the psychiatric field to overlook or underemphasize the many environmental factors that play an important role in the development of psychiatric disorders. He concludes that psychologically traumatic events and environments have far more impact on development than do genetics and states (2006) and that it is "unlikely that genes for the major psychiatric disorders exist" (p. 13).

Ultimately, in the nature vs. nurture debate, it might be more helpful to conceptualize that both nature "and" nurture contribute to symptom formation. I believe that even if there was a genetic component to the development of eating disorders, the narrow view of eating disorders as a "brain-based illness" does not take into consideration the impact of the environment and human variation. The geneticist, Richard Lewontin, believes the value of identifying genes is limited, since many disorders are "the result of complex developmental and physiological causes that involve many interacting processes" (2011b). Perfectionism, rigidity, and impulsivity have been correlated with eating disorders (Goldner et al., 2002; Cassin & von Ranson, 2005), but there are many perfectionistic, rigid, and impulsive people who do not develop eating disorders. Genes, thoughts, interactions with people, and other environmental circumstances also impact behavior. The unpredictably complex interplay of all these factors leads to the development of eating disorders.

Another popular "brain-based" explanation for eating disorders, particularly binge eating disorder, is the notion of food addiction. Proponents of the addiction model have studied the neurotransmitter dopamine and its impact on food intake, concluding that people binge because of biological factors in the brain. According to food addiction theory, people who overeat are at risk for both decreased dopamine levels and diminished activity in the prefrontal cortex, both of which lead to overeating.

Dopamine mediates pleasure in the brain and when people repeatedly overeat certain types of hyper palatable foods, dopamine receptors begin to down-regulate, meaning the brain decreases dopamine to keep things balanced (Gearhardt et al., 2011). When there are fewer dopamine receptors, people need more dopamine to get the same effect and eat more food to reach the same level of dopamine reward as before. A 2008 study (Volkow et al.) found that individuals with fewer dopamine receptors also have less activity in the prefrontal cortex, the area responsible for executive function, which oversees the regulation and control of cognitive processes, including memory, reasoning, and problem solving. The prefrontal cortex also governs impulsivity, which has implications for binge eating.

On the surface there appears to be a connection between brain changes and binge eating, but a closer examination reveals a far more complex issue. Sugar and junk food do change the brain, as do certain drugs. Indeed, any activity involving pleasure, including sexual activity, exercise, and spending time with friends, raises dopamine levels. One study (Salimpoor, 2011) showed that listening to music had the same impact on the brain as cocaine. Focusing on the brain without considering the complex interaction of physiology and psychology perpetuates a Cartesian dualism in which the mind and the brain are perceived to be separate entities. In actuality, the brain does not operate alone, nor does the mind function independently of the brain.

In recent years our increasing ability to map the structure of the brain has allowed scientists to research the impact of attachment experiences on the developing brain. The early attachment work of John Bowlby (1965) first explored the connection between certain styles of family dynamics and child development. He examined how early interactions with caregivers influence a child's self-concept, which impacts self-esteem and shapes expectations of relationships and of people. Using a psychobiological model that included both psychoanalysis and biology, Bowlby suggested that an infant's inter-action with a primary caregiver, usually the mother, created either secure, avoidant, or resistant patterns of attachment. Margaret Ainsworth (Ainsworth & Bell, 1970) amplified this idea and further developed specific types of attachment styles with others. Insecure and avoidant difficulties have been correlated to eating disorders (Armstrong & Roth, 1989).

Contemporary neuroscientific research (Schore, 2000, 2002, 2010) confirms that our experiences with early attachment figures impact brain development. Alan Schore, a neuroscientist and psychoanalyst whose research melds both disciplines, has conducted extensive research (Schore & Schore, 2008; Schore 2010a, 2011) on how early attachment patterns with a primary caregiver influences the orbitofrontal cortex, an area of the brain involved in self-regulation, managing stress, regulating mood, and also recognizing the emotional states of others. In a 2001 interview, Schore ("Thinking Through the Body") observed:

> What human beings learn in their first interactions with other human beings, in the mother infant relationship, (is) central to the formation of self concept, of positive and negative concept, of self regulation, of the ability to regulate internal bodily states . . .

Our ability to manage emotions is tied to our early interactions with caregivers, and these early attachment experiences can also impact us physiologically. Moriceau and Sullivan (2005) suggest that an infant's brain is not an immature version of the adult brain, but is uniquely designed to optimize attachment to the caregiver. Louis Cozolino (2006, 2014) notes that children of depressed mothers show "a disruption in the development, connection, and integration of the frontal lobes" (p. 262) and a decreased ability to regulate emotions. In the early 1950s, a sample of Harvard undergraduate men participated in a study that investigated the warmth and closeness they felt with their parents. Thirty-five years later, a follow-up study (Russek & Schwartz, 1997) showed that 91 percent of those original participants who did not perceive their relationships with their mothers as warm had been diagnosed with diseases such as hypertension, ulcers, and alcoholism, in contrast to 45 percent of the participants who perceived warm and loving relationships with their mothers. A similar connection between perceived warmth and future disease was found with fathers. The research suggests that the perception of parental love and caring impacts biological and psychological health throughout the life span.

Again, research that focuses exclusively on the brain as the primary source of the behavior ignores the powerful influences of the unconscious mind on the brain, as well as the familial, social, cultural, and other influences that impact development.

A safe therapeutic relationship offers a new experience, affecting the complex interplay of brain and mind, and leading to behavioral change. As Klaus Grawe (2007) puts it, "Processes in our brains influence experiences, and conversely, experiences create processes in the brain." *Psychoanalysis addresses underlying conflicts and creates changes in both mind and brain, in part by offering a new attachment experience through the therapeutic relationship.* These attachment experiences impact our brains, leading Nancy Andreasen (2001) to state, "Psychotherapy . . . is in its own way as 'biological' as the use of drugs" (p. 31).

Blame It on the Media

> You've gone thin.

In Western culture, such a remark would likely be considered a compliment and acknowledged by the recipient with pride. In Fiji, prior to the advent of television in the late 1990s, this observation expressed disapproval (Becker, 1995). The traditional Fijian view on body image was the opposite of Western culture, privileging a round physique as the ideal body type and disdaining thinness. A robust, healthy appetite and plumpness were highly valued and considered positive attributes. This began to change in 1995, shortly after television was introduced to Fiji. As anthropologist Ann Becker (Becker et al., 2002) observed, the influence of Western media in Fiji radically altered the cultural ideals of beauty in a remarkably short period of time. Only three years after television arrived in the country of Fiji, 83 percent of adolescent girls reported that their views of their bodies had been impacted by what they watched. They did not feel good about the larger, rounder bodies they previously viewed as the ultimate in femininity (Becker, 1995) and 69 percent of the survey respondents indicated that they recently had been dieting.

This radical shift in social values in Fiji points to the strong impact of the media on body dissatisfaction. In Western culture, evidence shows that magazine and advertisement images of young women and men, many of which have been significantly photo-shopped and altered, influence the self-concept and self-esteem of readers (Irving, 2001). Contemporary standards of attractiveness privilege tall, thin, young women and chiseled, muscular young men as the ideal body type. These unrealistic images are definitely associated with body dissatisfaction and may facilitate a preoccupation with weight and appearance.

Body dissatisfaction pertains to a negative view of the body, and usually involves a perceived discrepancy between a person's subjective evaluation of his or her body and the body image that is held as an ideal (Szymanski & Cash, 1995). Sarah Grogan (2007) broadly defines body image as "a person's perceptions, thoughts and feelings about his or her body" (p. 3). Paul Schilder (1950) was among the first to develop the idea that body image is a fluid concept that shifts along with our interactions with people. Thus we may have a sense of heaviness at times, or feel smaller or bigger according to the people and situations with whom we are interacting. Several patients have described this phenomenon to me. One woman explained that she looked in the mirror and thought her reflection was, "okay, not perfect, but somewhere in the range of acceptable" and yet an hour later, the same image seemed distorted, huge and ugly.

Boys and men are not immune to body image issues. The rate of body dissatisfaction among men has increased dramatically in the last few decades and men are now just as likely as women to be unhappy with their appearance. Up to 43 percent of men are dissatisfied with their bodies (Garner, 1997; Goldfield et al., 2006; Schooler & Ward, 2006). For men, body dissatisfaction often has to do with not being muscular or tall enough, and is associated with lack of muscularity and size. The term "bigorexia" was coined to describe a type of body dysmorphic disorder called "muscle dysmorphia" in which males perceive themselves as being too small, weak, and not muscular enough, regardless of their actual physical appearance. This phenomenon has been referred to as "reverse anorexia" because the perception of having inadequate musculature is analogous to an anorexic's view of their bodies as too big.

The fashion industry is beginning to respond to the public perception that advertising is destructive to self-esteem. In 2013, Israel instituted a ban on underweight models and legislated photo-shopped images in an effort to protect the health of the models and change the cultural standards of beauty. France passed a similar ban two years later, touting the law as a way to prevent anorexia. Proponents asserted that because girls and young woman want to emulate the underweight models, a lack of exposure to those images would lessen body dissatisfaction. French lawmaker Olivier Veran stated, "This will also help protect our adolescents at risk, because teenagers are under social pressure from the image these models convey to always be thinner and thinner" (National Public Radio, April 6, 2015).

The ubiquity of extremely thin models in the media certainly causes body dissatisfaction and may lead to dieting, which has been associated with the development eating disorders. Correlation, however, is not the same as causality. Correlation is the measure of the strength of association between two variables, whereas causality refers to the direct cause and effect between one thing and another. When two or more events happen at around the same time they may be associated with each other, but they are not necessarily connected by a cause/effect relationship. Research (Wadden et al., 2004) shows that dieting is not the sole factor in the development of eating disorders. If there were a causal relationship between dieting and eating disorders, far more people would suffer from eating disorders, since it is estimated that 108 million people in the United States are on a diet at any given time (Marketdata). A 2012 study in Britain revealed that the average woman in the United Kingdom has tried sixty-one diets before the age of forty-five (*Huffington Post*). Body dissatisfaction and dieting are thus correlated with eating disorders but there is not a cause-and-effect relationship between them. I have treated many individuals who developed body dissatisfaction and significant eating disorders, despite living in environments in which they were not exposed to media images. Eating disorders are complex and not limited to the population of young women (or anyone, regardless of gender) concerned about their appearance.

Blame It on the Family

In his 1967 book on the treatment of anorexia nervosa, Helmut Thomä observes, "We must also refrain from characterizing the family environment of the anorexia nervosa patient and its etiological influence on the pathogenesis of the symptomatology. Of course our observations about the mother-child relationships of these patients would be worthy of mention in the case histories, but they cannot be generalized" (p. 238).

In contrast to Thomä's recommendation not to generalize, other writers (Bruch, 1963, 1973; Blinder et al., 1988) suggest that specific patterns of interaction in families are a primary factor in the development of eating disorders. In some cases, disturbed family relationships are definitely a key element in the development of eating pathology, which was the case in the anorexic families described by Salvador Minuchin (Minuchin et al., 1978). However, eating disorders are not always explained by external events and environmental disruptions. S. Freud (1912) sets forth four reasons that people develop problems. The first reason is that symptoms develop as a result of actual lived experience. The second is that the facilitating factor in symptom formation is a disturbance in a developmental process. The third factor, which is closely related to the second, is that an inhibition in development causes these symptoms; people reach a certain age or developmental level and are conflicted about moving past that stage, causing them to remain stuck at that level of development. Last, Freud recognizes the combination of biological and psychological elements that cause distress at certain stages, such as the simultaneous developmental and biological changes of puberty and menopause.

Thomä reminds readers that Freud also writes, "we must give up the unfruitful contrast between external and internal factors, between experience and constitution . . . we shall invariably find the cause of the onset of neurotic illness in a particular psychical situation which can be brought about in a variety of ways" (pp. 237–238). When it came to symptom development, we must not privilege one cause over another, neither the external environment over internal genetic/biological factors nor vice versa, as symptoms are caused by a number of factors and that have to do with both the biological and the psychological.

Each person develops an eating disorder for different reasons, given his or her unique constellation of constitution, temperament, genetics, and cultural and social factors. When I was in graduate school, one of my professors differentiated between psychology and psychoanalysis by stating that psychology is the study of what affects the most people, whereas psychoanalysis concerns itself with what impacts one individual. Honoring the unique history, personality, experiences, wishes, and fears of each individual is vital to the process and outcome of psychoanalytic treatment.

Blame It on Cognitive Distortions

Early in my career I interned at an intensive outpatient program for eating disorders. The clients (as they were called in that program) were mostly adolescent girls, and my job was to help them stop their self-destructive behaviors by identifying and correcting their cognitive distortions. The treatment philosophy was grounded in cognitive-behavioral theory, which posits that these clients had core beliefs that led to their difficulties with food and relationships. The expectation was that once these maladaptive beliefs were identified and challenged, altering thought patterns, clients would feel better about themselves and stop being self-destructive. Thought modification was thus expected to lead to behavioral change.

There was no question that these girls and young women had patterns of thinking that created a great deal of anguish. They overgeneralized, magnified the importance of certain situations, events, and emotions, minimized others, intellectualized, exhibited dichotomous thinking, personalized external events, and more. All-or-nothing thinking was the norm, as exemplified by the girl who told me, "I ate a cookie, so the whole day was ruined. I thought, whatever. I might as well eat the whole box."

For many clients, an extra three pounds was experienced as catastrophic but an abnormal EKG or vomiting blood was "not a big deal." I was often struck by how these young women minimized their health risks and magnified the significance of a few pounds.

One of the initial goals for anorexic clients was weight restoration. This is always a crucial part of the recovery process in the treatment of anorexia, since there are so many medical risks associated with restricting and/or the purging that often accompanies anorexia. A starved brain cannot think rationally, and the resulting inability to reflect impedes the effectiveness of therapeutic intervention and progress. Thus, for psychological as well as physical reasons, weight restoration is crucial.

I noticed that the anorexia sufferers did not get better once their weight had been restored. Instead, they often said they felt worse than ever. A common complaint among these girls and young women was that after they gained weight, friends and loved ones assumed that they had restored their mental and emotional well-being along with their physical health.

"My family and friends think I'm fine because I gained weight. But I'm not fine at all," asserted one young woman. "Inside I feel exactly the same as before."

Although the eating symptoms had diminished or stopped, the underlying depression, anxiety, and issues of self-criticism and self-hatred remained. There was an extremely high level of relapse at this program; many clients had already cycled through several other inpatient, outpatient, therapy, twelve-step, and other programs, while others had experienced months or years of relief from their eating disorder behaviors, but they all slid back into a pattern of using food in a way that was harmful to their physical, emotional, and mental health. There was no question that food was a way of managing dis-regulated states that resulted from these thought patterns, yet it seemed to be only a piece of the eating disorder puzzle. I often wondered how these problematic thoughts developed in the first place.

Cognitive behavioral therapy (CBT) is widely touted as the treatment of choice for eating disorders, as it is "evidence-based" and therefore considered reliable, but this assertion lacks scientific basis. A 2012 study (Waller et al., 2012) revealed that half the clinicians who claim to practice CBT do not adhere to the techniques outlined in treatment manuals and include non-CBT methods, such as identifying defenses, using the therapeutic alliance as a means of identifying relational dysfunction, and other strategies in their sessions. Jonathan Shedler (2010) points out that these methods, especially utilizing the therapeutic relationship and identifying implicit feelings and meanings, are among the most basic tenets of psychoanalytic treatment, and lead to the most successful outcomes in cognitive therapy (Castonguay et al., 2014). Focusing on cognitive distortions was actually a predictor of poorer outcomes.

Shedler (2010, 2015) writes extensively about "evidence-based" treatment, pointing out that the scripted and manualized treatment protocols of CBT are only empirically validated compared to control groups that either did not have psychotherapy or received alternative nontraditional therapies. Thus, these ostensibly empirically validated studies, from which the term "evidence-based" is derived, only prove that CBT is better than nothing, or is more effective than pseudotherapy, rendering the scientific edge asserted by CBT researchers as misleading at best.

When manualized treatment is compared to psychotherapy with licensed clinicians, there is no evidence that CBT is more effective than traditional psychotherapy (Minami et al., 2008; American Psychological Association [APA], 2013b). Shedler (2013) observes, "Academic researchers have been selling a myth—one that enhances the careers and reputations of academic researchers, but not necessarily the well-being of patients" (Psychology Today website). The APA (2013b) also recognizes that so-called evidence-based psychotherapies have not shown greater effectiveness than traditional psychotherapy.

My observations while working at the eating disorder outpatient program, along with my subsequent training as a psychoanalyst and experience in private practice, indicates that *eating disorders are a symptom of the problem, not "the" problem.* The behavior is always a means of expressing, comforting, or enacting conflicts that may or may not be available to conscious awareness. The psychoanalytic goals of treating people with eating disorders include but are not limited to decoding the behavior and identifying what is unconsciously being expressed or communicated; determining the genesis of this way of relating to self, food, and others; and cultivating new ways to respond to thoughts, emotions, and conflicts. Restricting, bingeing, purging, obsessing, calorie counting, and compulsively exercising all serve to express what cannot be expressed in words. By translating the language of the body into words, the fears, wishes, defenses, and conflicts that lie beneath become available for working through. Patients are able to understand themselves on a deeper level, creating a shift in the way they relate to themselves and others and obviating the use of eating disorder behavior.

Chapter Two

Overview

This chapter provides an overview of psychoanalysis and of eating disorders, both disorders that fall within the guidelines of clinical diagnoses (binge eating disorder, bulimia, anorexia) and those that are subclinical in nature, such as orthorexia and disordered eating.

PSYCHOANALYSIS

Psychoanalysis is a theory of the mind as well as a therapeutic modality. Although commonly associated with Sigmund Freud, the "father of psychoanalysis" who first developed the theory and practice of psychoanalysis, much has changed in the last 100 years. Equating Freudian theory to contemporary analysis is like comparing a turn-of-the-century telephone to a smartphone, and furthermore imagining that phones are the only mode of communication. Current analytic perspectives have their roots in early Freudian tenets, but modern thinking and technique has expanded to include multiple and divergent perspectives under the rubric of psychoanalysis. Psychoanalytic theory includes, but is not limited to, classical theory; ego psychology; relational, intersubjective, and object relational perspectives. Each theoretical modality has a different philosophy about the working of the mind and what is curative. What all these modalities have in common is the deep interest in alleviating suffering and facilitating healing, so people can live their most authentic and satisfying lives.

Psychotherapies such as behavioral, cognitive behavioral, dialectic behavioral, EMDR (eye movement desensitization and reprocessing), and family systems primarily aim at symptom relief. Psychoanalysis seeks to go beyond symptom relief; yes, the work of analysis is concerned with alleviating the symptoms, problems, and suffering that bring people into treatment, but its aims are deeper and go far beyond crisis resolution to change the very structure of how a person relates to self and others. It also differs from other psychotherapies in its focus on the unconscious and on the conflicts, repetitions, identifications, defenses, and transferences that impact people's relationships to themselves and others.

As I have stated elsewhere (Savelle-Rocklin, 2015):

> The goals of psychoanalysis include explaining why people behave in ways that are self-destructive or why they may fail to act in their own best interests, identifying how the past impacts their current distress, and working through their hopes and fears about change, all in the service of helping them live more freely and authentically. (pp. 3–4)

Eating disorder behavior is a symptom of an internal psychological problem expressed through the body, but is ultimately not only about the body or about food. Since the destructive relationship to food and self is embedded in internal conflicts, one task of treatment is to create a language for thoughts, emotions, needs, wants, wishes, fears, and anxieties.

Individuals who struggle with eating disorders often lack a vocabulary for their feelings. They experience anger, sadness, frustration, and hostility as inchoate, unbearable states that cannot be named and therefore cannot be processed. They often exchange one affect for another, for example, crying when they are angry or showing explosive rage when they are actually sad. Getting to the root of the eating disorder can be difficult, as the behaviors serve to hide and disguise those conflicts.

Psychoanalysis helps decode the eating disorder symptoms and translate them into their true underlying meanings. Determining the beliefs and ideas that cause distress, and furthermore recognizing the source of these beliefs, is an essential part of the process. Identifications with primary caregivers or other significant people, such as siblings, often lead to internal conflict that is expressed via eating disorder symptomology. What starts as a relational issue between two people may eventually be internalized and continue as a conflict between parts of the self. In this way, a child may rail against a rigid or critical parent during childhood, but simultaneously internalize that parent and become rigid and self-critical toward both self and others.

An exploration of the family's attitude toward emotions and appetite—not just for food, but the appetite for life—also must be explored. Messages received about wanting, yearning, and needing have significant impact on a person's ability to both identify and meet those needs and wants. The treatment must address early traumatic experiences, especially sexual abuse, that may not have been mourned or fully processed.

Conflicts relating to dependency and trust are also common. After a therapeutic bond has been established and patients have insight into what is causing the symptoms that brought them to treatment, the "working through" process occupies most of the treatment. This working through refers to recognizing how the past impacts the present, mourning that which has not been grieved, dealing with the unresolved relationships, and arriving at acceptance. It involves "repeating, retreating from, and finally consolidating and 'owning' the new combination (or recombination) of feelings" (Shengold, p. 160). In this way, psychoanalysis helps people understand why they do things they don't want to do, and why they fail to take actions they want to take. The analytic relationship provides a new model of relating, one that patients can take out of the consulting room into every aspect of their lives.

The Unconscious

One goal of psychoanalysis is to bring unconscious conflicts into conscious awareness. The concept of the unconscious is often misunderstood. The conscious mind is that which we are aware of at any given moment, both in terms of our environment and our thoughts. Some mental contents are out of immediate awareness, yet they remain accessible to us. For example, if you are talking to a friend about your weekend plans, your mother's maiden name is not in the forefront of your mind. Yet the next time you fill out a government form that asks for your mother's maiden name, it will immediately come to your mind. In psychoanalytic terms, those mental contents that can be readily brought into consciousness are collectively called the preconscious, but more commonly are referred to as the subconscious.

Other parts of the mind are completely outside conscious awareness. They cannot readily be recalled or even known and remain completely elusive. The obvious question is, if they are not known, how do we know that they actually exist? Since the unconscious is out of awareness but not out of operation, there are various ways to infer its existence. Some of these methods include the exploration of transference, dreams, parapraxis (Freudian slips), negation, derivatives, and sudden solutions to problems, which will be explored in more depth in subsequent chapters.

The notion that parts of our minds are out of our awareness can be quite disconcerting. As one woman put it, "It's like thinking you're in the driver's seat and discovering you're actually a passenger being chauffeured through life by a mysterious and unknown driver." Psychoanalysis illuminates the existence of this secret driver, allowing for its motives, wishes, fears, and anxieties to be worked through, thus restoring or creating a sense of ownership over one's life.

With respect to eating disorders, focusing on what's going on with food is like weeding a garden by simply pulling out the weeds. As any gardener knows, to truly eliminate a weed, one must remove the root. Dieting, restricting, bingeing, and being obsessed and preoccupied with one's weight are analogous to weeds; each behavior is the result of deeply rooted conflicts. The parallel to the human psyche is that the unconscious is also, in a sense, underground, unseen, and yet powerful. By unearthing the proverbial roots of what is going on inside people's minds and hearts, which are often hidden, tangled, and complex, and digging those up through the process of working through, they are removed for good.

The Analytic Relationship

Many eating disorder patients have experienced some form of relational trauma, causing them to have mixed feelings about the analytic relationship. They may experience both a wish for closeness and a concurrent terror of losing themselves in a therapeutic relationship. They may feel an urgent wish to be known, seen, and understood, yet simultaneously fear dependency. Being in a dependent state is often associated with negative experiences such as loss or humiliation. One patient, who had a history of sexual and emotional abuse in childhood, announced at our initial consultation meeting, "I don't want to need you." Her expectations of relationships were based on the horrific experiences of her childhood. She imagined that needing and depending on another person inevitably led to pain, disappointment, and loss. A male patient who was initially very reserved and distant finally let down his guard and shared some of his secret fears. Afterward he was partly relieved, yet regretful. He worried that now I "had the goods" on him, information I would somehow use to my benefit, and he found it difficult to trust that I truly wanted to know, understand, and connect with him.

Many eating disorder patients have an empty place inside where ideally they would have access to warmth, love, and nurturing. They use food as a way of filling that emptiness, or expressing it, and managing profound aloneness. In psychoanalysis, the analyst and the patient explore the internal world of the patient through the methods of transference, countertransference, use of the couch, and the interpretation of dreams, all of which facilitate the discovery of unconscious ideas, fantasies, conflicts and other material, and allow the treatment to unfold.

EATING DISORDERS

A great deal of psychoanalytic literature focuses on either anorexia or bulimia, with very little exploration of binge eating or subclinical forms of eating disorders. As stated earlier, each individual develops symptoms for different reasons, yet I've noted certain similarities among them. As a clinician,

I've treated girls, boys, women, and men from many different walks of life and varied backgrounds. Despite the range of differences in ages, ethnicities, histories, and personalities, I consistently find several commonalities:

- A marked inability to self-soothe
- Difficulty identifying and expressing affects, which remain undifferentiated and diffuse
- A primary relationship with their bodies rather than other people
- A high degree of somatization, the conversion of psychological conflicts into physical symptoms
- A history of trauma

Patients with eating disorders develop a variety of ways to deal with intolerable emotions, conflicts, and wishes. Whatever the symptomatic behavior, it is important to recognize that the eating disorder behavior serves a protective measure that gives "patients respite from distress" (Abbate-Daga et al., 2013, p. 2). As difficult as it is to suffer, the eating disorder also functions to relieve other painful states. One patient called her eating disorder a "frenemy" because it was both a friend and an enemy. As a friend, it served to help her calm down, numb, and feel comforted. As an enemy, it caused emotional and physical pain and damage.

The term "defense mechanism" has become a common expression in our cultural vernacular. As defined by Freud (1894a, 1896) a defense mechanism is a means of avoiding anxiety or warding off impulses or conflict. His daughter, psychoanalyst Anna Freud (1937), expanded on this idea, elucidating the many ways people use defense mechanisms to keep uncomfortable emotions, wishes, urges, ideas, and/or conflicts out of awareness. Jerome Blackman (2004) points out that defenses may be "part of the solution to intrapsychic conflicts" (p. 11). Intrapsychic conflicts are those that exist within different parts of an individual, as opposed to interpersonal conflicts that exist between two people.

Whether individuals present with anorexia, bulimia, binge eating, or some other subclinical form of disordered eating, the goal of treatment is to identify what is unconsciously being expressed or communicated through food, identifying the genesis of this self-organization, and finding new ways to respond to thoughts, emotions, and conflicts.

Binge Eating Disorder

Binge eating disorder is the most common eating disorder, impacting as many as eight million people in the United States (ANAD website) alone. Only recently classified as an eating disorder in the *Diagnostic and Statistical*

Manual of Mental Disorders (*DSM-5*; American Psychological Association [APA], 2013a) it is estimated that in the United States 1.6 percent of women and .08 percent of men (p. 351) have binge eating disorder.

Binge eating disorder is defined as "recurring episodes of eating significantly more food in a short period of time than most people would eat under similar circumstances, with episodes marked by feelings of lack of control" (APA, 2013a, p. 350). This behavior occurs, on average, at least once a week over a period of three months. People who binge are often deeply ashamed of their behavior, and the resulting guilt, embarrassment, and disgust causes significant impairment in self-esteem.

In the psychoanalytic literature on disordered eating, little has been written about compulsive eating or bingeing, independent of purging and without the accompanying obesity. Most authors who explore bingeing (Bychowski, 1950; Glucksman et al., 1978; Glucksman, 1989; Rand & Stuckard, 1977) do so in the context of obesity. Their patients ate compulsively, and consumed immense quantities of food, but did not use compensatory measures such as dieting or exercising to manage their weight.

Pietro Castelnuovo-Tedesco and Lynn Whisnant Reiser (1988) viewed compulsive overeating as an impulse disorder, primarily a self-soothing activity that provides "substitutive gratification" (p. 163) as a way of replacing lost or disappointing love objects and recreating a preverbal attachment to the mother. Their pithy phrase, "when the love of food replaces the food of love" (p. 168) is striking, but for me it fails to capture the experience of people for whom compulsive eating is not at all pleasurable, but rather a highly unpleasant and painful experience, marked by regret and self-loathing.

A common assumption is that people who struggle with binge eating disorder are overweight or obese, which is a misconception. People with binge eating disorder may be obese, overweight, or within a normal weight range. Obesity is a physical condition that may or may not be the result of binge eating disorder. Obesity may result from many factors, including poor eating habits, heredity, and culture. Some individuals make poor food choices or do not have the time or knowledge to prepare nutritious food, which may lead to weight gain. They may eat meals high in calories and fat, or may not get enough exercise, or some combination of both. Other people may be genetically prone to being at a heavier weight. All these factors can cause obesity, but they are not indications of disordered eating.

Binge eating disorder, in contrast, is a complex psychological condition. People binge for many different reasons, including denying, avoiding, or enacting painful or upsetting thoughts, emotions, and conflicts. Some patients with binge eating disorder wish to be thinner; for others, their weight may serve a protective purpose. As reported by Castelnuoveo-Tedesco and Reiser (1988), many obese individuals do not yearn to be thin;

instead, they unconsciously fear thinness and need to stay overweight or obese for a variety of different reasons, depending on their conscious or unconscious conflicts. Consciously, they very much want to lose weight. Unconsciously, they may fear being objectified and becoming a sexual object to others. They worry that they will lose some essential part of their identity by losing weight. Many fear of reaching a goal weight and finding, to their dismay, that they feel exactly the same. "As long as I have a hope that losing twenty pounds will make my life better, I'm happy," one patient realized. "But if I lose weight and my life doesn't get better, I'll be crushed. It will be the end of hope."

The terms "overeating" and "binge eating" are often used interchangeably, but there is a significant difference. Nearly everybody overeats at some time or another, since overeating essentially refers to eating too much. There are varied causes of overeating that generally have to do with food itself, not feelings. Many Americans overeat on Thanksgiving, when eating to excess is celebrated as part of the holiday. Other people do not eat enough during the day, which causes them to be ravenously hungry at night, and their physiological need for food eventually leads to overeating. What differentiates bingeing from overeating is the intensity and scope of the binges themselves, which are usually not pleasurable, and have a driven, compulsive quality. They are usually followed by remorse and self-recrimination.

Bingeing in the context of binge eating disorder may or may not be tied to the experience of physical hunger. Sandor Rado (1928) suggests that hunger is a physiological manifestation of the psychological experience of emptiness. Fullness represents the experience of being loved, and emptiness, yearning for the mother, represents a loss of maternal love and affection. Most people who binge report eating when they are not physically hungry, and they continue to eat well after the point of satiety. The origin of their hunger is not physiological, but psychological, a concept exemplified in the following example:

"Resistance Is Futile"

"Why food? Why is food my thing?"

Emily, in her late twenties, gained and shed 30 pounds repeatedly throughout her life. She calculated that she lost at least 300 pounds in total since she went on her first diet at age ten. She joked that she "always found those lost pounds." In other areas of her life, Emily was doing well. She worked as an assistant literary agent for television writers and was in line for a promotion. She often socialized with a group of friends she'd known since elementary school and she saw her family regularly. Emily struggled to understand her strong compulsion to binge. She reported a ravenous need to eat that had nothing to do with physical hunger, often bingeing until she was in acute physical pain.

"It doesn't make sense," she said, exasperated. "I want to lose weight. To do that, I know I have to stop bingeing, but I can't. I have no willpower and I'm a food addict."

Emily's weight was a source of consternation to her and a focus of her family's attention. Both her parents were physically active and participated in various sports, but Emily did not share their enthusiasm for outdoor activities. As she put it, "I didn't inherit the sport gene."

In contrast, her older sister Mandy was a competitive athlete. Emily described her sister as having the Midas touch, since everything she did was golden. Their father often made comparisons between the two sisters, complimenting Mandy on her athletic build and excellent grades. Mandy also had a calm personality that was similar to the easygoing nature of their parents. In contrast, Emily was labeled as the "emotional" one, perceived as oversensitive and dramatic. The family experienced Emily's emotions as too much to handle. This notion of being "too much" was converted to viewing herself as literally too much, too big, too fat, and therefore a burden.

Emily often expressed curiosity about the "others" who came to see me. She wondered if I liked and cared for my other patients more than I did her, fearing I thought of her as difficult and too much trouble. She feared that I dreaded the analytic hour I spent with her but simultaneously hoped I appreciated her uniqueness. I interpreted to Emily that the experiences of her childhood had been transferred to the analytic situation. The "other" patients were imagined as representations of her sister. Emily yearned to feel special but feared that I liked other patients better than I liked her, just as she thought her parents preferred her sister. Invariably our exploration of the early relationship difficulties and their impact on her expectations of relationships, particularly as they played out in the treatment, was interrupted by attacks on her weight.

One day she started the session by announcing, "I'm feeling really bad about my body."

A few nights earlier she had attended a birthday party, catching up with friends and enjoying herself. Then, as if a switch had suddenly gone on, she was drawn to the dessert table, which was laden with a huge birthday cake, platters of cookies, brownies, and other sweets. She compared it to a scene in the original *Star Wars* (1977) movie, at the point at which the protagonist's spacecraft was pulled into the *Death Star*. Emily felt trapped by an invisible force that pulled her inexorably toward the dessert table.

"Resistance was futile," she sighed.

Emily often referenced movies as a way of expressing her inner conflicts. The phrase, "Resistance is futile," is from a *Star Trek* film in which the protagonists fight an enemy known as the Borg, an alien life form that has a collective mind. The Borg is analogous to a hive of bees, a colony of individuals that act as a single organism, resulting in a complete loss of individuality.

Emily sampled various cakes, chocolates, and cookies, eating more and more, feeling unable to control herself. She felt self-conscious and wondered if people were noticing how much she was eating. She snuck a few brownies into a napkin and hid them in her pocket, taking refuge in the bathroom so she could eat them private.

"It was horrible," she said. "I could not stop stuffing the stupid brownies into my mouth. I was crying, and barely tasting anything, but I couldn't stop."

Emily woke up the next day feeling bloated and sick. Positive she had gained weight, she called in sick to work and stayed home. She vowed to fast for two days as a way of nullifying the caloric intake from the day before. Her determination failed by the afternoon, when she became ravenous. She drove to a local fast food restaurant and ordered a super-sized meal. She ate quickly, feeling worse with every bite.

"I hate myself today," she said. "I am feeling so bad about my body."

I asked Emily to describe what was happening immediately prior to the moment she felt so inexplicably drawn to the dessert table. She had been having a good time, connecting with other guests and generally enjoying herself. Then her ex-boyfriend showed up with his current girlfriend, a successful young woman who was a few years older than Emily. This new girlfriend was thinner than Emily and had recently landed a producer position on a network television show.

"It's okay," Emily shrugged. "What happened with Henry is ancient history. We're all good, now."

She was quiet a moment. "To be honest, it was hard to see him with someone new. Especially her. She's so perfect."

She added, "I feel so gross and disgusting. I hate my body."

Feeling bad about her body was Emily's way of expressing or distracting from other "bad" feelings: seeing her ex-boyfriend with someone new activated Emily's rivalry with her sister and revived painful feelings about not fitting into the family. The girlfriend reminded her of her sister, since she was older and more successful. Emily felt "empty" and disconnected when it came to her relationship with her family, so filling up on dessert was a way of managing that emptiness. By eating until she was stuffed and in physical pain, she also converted her emotional pain to physical.

As we translated her behavioral symptoms into psychological conflicts, Emily was able to process her family issues. Although she had believed herself to be "over the past" and did not want to dwell on things that were "over and done with," she came to realize that she was still haunted by events of her childhood and that she was actually re-experiencing the most painful dynamics of the past. Emily was relieved that her problems with food had nothing to do with willpower. She cultivated the ability to consistently use words for soothing, and to express her loneliness and resentment by talking, journaling, or talking. She eventually stopped bingeing and no longer felt bad about her body.

Like Emily, nearly everyone who comes to my office seeking treatment for binge eating is initially convinced that the problem is willpower. They declare that they are preoccupied with food, and they cannot stop thinking about what they will eat or not eat, and report that all their attempts to eat normally always fail. They believe themselves to be addicted to food, usually white flour or sugar, or both.

But, is food addiction real? As noted earlier, various studies (Gearhardt et al., 2009a; Volkow et al., 2013) appear to make a case for the reward theory of food addiction, which correlates certain foods with increased dopamine levels. Dopamine is the chemical that mediates pleasure and motivation in our brains. Sugar, fat, and white flour activate the release of dopamine. People eat these foods, get a dopamine rush, and feel good. They want to keep eating in order to get that dopamine release. Researchers point out similarities between food and other substances, including the fact that food shares common drug pathways in the brain. Some foods activate reward neurons and dopamine receptors, and the anticipation of eating activates the same areas in the brain as drugs do.

Too much dopamine ultimately causes a depletion of dopamine. The theory around food addiction is that people crave more and more sugar, as an example, to get the same good feeling they previously were able to feel with lesser amounts. Sugar does indeed change the brain, as do certain drugs. Any activity involving pleasure does so, including sexual activity, exercise, and spending time with friends. Psychotherapy also changes the brain and has shown to be more effective than medication (Hunsley et al., 2013).

Other studies (Ziauddeen et al., 2012, Ziauddeen & Fletcher, 2013) challenge the notion of food addiction, identifying fundamental limitations, weaknesses, and inconsistencies in other studies from a neuroscientific research perspective. Ziauddeen concludes, "The rather damning conclusion with respect to the FA (Food Addiction) construct, is that successful therapeutic to treatment of, for example, binge eating, are quite different from what would be proposed were the condition to be meaningfully explained by an addictive process" (Ziauddeen & Fletcher, 2013, p. 14).

There are several alternative explanations of the neurobiological response to food. Evelyn Tribole (2011) points out that food is meant to be rewarding, which is why the reward centers of our brain light up and that normal hunger increases neural activation. She also discusses the impact of behavioral conditioning on eating and points to other studies (Smitham, 2008; Kristeller & Wolever, 2011) in which people who binged were asked to eat their "forbidden" foods. This caused a decrease in binge eating, the opposite of what would be expected from a food addiction model. Clearly, in addition to biological processes there are psychological factors that have even more impact on behavior.

This may have little relevance to a person who feels like an addict. As a patient recently said, "The science doesn't matter. Even if you tell me I'm not technically a food addict, I still feel like I need a fix."

Feelings, however, are not facts. The deeper we dig below the surface, the more the roots of the compulsion to eat become apparent. Patients discover that their behavior serves a purpose. When they identify what that purpose is and find new ways to respond and resolve their internal conflicts, they stop bingeing. This was the case with the following two patients, who also considered themselves food addicts.

"My Sister's Keeper"

"It's a chemical thing. I'm completely addicted to carbs," said Laura, 38, as she described a recent binge. She had been enjoying a rare afternoon at home alone while her husband and children were at a movie. As she relaxed by the pool, reading a book, she felt an urge to eat potato chips. She tried to resist the temptation but couldn't stop thinking about chips. She decided to "only have a few" to satisfy the craving. She ate one chip, then another, and ended up devouring an entire family sized bag of chips.

Laura was very upset with herself as she related this experience. She was at a loss to understand her behavior. She noted that nothing was bothering her and therefore she wasn't eating for emotional reasons. She said, "Obviously, I'm addicted to potato chips. I'm so disgusted with myself."

Indeed, there were no apparent issues in Laura's life. Her marriage was solid and loving. She worked in a profession that she found to be a source of satisfaction. She was happily married and her children were bright, happy, and doing well both scholastically and socially.

I asked what book she was reading before she felt the compulsion to eat cookies.

The novel was titled *My Sister's Keeper*, the story of a girl who is conceived to help save the life of her dying sister. In the book, the young protagonist is forced to donate an organ to save her sister's life and takes legal measures to prevent this from happening. Inherent in the narrative are some parallels to Laura's personal story. Laura was born after the accidental death of an older sibling, a sister who drowned at the age of three. Throughout her life, she felt haunted by the ghost of this dead sibling. She experienced a subtle pressure to enjoy the same things that her dead sister had enjoyed, to be what George Pollock (1970) expanding on the what Cain and Cain (1964) termed a "replacement child," a child conceived by his or her parents to replace a dead child. This definition has been expanded to include any child born either to replace a child who has died or a child born after the death of another child, especially in the presence of continuous and unresolved parental grief. When the loss of a child is not sufficiently mourned and accepted, parents may subtly convey a wish for the living child to behave like the dead child (Volkan, 1981). The more Laura resembled and acted like her dead sibling, the more it would seem to others that her sister had been brought back to life.

Laura was quite different from her sister in both temperament and appearance. She simultaneously felt torn between feeling guilty that she was so dissimilar and conversely wishing to be as different as possible. She also felt sorry for her parents for having lost their first-born daughter. She knew they were not purposely pressuring her to be like her sister. Therefore, she reasoned, she did "not have a right" to be upset.

Laura's compassion for her parents nullified her responsibility to herself. Reading the book had activated uncomfortable feelings over the covert pressure to replace her sister. Before these feelings came into her conscious awareness, Laura's mind turned to chips as a distraction. By getting angry with herself for eating chips, she further displaced the resentment she had about her parent's covert wish to make her like the dead sister and turned that anger on herself.

There was an additional factor of survivor guilt that added to her binge eating symptoms. Laura had lived and grown up to adulthood, whereas her sister had died in childhood. Schwab (2009) notes the commonality of survivor guilt in replacement children, who feel their lives are owed to the death of their sibling. This guilt was a factor in Laura's behavior with food. She felt guilty for eating the wrong food, or eating too much, transforming the guilt for living into the guilt of eating.

It is important to note that Laura's anxiety was completely out of awareness. She was simply trying to enjoy a peaceful afternoon, unaware of the internal conflicts that were roiling within her mind. If the word "addiction" could be used, it would be in terms of an addiction to the *behavior*, an eating addiction rather than an addiction to the substance of food. In this context, Laura was not addicted to the chips; she was addicted to eating chips to avoid the intolerable conflicts and feelings. Our challenge was to figure out what was eating "at" her when she wanted to binge, and then finding new ways to respond other than with food.

"Sugar Is My Own Personal Crack"

Belinda, 38, a stay-at-home mother with a lifelong history of weight problems, began planning her meals the moment she awoke and remained preoccupied by food throughout the day. She obsessed about "being good" and not giving in to temptation. When she was not eating, she was thinking about the next meal. She felt as if she were "in a love–hate relationship" with food, particularly with sugar. She confessed that baking cookies with her young daughter, she often sent the child out of the kitchen on some pretext so she could eat cookie dough alone. She constantly fought the overwhelming compulsion to eat more cookie dough and referred to sugar as "my own personal crack." She concocted elaborate excuses to explain the missing dough, pretending to have dropped the mixing bowl, or saying that she had accidentally used salt instead of sugar. Later, she felt intense remorse and self-loathing.

In treatment, Belinda came to realize that her obsession with food distracted her from deeper concerns. She grew up in a conservative religious community where dissent was forbidden and compliance expected. She learned to stifle her natural inquisitiveness and did what was expected of her. She married within the community and tried to get on with life and make the best of her situation. Belinda told herself she had done the right thing but her life felt wrong. She struggled with profound restlessness and dissatisfaction. Food provided a temporary panacea. Thinking about food and weight distracted from wishing for a more authentic life. Belinda did not have enough figurative sweetness in her life and food was the primary means by which she was able to experience pleasure.

If people do not have enough pleasurable activities in their lives, they may become overly reliant on food for their sense of enjoyment. Conversely, the greater the levels of pleasurable activity, the less likely they are to use food for that purpose. Belinda eventually got a job she enjoyed, started taking pottery classes and made some new friends. She found that she could bake cookies without bingeing on cookie dough. She ate cookies in moderation, without the craving and guilt that had tortured her for so many years.

How was this possible? Belinda did not understand the change. She asked, "A recovered alcoholic can't have just one drink, so how can I eat a couple of cookies and stop?"

The reason is that we have brains, but we also have *minds*. Belinda did indeed feel a rush when she ate cookie dough—a biological response to sugar, which created a pleasurable response in her brain. From a psychological perspective, she was also distracting from her problems and displacing her helplessness over her relationships and work onto food. That had to do with her mind. Once these unconscious motivations were identified and the root issues of helplessness and dissatisfaction worked through, Belinda stopped using food as a means of escape, or to numb, distract, or express her thoughts and emotions. She realized she was not physiologically addicted to the substance of food.

Human beings are capable of learning new methods of relating and responding to themselves and others. When we identify and process their

internal conflicts, and when we create new ways of understanding and reacting to thoughts and emotions, we change their relationship to ourselves—and
to food.

Bulimia

Many patients report that bulimia started as a seemingly magical solution to
overeating or bingeing. They got rid of what they had eaten by vomiting, fasting, or over-exercising and viewed that as a way of erasing what they ate and
zeroing out the calories. They believe bulimia is a habit that they are unable,
or unwilling, to break. The reality is that bulimia is a far more complicated
condition than a deleterious habit. Bulimia is a symptom that contains and
expresses a plethora of meanings; it can be understood as a defense against
painful emotional experience, an expression of ambivalence, an attempt at
mastery, and a means of self-regulation.

As stated in the *DSM-5* (APA, 2013a) the essential features of bulimia
nervosa are "recurrent episodes of binge-eating, recurrent inappropriate compensatory behaviors to prevent weight gain and self-evaluation that is unduly
influenced by body shape and weight" (p. 345). Bulimic individuals typically
binge on huge quantities of food and purge through vomiting, laxatives, or
diuretics. Those in the "non-purging" subtype use compensatory behaviors,
such as fasting or exercise, to get rid of the extra calories. Most are within
a normal weight range or overweight, but usually not obese, and exhibit
extreme preoccupation with body shape and weight.

Bulimia may simultaneously hide and express certain affects such as
aggression and anger. Patients often describe how they shove fingers or
other objects forcefully down their throats in their effort to purge, acts of
aggression that take the place of words. As Reich and Cierpka (1998) state,
"vomiting, has the function of erasing the eating binge, restoring the desired
body weight or shape, cleansing away filth and inadequacy, and eradicating
violation of interpersonal boundaries or penetration and aggressive or auto
aggressive impulse" (p. 394). I also find that many bulimic patients launch
vitriolic attacks on themselves, disparaging the slightest perceived mistake or
imperfection. They are mercilessly harsh and cruel toward themselves, but
often are deeply sympathetic toward the plight of others.

Bulimia is often rooted in conflict between opposing currents of two different wishes. Food is a symbol of a nurturing, reliable presence. For those who
have not been able to take in a soothing, loving presence of another, the wish
for comfort and connection may cause distress. Yearning for and wishing
for a response that does not materialize is painful. Eventually those wishes,
wants, yearnings, and needs become a consistent source of humiliation rather
than satisfaction. This is enacted in bulimia—the taking in of food represents

wanting something or someone, and purging represents a turning against those desires. With the taking in of food and the purging of it, feeling states are symbolically first owned and then disowned (Lunn & Poulsen, 2012).

The term "introjection" refers to the symbolic taking in of another person, a defense mechanism that is used constructively as a part of the natural path of development. For example, a baby introjects the soothing voice of a parent and gradually learns to soothe herself; in this way, introjection is an adaptive means of developing a capacity for affect regulation. If that baby is not soothed with words or if there is a fundamental misattunement in the bond, the absence is what is internalized, instead of the presence of soothing. This internalized absence diminishes on the capacity for self-soothing with words and leads the baby to depend on other sources of comfort, such as food, which can be taken in and expelled at will.

When needs are not met, or are inconsistently met, people turn against those needs rather than suffer the humiliation of staying "hungry" for love, attention, affection, responsiveness, and connection. Bulimia is a way of representing the dilemma of wanting connection, safety, and closeness, yet simultaneously fearing that closeness. Instead of turning to another person, many of those with bulimia turns to food as a mental representation of a person. Embedded in the frenzied action of the binge, in which more, more, and more is taken in, is a ravenous wish for more fulfillment, more of something or someone that may not be known or articulated in words. The purge is a means of repudiating desires and indeed driving them from conscious awareness. As Latzer and Gerzi (2000) put it, bulimic patients are "overcome by the message of 'I don't need anything or anyone—I can vomit you and put you at a distance" (p. 36). When I consider this, I recall countless times when patients expressed trust and I sensed they were taking in my kind, loving, and compassionate view of them, only to feel symbolically purged when they cancelled subsequent sessions or withdrew in other ways, reacting to closeness by creating distance.

Bulimia may also be understood as an attempt to gain a sense of mastery over certain aspects of life, while simultaneously expressing powerlessness. This was articulated by Reich (Reich & Cierpka, 1998) who states, "Bulimic symptoms are action symptoms, and as such, they correspond with the individual (and familial) defense system; they work by reversing passive to active, by taking action." Powerlessness is often an underlying theme of psychic conflict. For some bulimic individuals, helplessness over some aspects of their lives is first expressed in feeling powerless over food and neutralized by purging, which temporarily gives a sense of empowerment and control. This doing and undoing essentially reverses true wishes; a wish for more is turned into rejection, an urge to take in something is converted to expulsion.

Other theorists examine the way bulimic patients use their bodies to either express their conflicts or to achieve self-regulation. Sugarman and Kurash

(1982) focus on what happens to the body during the act of eating or binge-ing, viewing the physical experience of eating as a means of experiencing the early maternal bond. Since our earliest experience of love, relationship, and bonding is the experience of being fed by a parent, food represents the rela-tionship between parent and child. Purging is therefore viewed as a way of repudiating the need for that bond by expelling food/mother (A. Sugarman & C. Kurash, 1982). Lidz and Lidz (1976) describe the powerful focus on the consumption and rejection of food as "supplies that do away with the unbear-able sense of emptiness . . . are substituted for the supplier; food that can be gorged is sought inside of the feeder" (p. 340). In this way, it is the food that is sought, rather than the person who supplies nurturing, and the push–pull of ambivalence is played out within the relationship to food, rather than to people.

Other writers (Goodsitt, 1983; Swift & Letven, 1984) focus on the physi-ological aspects of bulimia and propose that the behavior is motivated by a need for self-regulation and to relieve internal tension. I find that this physi-ological release of tension and sense of relaxation is a common experience among bulimic patients but not the primary motivator.

Bulimia is thus a means by which thoughts, emotions, conflicts, wishes, and other aspects of mental activity are expelled from the mind and trans-formed into a bodily experience. Whether purging through vomiting, laxa-tives, or exercise, bulimic behaviors serve to disguise internal conflicts that often remain hidden from consciousness. Bulimia may be an unconscious strategy to express or symbolically eject disavowed conflicts and emotions, particularly rage (Chessick, 1984), to symbolically clean internal messi-ness (Reich & Cierpka, 1998), and to have mastery over needs and wants (Schwartz, 1986).

"My Totally Insane Behavior"

"I know exactly why I started throwing up," announced Katie, 42, a slim, attractive woman with the demeanor of a news anchorwoman. "It was a way of having my cake and eating it, too. It just got out of hand."

Katie came for treatment after nearly two decades of being bulimic. She described her struggle with bulimia as "my totally insane behavior" and finally sought help because bingeing and purging was affecting her physical health.

Katie married shortly after college graduation. She recognized that mar-riage was her means of escaping an intolerable family situation. Her father was physically and emotionally abusive and lived by the motto, "Children should be seen but not heard." If Katie or her siblings dared to disagree with him or speak without permission, he screamed obscenities at them. He often beat them with a belt for minor offenses. When Katie cried, got angry, or had any kind of emotional reaction, he became enraged and hit her, yelling, "I'll give you something to cry about." Her mother blamed Katie for provoking her father, since she "should have known" how he was, and therefore had brought the abuse upon herself.

Katie's solution to her abusive and neglectful circumstances was to please and appease her father. By catering to his every whim, cooking his favorite food, and being compliant whenever possible, she escaped his abusive outbursts and punishments. She learned to see herself only in terms of how she impacted other people, and came to disregard her own thoughts, ideas, emotions, and perceptions. As a child she was told she must be "seen but not heard." As an adult she could neither see nor hear herself.

At the time she began treatment for bulimia, Katie's two children were in college. The first time she purged was shortly after her first child was born, when her mother commented on how much weight Katie had gained during the pregnancy. Katie felt an acute sense of shame and immediately went to the bathroom, forcing herself vomit. Afterwards, she felt much better, describing the ensuing physical relief as a "fresh start." We came to understand bulimia as a way of symbolically purging bad feelings about herself and her resentment toward her mother, who "served me up on a platter to my father." Katie had difficulty getting in touch with feelings of betrayal at the hands of her mother, who did nothing to protect her children. She felt "mean" whenever she talked about how her mother had allowed the abuse to happen. She immediately attacked herself, criticizing her weight and appearance.

At our first meeting, Katie told me she had a lot to be grateful for in life; she lived in a lovely home in a guard-gated community and her husband made a good living as an executive at a successful accounting firm. She could not understand why she had such difficulty giving up her "habit" (which is how she described bulimia) of throwing up nearly everything she ate or drank. When I asked her to describe her relationship with her husband, she described their marriage as "fine" and then casually mentioned that her husband was "good with numbers, not people." As soon as she spoke the words, she apologized for "sounding mean" about her husband. Katie apologized for everything: she was sorry she was late to a session, sorry when she cried or blew her nose, sorry for not making faster progress.

Katie also went on shopping binges and later returned everything she bought. These were analogous to the bulimic episodes she experienced daily. She took in food or made purchases, only to get rid of all of it. Furthermore, she wondered if I wanted to get rid of her. She frequently asked if I was tired of her repeating herself or frustrated with her perceived lack of progress and feared I would "fire" her from my practice, thereby configuring herself as an employee rather than a patient.

We explored bulimia as a way of coping with upsetting or painful ideas, emotions, and situations, rather than a "totally insane behavior." As a child, Katie learned to take care of her abusive father at her own expense. She continued this behavior in adulthood, relating to friends, family, and even strangers in the same way she had related to her father. Katie volunteered for several charity organizations and felt passionately about helping others who were down on their luck. Most of her friends were people who needed some form of financial or emotional support. She sacrificed her own well-being to help others, cancelling plans to babysit for a friend, treating people to expensive dinners and buying them designer clothes—although she would not treat herself to nice dinners or clothes. She felt good about being so helpful to others, and was unconcerned with the lack of reciprocity. All her relationships lacked mutuality and were based on giving–taking patterns of relating.

At one point she took in a homeless family, a young couple with a baby that she recently met and barely knew. They lived in her home for nearly six months without paying rent. Interestingly, her husband accepted the intrusion of this family into the household without comment. The family was initially grateful and tried to help out around the house, but Katie insisted that they were guests and would be treated as such. She set to work preparing their favorite meals and helping them find jobs. In time they came to expect her to cook for them and take care of all their needs. Katie took great pleasure in taking care of this needy family of three babies, who fed off the milk of her human kindness.

Katie's tolerance of the growing demands of these houseguests, and her unconscious solicitation of their greed and egregious entitlement, is less puzzling when viewed through the lens of what Anna Freud (1937) terms altruistic surrender (p. 132). This is the tendency of some people to disavow their own needs but meet the needs of others, even encouraging those needs, as Katie did, and then vicariously living through them.

When I observed that Katie did not allow herself to recognize or meet any of her needs, but was comfortable meeting the needs of others, she protested that, "having needs was the same as being selfish." She did not experience others as selfish, but as appropriately entitled to get what they wanted. As we began to talk more about this disconnect between how she perceived her own needs versus those of others, she grew quiet and was silent for several minutes. She finally broke the silence with a heavy sigh. She said, "I'm wondering if I got all the food out of my stomach the last time I threw up."

This change of subject revealed Katie's coping strategy; when she felt uncomfortable, her thoughts turned to her body. Whenever Katie accessed any meaningful emotions or conflicts, she redirected her thoughts from the emotional to the physical. She hoped that by getting rid of the food, she could get rid of her uncomfortable feelings.

In this instance, musing about whether or not there was still food in her stomach was an oblique response to our discussion. She repudiated her most basic needs, for food, for understanding, for security and love. She found it nearly impossible to bear painful thoughts and emotions, since she had no paradigm for taking care of herself. Her solution to any emotional discomfort was to change her focus, in effect purging her thoughts by either thinking about food, weight, and her body, or bingeing and purging.

Six months after she took in her homeless houseguests, Katie started to become annoyed by what she had come to view as their grandiose entitlement. She recognized that in some ways she "had created a monster" by encouraging the family to rely on her for shelter, food, and even money. Finally, she made up an excuse to force them leave her home. It took her some time to communicate the news that she wanted them to leave. She worried about how they'd feel, fearing that she would be seen as "the bad guy." She was wracked with guilt and could not stop purging, trying to symbolically get rid of unwanted emotions.

By challenging the idea that her sense of self was based on taking care of others at her own expense, and cultivating the ability to tolerate affects, Katie learned to express a range of emotions. She also got in touch with the rage she had repressed but enacted through her desperate need to clean out her stomach, and to sanitize her thoughts. When she expressed her anger with words and affect, she was finally able to relinquish the symptom of bulimia.

Anorexia

The first clinical reference to anorexia were found in 1694, when physician Sir Richard Morton described two adolescent patients—one female and one male—who suffered a self-induced starvation he labeled "nervous consumption." His detailed account matches the clinical criterion for anorexia nervosa, long before the current media influence of skinny and airbrushed models. He describes the physical aspects of the disease and writes, "this Disease does almost always proceed from Sadness, and anxious Cares" (Morton, 1694, p. 8).

As noted by Caparrotta and Ghaffari (2006), "He distinguished this disorder from other wasting maladies and believed it to be amongst others the product of 'violent passions of the mind'. Moreover, after observing that the psychopathological process lay between the patient and the family, he advocated the removal of the patient from the family" (p. 177). In historical examples, such as that described in Rudolph Bell's book *Holy Anorexia* (1985), saintly women stopped eating as a way of embracing moral cleanliness, to find a perfect union with God. In our contemporary society, women and men restrict food in a conscious effort to have perfect bodies and therefore—or so they believe—perfect lives. The motivations are different, but the use of the body to resolve a psychological conflict or wish is the same. The body expresses what the mind cannot think about or recognize.

The clinical features of anorexia nervosa found in the *DSM-5* (APA, 2013a, pp. 338–339) are an intense fear of gaining weight or of becoming fat, or persistent behavior that interferes with weight gain, disturbance in the way one's body weight or shape is experienced, undue influence of body shape and weight on self-evaluation, or persistent lack of recognition of the seriousness of the current low body weight. The subtypes are restricting type and binge-eating/purging type.

Although physicians throughout the centuries were familiar with anorexia, it was not until Hilda Bruch wrote *The Gilded Cage* in 1978 that the public began to be familiar with the disorder. The death of the popular singer Karen Carpenter five years later brought eating disorders further into cultural awareness. Like binge eating and bulimia, the condition of anorexia is the result of a complex and individual interplay of social, cultural, and familial factors. It is estimated that 1.0 to 4.2 percent of women have had anorexia in their lifetime (Eating Disorder Hope).

Anorexia literally means "without appetite," but this is a misnomer. Anorexic patients are hungry, often ravenous—for food, for life, for connection—but they turn against their hunger, denying wishes for emotional and physical nourishment. An anorexic woman once told me with great satisfaction that she did not need anything or anyone. She proudly stated that she had no needs at all and that her mind had taken control of her physical body. She was starving yet would not allow herself to eat, finding perverse gratification in her ability to deny her biological needs. Her tone bordered on gleeful as she related this dominance over her body.

A male patient confided that he would not eat when he was hungry and resisted sleep when he was tired. Additionally, he would not urinate when he needed to do so, putting it off as long as possible and refusing to "give in" to his body's need to eliminate waste. To him, this refusal to eat, sleep, or go to the bathroom was proof that he was strong and powerful. He was at war with his body, which he had cast as a "not me" thing, and over which he could triumph by repudiating his basic biological needs.

From a psychoanalytic perspective, anorexia is often associated with denial of basic needs, conflicts over development, and issues of control and identity. Much of the earlier literature on anorexia focused on adolescents, viewing anorexia as a pathological response to the vicissitudes of growing up and thus considering it the result of a developmental crisis. Bruch (1978) and others (Lomas, 1961) speculate that anorexics experience anxiety about the psychological, social, and sexual aspects of adulthood and use their bodies as a means of regressing and reversing the maturation process. I once treated a high school senior who was only able to eat when her mother fed her "like a baby" and gave soothing reassurances that she was going to be okay. This teenager's symptoms started shortly after she started studying for the college entrance exams. When the goal of graduating high school and moving on to college became real, she began focusing on her weight and became hyper-vigilant about every calorie and fat gram consumed, terrified of being fat. Her solution to the anxiety about moving out of the house and going to college was to regress into a baby state, needing to be spoon-fed and returning to an earlier time when she felt safe in the cocoon of the family.

For some patients, anorexia functions as a way to manage relationships and navigate the stormy waters of identity. The slowly disappearing body of a person struggling with anorexia often results in increased attention and focus. The wish to be left alone that is commonly seen in anorexic patients can disguise a wish to be seen, to be recognized, to be separate, and to assert autonomy.

Early attachment patterns are associated with disruptions in the ability to regulate emotions and relationships. Daniel Stern (1977) describes extremes in the mismatch that sometimes occurs between parents and infants, giving the example of an intrusive mother who is not attuned to her child's need for space or needs. He calls this a "misstep in the dance" and notes that such missteps may be "valuable because the manner of negotiating repairs" (p. 157). If such reparations are not made, however, those missteps may lead to patterns of relationship and attachment that are destructive. As noted earlier, Schore's (2000, 2002, 2010) research in such misattunement in parent–child interactions leads to insecure attachment and affect disregulation.

Salvador Minuchin, a family systems theorist with a background in psychoanalysis, developed a model of what he termed a "psychosomatic family" (Minuchin et al., 1978) in which family members are enmeshed and the boundaries between individuals become blurred. The families he studied shared characteristics of enmeshment, overprotectiveness, rigidity, and avoidance of conflict and lack of conflict resolution. Enmeshed families have weak boundaries between members; there is intrusion on feelings and actions, lack of privacy, and there is covert pressure to conform to the family way of being and thinking, rather than to cultivate a sense of individuality and separateness. The mother of an anorexic patient expressed shock that her daughter was a Democrat. "You can't vote for the other side," she said, dismayed. "We're Republicans."

For this anorexic young woman, her refusal to eat was a rebellion against the intrusive expectations of the family, a manifestation of her refusal to "swallow" (as she put it) their ideals.

Other studies suggest that overprotective parenting in early childhood is associated with the development of anorexia. A controlled study on overprotectiveness and anorexia in the *British Journal of Psychiatry* (2000) found that mothers of anorexic teens rarely allowed others to care for their daughters as infants and children, experienced distress when separated from their children, and had high levels of anxiety when their daughters spent a night away from home.

Although much of the research and literature focuses on adolescents and young women, I treat many adults of middle age or older who struggle with anorexia. Yvonne, 53, spent twenty years in a power struggle with her husband, who "reminded me of my mother." Yvonne's mother put her on a diet when she was in kindergarten. She was a chubby child and her mother began monitoring her food and becoming overinvolved in her food choices. Most of Yvonne's interactions with her husband revolved around whether or not she was eating, a reversal of her childhood fights with her mother about her weight. Yvonne refused to eat, drawing her husband into an enactment of her childhood dynamic. Their relationship devolved into a power struggle, based on negotiation rather than mutuality. For Yvonne, to stop restricting was akin to giving up her power in the marriage.

Rigidity is another characteristic common to anorexic families and has also been found to be a trait common to many anorexic women (Sato et al., 2013). Rigidity preserves the family patterns at times when there should ideally be more flexibility, such as during adolescence, when accommodation and change must take place in order for development to proceed. Avoidance of conflict and lack of conflict resolution does not allow for the working through of problems or difficulties, and therefore children from these families do not develop the tools to tolerate conflict, either relational or internal.

My experience with anorexic patients is that anorexia gives an illusion of being self-contained and autonomous. The symptoms may take on a life of their own and become something of an identity, one that is initially cherished but difficult to relinquish. When friends and family members express concern, they are often summarily rejected by the anorexic, thus creating a pull–push dynamic between food and family. The anorexic behavior appears to be about weight, but actually expresses a myriad of wishes, fears, and conflicts. Too often, it is mistakenly thought to be about "control" but this is often not the case, as in the following examples.

"It's All about Control"

Taylor, 20, was pale and thin to the point of emaciation. She looked fragile and spoke haltingly in a soft, quiet voice, as if every word took tremendous effort. At our first meeting, she told me that she understood exactly what her eating disorder was all about. She knew she should not listen to her "anorexic voice" but it was very loud in her head. Since developing anorexia four years earlier, she had cycled in and out of many eating disorder programs, both inpatient and outpatient, and experienced a plethora of therapists, groups, dietitians, and intensive outpatient programs.

I invited her to tell me what she thought her eating disorder was all about.

She lifted her shoulders in an exaggerated shrug. "Control," she said. "I have no control over my life . . . so I control food instead."

Her voice was flat and lacked inflection. She might as well have been describing a science experiment.

"And, what are your thoughts about that?" I asked.

She appeared to be taken aback by my question. "Well, it has to be control. That's what it always is, right?"

Taylor developed anorexia when she was sixteen years old, around the time that she began taking a preparatory course for the college entrance exams. Consciously, she was terrified of "getting fat" and was motivated by a strong desire to attain physical perfection. She imagined that life would be perfect if she reached a perfect weight. This obsession was carefully detailed in her journals, in which she catalogued every calorie and fat gram.

Taylor was the oldest of four children in the family, and the only girl. She described her household as chaotic and overwhelming. From an early age she was expected to help her mother with the other children. She described her siblings as running around "in a pack" and their hyperactivity was a constant source of consternation to her parents. Taylor became her mother's helper, essentially taking on a co-parenting role and helping out "with the boys." She didn't feel like a child of her parents, but functioned as a kind of daughter–mommy. Her mother was grateful for the help and often exclaimed, "What would I do without you?" Taylor enjoyed feeling as if she was special to her mother. When she started to think about going away to college, she began to "freak out" about her weight.

Instead of going to a university, Taylor entered a series of inpatient programs. She improved during each stay in residential treatment but regressed into anorexia shortly after each discharge. These inpatient programs provided a sense of being held, replicating the structure of childhood. The doctors and nurses on staff, readily available twenty-four hours a day, represented parental attunement and provided the round-the-clock care that are normally reserved for infants. In this way, Taylor transferred the role of parenting to the doctors and nurses at the inpatient programs. What she had not adequately obtained in childhood, she received from medical personnel. Giving up the need for care was tantamount to giving up the experience of feeling loved, which is why she could not continue her recovery after she left the hospital. The anorexic symptoms were not, therefore, about control. Her unconscious wish to be small and to be taken care of was actualized by anorexia, in which her ever-shrinking body received care by the medical establishment.

Taylor's challenge in treatment was to mourn what she had not experienced in childhood, so that she could continue in her development into adulthood. She learned to bear the disappointment at what she had not received, to grieve the fantasies of what she had not gotten. She accepted what she had experienced and what she had, so she could ultimately give herself that which she longed to receive from others, the nourishment of her body and soul. Since being in need of care and feeling loved were so fused in her mind, Taylor also constructed a new definition of love that was based on mutuality.

"Making Weight"

Liam, 32, developed an eating disorder during freshman year of high school, when he was required to "make weight" to stay on the wrestling team. He and his teammates starved, sweated, purged, and restricted liquids to meet their weight goals.

As he put it, "That was the start of my manorexia."

The term "manorexia" has recently become popular to describe male anorexia, giving the incorrect impression that it may be distinct from anorexia nervosa in girls and women. As stated earlier, eating disorders do not discriminate, and people who struggle with anorexia may be male, female, young, old, and of any ethnicity and socioeconomic background. Like other eating disorders, it is not about food. Food is the means by which a person of any gender, age, or ethnicity may use anorexia as a means to express thoughts, fears, wishes, and conflicts. By presenting the case of Liam, I hope to convey the ubiquity of anorexia.

Liam was an only child, born to his parents late in life. As far back as he could remember, his mother peppered him with questions about the specifics of his day. What did he learn? Who did he sit next to at lunch? Who was his best friend? Had anyone hurt his feelings? What did he want for dinner?

"It was too much," he recalled. "I couldn't get her to leave me alone."

Liam experienced his mother's incessant questioning as deeply intrusive. He was unable to stave off the steady avalanche of words. As he told me about this verbal barrage, my own association (which I did not share with Liam) was to recall an occasion when I was a guest at a banquet in Beijing. A parade of tuxedoed waiters brought platter after platter of food, filling the table with exotic dishes, cramming every inch of table space with meat, buns, noodles, vegetables, and unidentifiable foods. As soon as one platter was empty, the dish was immediately replaced with a new platter of food. This constant procession of food felt more like an intrusion than a gift, and made me feel overwhelmed and claustrophobic.

I wondered if Liam had experienced his mother's questions in a similar way. Like the endless procession of food at my Chinese banquet, her ceaseless questions were a steady stream of words that she stuffed into his head. Liam could not shut off his ears so he shut off his mouth instead. This displacement from ears to mouth served as a way of putting up a barrier. In "making weight" for his wrestling team, Liam found a way to give expression to his wish for privacy, and his sense of violation by his mother's endless questions.

A theory proposed by Gianna Williams (1997) is that some patients reject food as a way of symbolically rejecting certain emotions, thoughts, fantasies, and expectations that were placed upon them in childhood. People who employ what she terms a "no entry" defense reject anything perceived as a penetration of their minds and internal worlds. Williams posits that these patients simultaneously lack a sense of containment and experience themselves as porous containers of their parents' expectations, ideas, experiences, and projections. Their solution is to ward off anything that comes in, whether literally with food and figuratively in terms of thoughts, ideas, wishes, and/ or expectations.

According to Williams, "the extreme and pervasive dread of being invaded and intruded upon in 'no entry' type of patients . . . may also be related to early very persecutory experiences of being at the receiving end of projections perceived as inimical" (Anderson & Dartington, 1999, p. 80). This fear of psychological intrusion may be expanded to a wider view of intrusiveness, as was the case with Liam.

Subclinical Eating Disorders

Many people have food, weight, and body image issues that do not fall within a clinically diagnosable category, yet the impact on their emotional and physical health is significant. Orthorexia, a preoccupation with healthy eating, is an obsession that causes acute distress. Steven Bratman (1997) originally coined the term as a way to categorize an unhealthy obsession with eating healthy food, deriving the term from the Greek *orthos*, which means "right," or "correct." Orthorexics appear to be motivated by health and obsess over the quality of their food, not the quantity. Unlike individuals who suffer from anorexia, people with orthorexia are not preoccupied with their weight. Bratman states, "While an anorexic primarily wants to lose weight, an orthorexic primarily wants to feel pure" (personal communication, July 2015). This is in line with my observation that the use of the term "clean" is a common way to describe food in those who are orthorexic, as is an obsession with cleanliness. Orthorexics appear to find moral virtue about their insistence on purity and cleanliness. In this respect, the syndrome may have more in common with the fasting saints described by Rudolph Bell in his book *Holy Anorexia* (1985), who expressed religious dedication by embracing purity through starvation, self-inflicted torture, and extreme self-denial.

Some researchers (Brytek-Matera, 2012) view orthorexia as a hybrid disorder with features of both anorexia and obsessive-compulsive disorder (OCD). OCD involves obsessions, which refer to obsessive thoughts, and compulsions, which refer to behaviors. These obsessions and compulsions are egodystonic, meaning unacceptable and inconsistent with one's self-view. People with OCD recognize that their obsessions are unreasonable and are often dismayed by their thoughts and actions. In contrast, anorexia involves preoccupations that are egosyntonic, meaning acceptable and consistent with one's personality and outlook. This is the attitude I have seen most commonly in orthorexics, who believe their preoccupation with clean eating is healthy and that concerned friends and family are overreacting.

The compulsion to eat "clean" serves the goal of trying to be as pure as possible. From a psychoanalytic perspective, the behavior serves to mask deeper conflicts and may be understood as a defense against impulses that are perceived as messy and impure, such as aggression and sexual desire. This reversal is a defense mechanism known as a reaction formation, in which anxiety-producing emotions and impulses are mastered by doing the opposite, often to an extreme. In orthorexia, clean food going into the body is a way of warding off any messy impulses or emotions.

Bratman notes the underlying aggression that often underlies the symptoms of orthorexia, reflecting that some men "act like monks to avoid being criminals . . . there is something very primal being shut down in orthorexia." Similarly, in discussing the nature of orthorexia with colleagues, several of them mentioned treating raw food vegans who appeared to suppress any aggression by concentrating on the ethics of veganism or limiting exercise to holistic practices such as yoga, which they also perceived as pure. I am certainly not suggesting that being a vegan or practicing yoga is a pathological choice or a sign of orthorexia; these behaviors become diagnostically significant only when individuals take clean food and bodily practices to an extreme level, usually to the point where the obsession takes over their lives.

As with people who suffer from other forms of eating disorders, those with orthorexia often have deep conflicts about their bodies. Rather than loathing their bodies and wanting to lose weight, orthorexics are intent on purifying their bodies. They do not hate their bodies; they fear their bodies. They wish to render their messy, bloody, intestinal tracts into clean and perfect structures, shining with metaphorical light in an attempt to attain spirituality through pure food. Bratman has referred to this as "kitchen spirituality" (personal communication, July 2015).

Like other eating disorders that start as diets, people with orthorexia transition from leading healthy lifestyles to being obsessed and grappling with disordered eating. The factors that cause these shifts are highly individual. For example, an acquaintance is confident that he will live until the age of

140 by eating clean food and taking the right supplements. He is obsessed with macronutrients and grows his own produce, limiting his caloric intake as part of his quest for longevity. For him, eating this way is a means of managing anxiety about mortality. This "cleanliness is closer to Godliness" attitude protects against the anxiety of mortality and the reality of death.

In addition to conflicts about aggression and mortality, many orthorexics become more attached to their diets than to people. They stop socializing because they cannot trust the food in restaurants or at other people's homes, and gradually their primary relationship is to their bodies instead of to others.

"I Like to Eat Clean"

Paige, 42, perched on the couch and read the notes she prepared for our first meeting. I noted her perfect manicure, glossy hair, and crisply elegant clothes as she recited details about her healthy eating habits, explaining the time and effort that went into selecting certified organic fruits and vegetables from a local farmers' market. She bought olive oil from a local farm that only sold to select markets and never touched anything made with white flour or sugar. She believed sugar to be poisonous and ate foods with only one or two ingredients. She took pride in "ever eating anything with a face" and considered veganism to be an ethical imperative.

Paige displayed little concern about her weight and thought she looked fine. Instead, she was obsessed with the quality of food and terrified of "putting anything in my body" that was not safe. She feared that unsafe foods would harm her, so she exerted incredible rigidity in the interest of "eating clean." Yet, no matter how perfectly she ate, no matter how "clean" the food was, she could not stop thinking about her digestive tract. She imagined food mixing together in her stomach and the notion of what she considered a "disgusting mess" caused her to feel physically ill. Paige was so preoccupied with the purity of food that she had stopped eating anything that was of uncertain origin. As a result, she no longer socialized with friends and spent hours planning her meals down the smallest micronutrient.

Paige entered treatment because she realized that her engrossment with health was increasing her anxiety and impacting her well-being. She was ambivalent about giving up her commitment to "eating clean," since orthorexia provided a sense of superiority and gratification that she felt loathe to relinquish.

As I got to know more about Paige, I discerned a possible unconscious motivation underlying her insistence on purity. Paige did not allow herself to get angry and she could not cry. When she was upset she got a stomach ache, converting emotional pain into physical, essentially experiencing a stomach ache instead of heartache. She described her emotions as chaotic and felt uncomfortable discussing them, telling me that she should be past her feelings. "After all," she told me, "I'm not a child. I should have outgrown this stuff."

She was dismayed by her body's gurgling, leaking, demanding unpredictability. Lacking an ability to validate her emotional experience and to be at peace with the idea of being a biological organism, she instead sought to neutralize the bodily mess by managing food. By putting only clean food into her stomach, she thought she could avoid the "disgusting mess" of messy, painful, upsetting emotions, a strategy that called for her to continue finding cleaner and cleaner food as a way of avoiding those chaotic feelings.

Paige feared that she might "blow up" in anger, imagining rage as volcanic lava that erupted and spewed forth, destroying everything in its path. This comparison further emphasized her unconscious connection between aggression, mess, and explosive destructiveness. She had fantasies of being a robot, with clean wiring and circuits, rather than messy organs and blood. She found going to the bathroom to be degrading and embarrassing, rather than a natural part of being human and having a body. Both her reticence to express anger and her humiliation over elimination were connected to a conflict about aggression. Sigmund Freud (1908), in his paper *Character and Anal Eroticism*, points out character traits in certain people who are "orderly, parsimonious, and obstinate" (p. 169). He describes orderliness as it pertains both to bodily cleanliness and other aspects of life, and observes that in some people being orderly is exaggerated. He found that many people who were obsessed with order were also frugal and fixed in their ways. Karl Abraham (1923), who noted that personality development is due to multiple factors, including basic temperament, disposition, and the environment, also observed that conflicts in the toilet training stage impact personality development, specifically with regard to aggression. Paige denied her wish to be explosive by repressing those wishes and turning against anything messy or difficult.

As Paige became more tolerant of her emotions, especially forms of anger such as annoyance, resentment, and frustration, she became more comfortable expressing them. Her rejection of her basic physicality and her emotional life gradually diminished. She began introducing forbidden foods back into her diet and one day proudly announced that she had eaten a piece of her son's birthday cake and pronounced it to be "absolutely delicious."

Disordered Eating

Many people express concern about their diagnosis and wonder if they have a "real" eating disorder. I tell them that diagnoses are based on the *DSM-5*, which did not recognize binge eating disorder as an eating disorder until

2013 (*DSM-5*; APA, 2013a) and until recently, males and post-menopausal women could not be diagnosed with anorexia because the criterion required the absence of at least three menstrual cycles. Women who exhibited all the other symptoms of anorexia but still menstruated were precluded from the diagnosis. From my perspective, the formal diagnosis is not as important as the level of distress and the impact on a patient. If the behavior bothers people and interferes in their lives and well-being, it needs their attention.

A Vicious Cycle

Many patients cycle through different types of eating disorders, oscillating from one to another in a seemingly endless cycle. Their symptoms have different meanings at different stages of their lives and serve a variety of purposes.

At my first session with Maya, then 17, she reported a history of anorexia that started just before she began her middle school, when her parents announced that they were getting divorced. A short time later, her father took a job in a different state and more or less disappeared from her life. Her mother responded to these circumstances by becoming anxious and self-involved. She was constantly on the phone with friends, talking about the divorce and its impact on her life. She was so caught up in her misery that she often forgot to make dinner. When Maya reminded her mother that it was time to eat, she felt as if she were doing something wrong by interrupting. She also found it "embarrassing" to ask to be fed.

The shame Maya felt for wanting attention from her parents was transferred to food. She turned away from food as a way of denying her wish to be prioritized. "I'm here, see me, hear me," her disappearing body silently communicated. By losing weight, she finally gained her mother's attention, and she began spending more time with Maya. In her senior year of high school, realizing she was hungry—ravenous—Maya began to eat again, and immediately started bingeing and purging on a daily basis. At this point she sought therapy.

When I asked about what was going on, she said, "I woke up one day and realized I was really fucking hungry. Starving. So I started to eat again and throwing up seemed like a good solution. I could eat and get rid of it."

Maya was also hungry for something that was far more intangible. She was starving for love and security. She wanted to feel like a priority to her parents because she was their child, not because she was struggling with an eating disorder. A part of her was hungry for emotional nourishment, and so she used food to fill up. Another part of her remained ambivalent about needs, so she purged, symbolically getting rid of what she was feeling.

She complained, "I wish I weren't so stupidly needy."

Like many other eating disorder patients, Maya believed that having needs was equivalent to being needy. I related a parable about a wolf that wanders into a vineyard filled with ripe grapes. The grapes look juicy and delectably sweet, yet hang tantalizingly out of reach. The wolf tries desperately to get to the grapes. He leaps, jumps, and tries to climb the vines, all to no avail. Finally, the wolf is forced to concede that the grapes are close enough to see and smell, but will remain forever out of reach.

"Well, those grapes are probably sour anyway," sniffs the wolf.

This allegory illustrates the humiliation of wanting, yearning, and wishing for something that is out of reach. The experience of yearning and of being left deprived is so shameful that people turn against that which they really want. The need for love thus is felt as neediness.

Maya had turned against her health and human need for love. As therapy progressed and allowed her to create a new relationship to her needs, she stopped purging. Her mother stopped worrying about her as much and they settled into a new routine. Maya continued to binge, however, gaining weight at a steady pace. Each week I could see her body swelling larger, growing almost visibly before my eyes.

In a family session, her mother finally stated the obvious. She said, "I've noticed there is more of Maya, lately. I'm worried."

I caught a flash of Maya's smile, a hint of triumph on her lips.

Through her weight and her size, Maya expressed what she could not convey in words. As a young teenager, she shrank her body to the point where her parents became alarmed and sought treatment for her. By getting smaller, she finally became more visible to them. Now, by taking up more space, she again made her mother look at her. She was *Alice in the Looking Glass*, growing smaller, growing bigger, stuck within the mirror of painful relationships.

Worry and concern formed the links of connection between Maya and her mother. Maya experienced her mother's anxiety about her weight as an expression of love. Anorexia, bulimia, and binge eating served to somatically articulate various internal conflicts and relational needs. Restricting was a way of communicating how deprived she felt, how alone and unhappy. Bulimia represented her conflict about needs. She wanted so much and hated the fact of her yearning, disparaging her wishes as "stupidly needy". Bulimia allowed herself to fill up on food the way she wanted to fill up on people, love, attention, connection, and recognition, and then symbolically purge the neediness. Finally, binge eating was an expression of her deep, restless, and ravenous hunger for connection and attention.

When Maya mourned the unavailable father and came to terms with the fact that her mother could not be both mother and father, she started communicating with words instead of through her weight, and stopped using her *Alice in Wonderland* method of capturing attention from others.

Part II

ORIGINS

In this section, I discuss the origins of disordered eating, drawing attention to how early relationships with caregivers influence the development of eating disorders, examining problems in the areas of symbolism, and exploring various dilemmas involving the body and relationships.

I also review the unconscious compulsion to repeat and analyze how the past continues to impact the present.

Chapter Three

Object Hunger

S. Freud (1938) writes, "A child's first erotic object is the mother's breast that nourishes it; love has its origin in attachment to the satisfied need for nourishment" (p. 118). I believe he meant that an infant's first experience of love is being fed, connecting and taking food from another. Food thus serves as a representation of mother, of mothering, and of love. The experience of being fed registers in our psyches as the first relationship with another person. If the maternal experience is unsatisfying and frustrating, people use food to express and enact that frustration: compulsive eating serves as a means of symbolically incorporating a lost maternal object; restricting is a way of denying need for nurturing; and bulimia expresses conflicts about needs and wants.

In psychoanalytic lingo, "object" may refer both to an actual person and to the mental perception of that person. In a thorough explication of the term, Salman Akhtar (2009) offers several interpretations, explaining that while the term "object" refers to a combination of external reality and internal factors that "gives shape to internal objects" (p. 192), some analytic theories privilege internal conflicts over external relationships and vice versa. For the purposes of this book, I refer to objects as both actual people with whom patients have relationships, and also as the mental representations of those people.

The term "object hunger" is used by a range of psychoanalytic writers and theorists (Sterba, 1934; Blos, 1967, 1974, 1983; Kohut, 1968; and others). Although the phrase has not been employed specifically in regard to disordered eating, it nonetheless has implications in terms of understanding the underpinnings of bingeing, bulimia, and anorexia.

Early writers viewed eating issues within the frameworks of oral fixation and unconscious wish-fulfillment. Sigmund Freud wrote a letter to Wilhelm Fliess in 1899 suggesting that a patient's "hysterical vomiting" represented a wish to rid herself of a fantasied pregnancy. He states, "By vomiting, she is deprived of food, wastes away and gets ugly, so that she cannot attract any lover, as a punishment" (Masson, 1985, p. 345). In this comment, he appears to view purging as a means of unconsciously avoiding pregnancy or sexuality.

Much has changed since this early attempt to understand eating problems. Otto Fenichel (1945, 1996) notes, "Many peculiarities of persons fixated at this stage can be explained by realizing that in this period, objects are not looked upon as individuals but only as food or providers of food" (p. 63). He viewed the eating of food as a way of unconsciously creating a "reunion with objects" (p. 63). From this perspective, yearning for a union with an "object" pertains to the wish for connection with a real person, the provider of nutrition and sustenance. There may even be confusion between food and people at some level. One of my patients was lonely while housesitting at a friend's large beach house. One night she wanted to go out on desk to watch the ocean, but she "could not go out there alone" and brought some hot chocolate to give her company. She anthropomorphized the beverage in order to feel as if she had companionship.

In subsequent decades, many other theorists sought to specifically understand the etiology of disordered eating. Hilde Bruch (1973) proposed that mothers who meet their child's every need with food, regardless of whether the child is hungry, sleepy, or anxious, hinder the infant's ability to differentiate between hunger and other needs and internal states. She also emphasized that hunger is not an innate function and must be learned, and posited that misattunement in the feeding process can lead to problems with separation and individuation. She thought that patients who struggle with eating disorders suffer "the basic delusion of not having an identity of their own, of not even owning their body and its sensations" (p. 50).

This fits with my experience with many patients who respond to all their bodily and psychological needs with food, eating when they are sleepy, angry, anxious, sad, and/or lonely. Many report that when they are exhausted they eat for energy. Others eat to relax and calm down. They commonly meet all their needs with food. When they are inevitably disappointed, they often eat more, thinking that a greater quantity of food will perk them up, or relax them. Inevitably this brings frustration and disappointment, and a sense of helplessness over their ability to manage their bodies.

Heinz Kohut (1968) suggests that a child's traumatic disappointment in his or her objects inhibits the development of an internalized representation of those objects, leading to an "intense form of object hunger" (p. 89). Kohut goes on to posit that individuals are subsequently dependent on others to make up for what is missing internally. He contends that for these individuals, other people become "a substitute for missing segments of the psychic structure. These objects are not loved for their attributes, and their actions are only dimly recognized; they are needed in order to replace the functions of a segment of the mental apparatus which had not been established in childhood" (p. 89).

Specifically with respect to eating, Murray Jackson (1993) states, "object hunger and greedy eating attests to the power of the phantasy of oral incorporation of the mother" (p. 124). This refers to the idea that the mother is symbolically devoured during eating, and that bingeing represents a way of taking in and holding that mother internally. If food is unconsciously experienced as symbolizing one's mother (or father), then one never has to feel alone. Even if mother is not present, food is there, and food takes the place of mothering.

"MY MOTHER, MYSELF"

Jane, the patient introduced in the preface, who imagined she would continue to binge until she had gained 135 pounds, the exact weight of her mother, provides a concrete example of this notion of internalization. Jane grew up in a chaotic household dominated by an alcoholic father and a depressed mother, both of whom alternated bouts of intrusive rage with periods of withdrawal and absence. She had one sibling, an older brother who was not much of a presence in her life and was usually playing sports or video games. Her mother was physically and emotionally abusive to Jane, but her older brother was never a target of rage or abuse. Jane told me that her brother was their mother's favorite, which she attributed to a preference for sons. When Jane was twelve, her newborn brother became the center of the family and a beloved new addition, obviating this gender theory of favoritism.

Jane used food for comfort while she was growing up. She became an obese child who turned to productivity and accomplishment as an attempt to win praise from her parents and authority figures. She played cello in the school orchestra and excelled academically. No matter what she achieved, her parents appeared not to notice or care.

Jane developed anorexia at the age of fourteen and was hospitalized multiple times over the next few years. She remained underweight into adulthood, mainly by exercising and restricting her intake of food. She began bingeing after losing a job where—notably—she felt as if she was part of a family. Losing the job and the associated sense of community facilitated an intense hunger for connection, which was expressed in her intense hunger in food.

Jane binged on enormous quantities of food, all food that she hated and her mother loved, and told me she would not stop until she gained 135 pounds—again, not coincidentally, the exact weight of her mother. By gaining the weight of her mother, Jane could unconsciously and symbolically carry her mother with her in an ultimate merger of herself and her mother, and thus maintain the connection. To give up food and the excess weight was unconsciously equivalent to giving up her mother. Losing weight, therefore, would be akin to losing the maternal bond.

Jane was in an impossible bind. For her to be independent and individuated, she had to give up her bond with her family; conversely, to feel connected to her family, she had to relinquish her autonomy and individuality. What is rational and conscious, therefore, has little to do with the powerful influence of unconsciously motivated behavior. In Jane's case, bingeing may be understood as an unconscious effort to take in or to incorporate early representations of those attributes of the m/other that were missing or unavailable, such as nurturing, love, and a sense of connection to another.

Additionally, it is important to recognize how aspects of the original disappointing or rejecting object/s manifest in the psyche, keeping individuals locked into the same disappointing, depriving, abusing, or rejecting relationships that they sought to escape.

"MOTHER, PLEASE TALK TO ME"

Rose, 58, entered treatment to address her problematic relationship with food, describing herself as, "currently in my anorexic phase." She had fluctuated between bingeing, anorexia, and bulimia for decades. Rose's only sibling was an identical twin sister with whom she had a moderately pleasant relationship but they were not close. They discussed clothes, the weather, and movies, but never connected on an emotional level. She described her childhood as alternately chaotic and lonely. Her father was prone to rages and unpredictable behavior, often yelling and raging in response to very little provocation. Her mother was depressed and emotionally absent. When her mother was upset with Rose, she responded with silence as a way to convey her disapproval. Rose recalled that these silences seemed to last for days and remembered tugging at her mother's skirt and pleading, "Mother, mother, I'm here, please talk to me."

Her mother merely went on with her activities as if Rose did not exist. The silence obliterated Rose's sense of self, rendering her invisible, unseen, unheard, and left with an overwhelming sense of longing, bewilderment, pain, and rage. The fact that these interactions happened in the kitchen while her mother was preparing a meal may have also created a connection in Rose's mind between food and withholding. She later withheld food from herself and effectively gave herself the silent treatment by not listening to her own needs, not hearing herself, and casting herself out as soundly as her mother appeared to have done.

Rose initially could not tolerate any silence in our sessions. She experienced even a few moments of quite reflection as an intolerable stretch of distance between us that felt interminable. Lief (1962) points out that, "silence is perceived in terms of the patient's prior experience. The patient who has been given 'the silent treatment' as a child will inevitably regard the therapist's silences as hostile and react to them accordingly. If talk equals love, withholding of it is equivalent to hate" (p. 82).

Significantly, Rose and her sister only referred to their mother as "Mother" but never "mommy" or "mom." Rose had a connection with a woman who was biologically her mother, but lacked the ability to listen, comfort, soothe, and respond to her. Early photographs of the family depict her mother looking blankly at the camera, a baby at each side held at arms length. When Rose showed me those photos I felt a rush of compassion for those two tiny babies who grew up with a mother but did not know the soothing, loving presence of a mommy.

Rose always felt as if she was too much for her mother. As a child, she never imagined that her mother might have been overwhelmed by the task of caring for twins, since that was an adult concept and not something a small child would consider. Whatever the reasons for the mother's silence, which was experienced by Rose as a hostile rejection, she did not experience her mother as a safe object, and therefore did not take in a safe, comforting internal representation of such a mother. Rose lacked object constancy, the ability to hold onto a consistent and safe representation of a nurturing parent. She did not have the experience of being nurtured and soothed and therefore did not learn how to soothe herself with words. Instead, she relied on food as a means of either stuffing down her feelings or expressing her deprivation, and her relationships with others were underscored by anxiety.

When the twins were ten years old, their uncle visited from out of town. Rose was outside in the yard playing in the pool with her uncle while the rest of her family was inside the house, when her uncle suddenly pulled down her tube top, exposing her chest. She remembered feeling startled and mortified, but could not recall what happened immediately thereafter.

Rose did not tell anyone about the incident but soon began to gain weight. For the next few years, she wore big, baggy sweaters and hid from the unwanted views of others. Men became a source of fear and shame until she went to college. At that point she became, as she put it, "like a guy" and used men for sex, avoiding romantic relationships but having sexual conquests. By doing this, she reversed the original trauma with her uncle and turned passive to active, becoming the sexual predator instead of the victim. A couple of years into analysis she revealed the "tube top incident" to a relative and learned for the first time that her uncle had a history of behaving inappropriately with women, impulsively touching their breasts or making sexual comments. Rose felt tremendous relief when she discovered this, since it alleviated her sense of responsibility for the encounter, as if she somehow brought her uncle's inappropriate actions upon herself.

Children are egocentric and blame themselves when things go wrong in their lives. A classic example is that children who are told their parents are getting a divorce typically ask, "What did I do?" When children are treated badly, they often feel as if they are bad and blame themselves for the bad treatment. Fairbairn (1941) explains this phenomenon by what he terms the "moral defence" and proposes that children cannot allow themselves to imagine that their parents, on whom they are completely dependent, are incapable of being good and reliable figures. Rather than contemplate disappointing or cruel parents, children decide that they are the ones who are not good enough. This provides the illusion of control and offers hope; a child unconsciously believes that if he or she can just figure out what's wrong with him or her and make it right, then he or she will earn the kind, loving parents he or she craves. Thinking that something is wrong with oneself is therefore a strategy for hope that becomes a conviction about one's likability and lovability that persists into adulthood.

Rose experienced a pervasive and constant sense that there was something "deficient" in her essential personality that caused her to be rejected by others. As a child, cast in the role of the bad twin/bad daughter, she held onto hope that things would change if she changed. She thought that she was a bad girl and hoped that if she made herself good, she could earn the love and acceptance that eluded her. She clung to this illusion through adulthood, finding men who were stand-ins for her original rejecting father and turning on herself when they rejected her. While her father was alive, she continued to do everything she could to earn his love and approval. His death facilitated a deep depression, because that loss signified the death of all hope that she could ever achieve a loving and secure bond with him. In the rejecting boyfriend, she found a father-like figure, and their relationship activated the hope that this simultaneously enticing and rejecting man would become loving and accepting.

Our work initially centered on Rose's anxious hope that she could achieve the recognition, love, and acceptance that had eluded from her, both from herself and in terms of her attitude toward herself. She developed an observing ego, a function of the mind that acts as a witness to one's own internal and relational dynamics. An observing ego allows people to step outside themselves and reflect on the thoughts, reactions, and interpretations they make, instead of reacting, and facilitates reflection. Rose was soon able to recognize when the familiar childhood reenactment was taking place. Eventually she was able to address the original psychological wound with her father in treatment, to work through the pain and rage of their unresolved relationship, which led to a sense of healing. She stopped seeking the kind of enticing/rejecting men who consistently led to such profound and familiar disappointment. Concurrent with this shift in her relationship to herself and others, she also stopped using food as a means of expressing her emptiness, anger, and pain.

FATHER HUNGER

Most literature on eating disorders focuses on the mother–daughter relationship, but the father–daughter bond is also important. Margo Maine (2004) explored the connection between eating disorders and paternal relationships, finding that fathers who remain absent, unavailable, or unsatisfying leave hungry daughters yearning to fill an internal emptiness. These daughters often turn to food to express their needs and conflicts, filling up the inner void with food or starving themselves as a way of expressing their deprivation. Sandra Yarock (1993) noted the prevalence of seductive fathers who alternate "special attention" with periods of rage, an observation that matches the experiences of many patients I see in my practice.

Father hunger refers to the void in people whose fathers were physically or emotionally unavailable and absent. As Margo Maine (2004) notes, "like physical hunger, unsatisfied emotional hunger does not disappear; it grows and grows" (p. 21). Fathers play a crucial part in a child's development. Tuttman (1986) traces the shifts in analytic thought from Freud's emphasis on the father as a source of love and support for the child, as well as a potentially punitive authority, to a contemporary focus on the importance of the maternal relationship. This shift essentially pushed aside the significant contribution of fathers in the area of child development. This is perturbing, since both parents contribute significantly to an individual's development. Problematic relationships with fathers are equally as significant as ruptures in the maternal bond. Conversely, good fathering can mitigate and heal the impact of maternal ruptures.

Babies attach to their mothers and fathers differently from the earliest moments of life. According to Salman Akhtar (personal communication, 2015), there are a number of developmental functions that a father performs. The father provides an alternate form of attachment; he has a different voice, a different look, and a different way of holding the baby. From an early age, the child learns that there are many ways of being in the world and that being with mommy is different from being with daddy. Akhtar further observes that in contrast to the mother's body, which is utilized for nourishment and as a safety haven, the father's body is used for testing strength. Fathers may arm wrestle, have tickle matches, or wrestling matches, and invite the child to test his or her strength. A father teaches the child that healthy aggression, such as that displayed in arm wrestling, is not destructive. When this does not occur, that aggression may be turned against the self, especially the body, which becomes a target of hostility.

Additionally, the father pulls the child from the enmeshment with his or her mother, both in early childhood and later in adolescence. Mothers tend to be more overprotective of their children than fathers. Paul Raeburn (2014) notes that despite changing gender roles in our culture, there continues to be significant differences in the way fathers relate to their children. Fathers are generally more physical and less protective when it comes to running, climbing on playground jungle gyms, and being physically independent. A male patient recalled being pleased after his teenage daughter passed her driver's test, and he immediately gave her the keys to the car. His wife, on the other hand, was a bundle of nerves every time their daughter drove the car, imagining all kinds of terrible things that could happen to her on the road. One role of the father, therefore, is to encourage the child to leave that maternal orbit and explore the world, promoting a sense of trust in the ability to navigate the exigencies of life.

If a father does not accomplish this task of facilitating separation from the mother, helping the child move from dependency to independence, children are left to navigate this shift to autonomy alone, and may use an eating disorder as a coping strategy. Kathryn Zerbe (1993) observes, "the very act of refusing food cuts off the symbolic umbilical cord to the provider of food, that is, to the mother, and as such is an autonomous statement par excellence" (p. 95).

Fathers are more likely to focus on the external than the internal. Whereas mothers introduce children to their internal worlds, naming their states as hungry, sleepy, bored, excited, sad, and so forth, fathers traditionally show children how to do things, to go down a slide, climb a tree, ride a bike, and do other things in the external world.

In the twenty-first century, fewer children are growing up in traditional homes. More children are now being raised by single parents and by same-sex parents. When a single mother is raising a child alone, she usually has a boyfriend or a male friend or there may be an uncle or a grandfather, or a friend, and these male figures often provide the child with an experience of fathering. Although there are fewer single fathers, the same is true of children who have a missing mother, and obtains mothering through maternal substitutes. In same-sex families, one person generally takes on the more maternal role and the other the more paternal role. Therefore the terms "mother" and "father" are not necessarily gender specific.

A father's physical or emotional absence has a huge impact on the development of self-esteem in children of both genders. A recent study (DelPriore and Hill, 2013) revealed an association between physical and psychological paternal absence and riskier sexual behavior in their daughters. When girls don't have a father or when their relationship with their father is compromised, they are vulnerable to feelings of inadequacy. Most of us want to be seen, noticed, and recognized as special by our parents. In contrast to being stared at, which is to be violated with a gaze and rendered an object, being looked at with affection and pride gives a sense of enjoyment. The sense of not being seen often creates a desperate need to be seen, a hunger to be seen that may cause an overvaluation on the body and diminished self-worth. Margo Maine believes the lack of father–daughter bond leads to body image issues, disordered eating patterns, and dieting. Bruce Ellis, an evolutionary developmental psychologist, has helped establish a connection between father absence and adverse outcomes for girls (Ellis et al., 2012), specifically with respect to early puberty and precocious and risky sexual behavior. Ellis speculates that boys might respond to a father's absence with a diminished ability in navigating relationships (Raeburn, 2014, p. 166).

If people do not successfully navigate developmental stages, they may find themselves stuck in a phase of life, in an attempt to get what they never got, creating a developmental arrest. Taryn, a successful professional woman in her mid-fifties, often talked referring to her "tiny" body and her "little tummy" as if she were a small child, rather than a capable adult woman. She talked about "my little feet," as if she were a tiny little girl in need of care, and associated being a little girl with getting help from men. For her, being little meant deserving the care and attention of others. By staying small and helpless, she could depend on a "big strong man" to take care of her.

Taryn lost her father early in life and transferred her father hunger to all men. She kept her body small and felt fragile and incapable, as a way of staying connected to this little girl self, remaining in need of care and attention but never truly recognizing or working through her feelings about having lost a father. By remaining a helpless little girl who had a succession of father substitutes rotate through her life, she never truly processed the loss of her father. Restricting food also served to express how deprived Taryn felt of the kind of care and nurturing she did not receive. The male substitutes she chose did not want to be her father, or did not measure up to her expectations of her fantasied "big strong man" and therefore were a source of constant disappointment.

Taryn had to come to terms with the loss of a father and face the reality that she would never get what she did not have in childhood. Only by mourning this loss was she able to finally embrace the reality of her womanhood and search for a true partner, not a father substitute.

As these clinical samples show, eating disorder behavior serves as the mind's way of protecting itself, a coping strategy that simultaneously communicates and hides unbearable thoughts and emotions from consciousness. By translating these hidden conflicts into awareness, patients are able to heal the past and transform their experiences of the present.

Chapter Four

Symbolic Representation

Dan, a successful professional in his late thirties, stretched rigidly on the couch, talking about his latest binge. The previous night he tossed cup after cup of dry oatmeal into a bowl, emptied brown sugar into the mix, poured in warm tap water, and shoveled it into his mouth. He choked down an entire container of Quaker Oats and a box of brown sugar, followed by cheese, unheated canned soup, dry cocoa powder, and other foods.

Then he went to the bathroom and forced himself to throw up.

"It was five days worth of food," Dan said. As he described the resulting physical pain, tears leaked from his eyes. He hastily wiped them away.

I felt a deep sadness and horror at the thought of that unpalatable paste of oatmeal, sugar, and tepid water, each bite both promise and torture. Dan had described similar binges before, and each time I reacted with both compassion and revulsion, as jarring a juxtaposition of emotion at the food combinations he created.

Dan often mentioned eating "five days of food" in one binge. He was in treatment five days per week, so the phrase was significant. When Dan was a young boy, a priest at his local church sexually abused him. Dan immediately told his mother, a single mom who relied on the church as the basis for her social life. She dismissed him, saying that he was "imagining" things and "making things up." Dan began using food for expression, filling himself up until he was in pain, somatically expressing his emotional pain. His binges also served as a means of enacting and perpetuating the abuse. He abused his body as the priest did, and ignored his emotional needs in much the same way as his mother had done.

Just as his mother had summarily dismissed the abuse, Dan dismissed my interpretations, my questions, and often, it seemed to me, my actual presence. Each session he arrived on time, talked about what was going on, wept, and essentially ignored everything that I said and asked. He regularly took in five days of food and then purged it. He could not connect with me; instead, he had a relationship with food as a substitute for me, taking it in, and then immediately getting rid of it and flushing it away. My analytic food was concretized into actual food, just as his desperate need for nurturing had been displaced onto food.

Sigmund Freud (1900) first introduced the notion of food as a symbol of mother (and mothering) when he writes, "love and hunger, I reflected, meet at the woman's breast" (p. 204). Ernest Jones (1918) elaborates on the nature of symbolism in his article, "The Theory of Symbolism," which was later summarized by Hanna Segal (1957) when she concludes, "when a desire has to be given up because of a conflict and repressed, it may express itself in a symbolic way, and the object of the desire which had to be given up can be replaced by a symbol" (p. 392). Segal, expanding on the ideas of Melanie Klein (1930), views symbolization as "a relation between the thing symbolized, the thing functioning as a symbol, and a *person* for whom the one represents the other" (1957, p. 392, italics by Segal).

Symbols are thus substitutes that represent the original object, in contrast to Hannah Segal's (1957) notion of a "symbolic equation" (p. 393), in which the thing symbolized is felt to be equal and the same as the original object. Unlike equations, which are used to deny the loss of an object, symbols are utilized to overcome loss. Segal underscored the shifting nature of symbolism and posited that in times of acute stress, a symbolic representation may unconsciously register as a symbolic equation. Unconsciously, this food = mother equation may be at the root of bingeing.

Donald Winnicott's (1953) concept of a "transitional object" (p. 89) that provides a maternal soothing function when the mother is absent or unavailable can also be understood as a type of symbol. The term "transitional object" was originally suggested by Winnicott (1953) to describe what he terms "the original not-me possession" (p. 91), such as a blanket or teddy bear, which symbolized a part-object, such as the breast, and "gives room for the process of becoming able to accept difference and similarity" (p. 92). He suggests that the blanket is a possession but not an internal object, and serves as both a symbol of the mother and the child, something that represents what lies between a child's sense of self and the child's actual experience of the mother.

This concept has often been misunderstood, as if the blanket or teddy bear itself represents the actual mother, and can be used by the child to feel connected to her in times of separation. Although a transitional object can symbolize the mother, it is more than a mental construct; it is an object that "does not exist inside or outside but rather is imaginatively 'created' in its meaning" (William Bauer, personal communication, 2011) and can therefore be simultaneously utilized in different ways, including soothing.

One of my patients, Elle, liked to curl up with a soft, cream-colored blanket that I kept on my couch. She snuggled in the blanket each session, telling me she felt safe and cocooned. During a particularly challenging period when she began to harm herself, cutting her arms and legs with a razor as a way of "feeling something else," I spontaneously gave her the blanket to bring home. That blanket was something tangible that represented not just me, but both of us; it was a symbol of the soft, safe, cozy, and warm connection that she experienced during our time together. Notably, when she cut, she left the blanket in another room. She could not harm herself in front of the blanket. The blanket became her lifeline to me, her "security blanket" in every sense, so that she could sense my presence when she was alone. Eventually, she felt my presence within her and stopped cutting to express her pain; instead, she used the blanket for comfort.

Winnicott (1958) also discusses the importance of developing "a capacity to be alone" (p. 416) with another person. This means that an individual is able to separate and individuate, can access an internal mother, and self-regulate. The capacity of being alone with another indicates the presence of a good internal object, something that is absent in many eating disorder patients. Unable to evoke or symbolize a positive representation of a soothing other, they binge when they are alone, only able to use food for soothing and self-regulation.

"BAD MILK"

Vicky, in her forties, married and the mother of three small children, was preoccupied with food. She worked in a restaurant, an experience that she found both compelling and torturous. She loved food and she hated food. Vicky grew up in a home environment that was alternately intrusive and depriving. She recalled that her mother always cooked too much, so food was the only abundance in a home environment in which love, comfort, and emotional nourishment were severely lacking. Her mother prepared several desserts at Thanksgiving, instead of only one or two. She made enough dinner to feed ten people instead of a family of four. Food became the primary symbol of the love for which Vicky longed, but which eluded her.

As a young child, Vicky was a picky eater. Her mother tried many different ways to make her eat but Vicky resisted all of these attempts. Finally, when she was seven years old, she made an effort to please her mother by eating seven bowls of cereal for breakfast while she was alone in the kitchen. When her mother came in the room, Vicky announced, "I ate breakfast," and recalled her mother's pleased face at this news. When Vicky shared how much cereal she had actually consumed, her mother's expression changed to one of dismay and horror. Vicky was confused by this reaction, believing that her mother would be happy. She imagined that if one bowl of cereal earned her mother's approval, surely seven would be even better.

In Vicky's childhood, food was love, but love often felt tainted and poisonous. She recalled an occasion in which her mother had made chocolate pudding with bad milk. She said, "She used powdered instant milk to make pudding. It had expired. She used it anyway, and we both (Vicky and her brother) got really bad food poisoning. We were both throwing up. To this day my mother laughs about it. She says, 'I'll never forget the time when you were both sick and you were fighting for the toilet.'"

This literal example of "bad milk" is an example of the dichotomous nature of food/love in Vicky's upbringing. Food was a symbol of both love and hate, with an amorphous boundary separating love and hate, so that they were almost interchangeable.

Shortly before starting therapy, Vicky was fired from her job at a restaurant. Her employers accused her of stealing a quart of milk and told her they had evidence on videotape. Although she consciously denied it, some nagging part of her mind wondered if she had indeed stolen the milk. She may have dissociated this theft, which suggests an unconscious belief that mother's milk must be stolen to be possessed.

The notion of food as a representation of mothering and parenting is one that contemporary writers and theorists conceptualize in very different ways. Self psychologists such as Alan Goodsitt (1983, 1997), Susan Sands (1991), and David Krueger (1989, 1997) conclude that infants and children who experience failure in empathic mirroring do not learn to self-soothe, failing to internalize the ability to identify and meet their emotional and physical needs. They turn to food when they feel anxious, depressed, lonely, or uncomfortable, because they lack the capacity to regulate these internal states. Food thus serves as a self-object, used for soothing by those who cannot trust that others can meet their needs. Unlike people, food is readily available, consistent, and may be taken in, or purged, at will. I think this viewpoint has some merit, in that food does provide soothing, yet this conceptualization fails to take into consideration those aspects of the psyche involved in repetition compulsion, because the food that people seek for comfort is often as unsatisfying, unfulfilling, and hurtful as the original bad objects.

Some theorists (Sugarman & Kurash, 1982; Glucksman, 1989; Krueger, 1989; Guinjoan, 2001) propose that food, or the patient's own body, serves as a transitional object, a representation of maternal function that cannot be given up. David Krueger (1997) writes, "Food, the first transitional object, is a symbol of all that the mother is or might have been, as well as a real, tangible, soothing substance which physiologically and emotionally regulates affect and tension states" (p. 618).

One critique of this perspective from Goodsitt (1983) is that a transitional object serves to facilitate development and an eating disorder does not promote development; therefore, the body or food cannot be viewed as a transitional object. Ideally, a transitional object serves the purpose of helping a child maintain a connection with an absent mother, a part of the separation and individuation process. Phyllis Sloate (2008) also disputes the notion of food or the body as a transitional object. I agree with Sloate, who views the patient's use of the body more along the lines of a fetish object, which "temporarily enhances a deficient and unstable body image and assuages separation anxiety, but does not promote progressive development" (p. 69).

Geraldine Shipton (2004) describes how a wish for a mother to help contain emotions or other painful affects is fused with the actual feeding experience, leading to the experience of food not only as a maternal representation but also as a "kind of controllable alternative to that person" (p. 76).

Other writers (e.g., Sands, 1991; Shulman, 1991) note the prevalence of dissociation in bulimic patients during the bingeing episodes. Diane Shulman (1991) proposes that bingeing recreates the experience of a mother without having to think about her, providing a means of dissociating from thought and reality while having a sense of maternal bonding. The patient thus creates a "retreat into a sensation-dominated world in which the bulimic creates an ever-present experience of the maternal object and/or a mindless, vacant state" (p. 333). This is consistent with what several of my patients have described as "zoning out" while eating. They refer to being "in the zone" or "going dead" or "numbing out," describing states of dissociation in which they are absent from themselves, often neither thinking nor feeling. This dissociative zone appears to be a means of returning to the bliss of nursing at a mother's breast (or with a bottle, regardless of the parent), of experiencing a connection with a parent in which nothing exists but that shared and blissful bonding.

Of course, not all feeding experiences are ideal. Alitta Kullman (2007) presents a theory of the "perseverant personality" as a new way of understanding eating disorders. She defines a perseverant personality as "a solitary and circular mode of being, thinking, and relating that is organized around a sustained physiological and psychological reliance on the feeding as a mode of thought-processing and affect regulation" (p. 718). Kullman suggests that infants whose mothers cannot connect with them during the feeding process might be hindered in their development, specifically with respect to connecting to the mind of another. This, in turn, impedes the ability to form links between their bodies and their minds.

These patients often "think" with their bodies instead of their minds, using food to regulate what cannot be mentalized and psychologically metabolized. Mentalization (Fonagy, 1991) refers to the ability to reflect upon one's own thoughts and ideas, and to discern the difference between perceptions and reality. Fonagy further defines mentalization as, "the capacity to conceive of conscious and unconscious mental states in oneself and others" (p. 641). In the absence of mentalization, eating becomes a method for trying to connect, when the capacity for thinking is not fostered. Purging serves the purpose of trying to relieve oneself of being a toxic container of uncontained affects. Many patients feel intensely uncomfortable but they are unable to ascribe a name to their intense emotions. I describe this as a "gray paint" feeling, as if the emotional experience is akin to messy, ugly gray paint, which is composed of an amalgamation of many colors. Only when the different colors are named and experienced as feeling states can people begin to reflect on their experience. In time, thinking replaces purging, and the behavior ceases.

FOOD AND AGGRESSION

In addition to using their bodies to talk about their internal conflicts in a disguised way, many people use their bodies as a primary target for their rage at others, castigating and disparaging their appearance when they are upset at other people or conflicted about relationships. Ritvo (1985), in a discussion at the Anna Freud Centre on the topic of "Fantasy and Body Representation in Physical Disturbances," states that, "aversion and rejection of the female body can be an expression of deep hostility to the mother, a dread of being swallowed up by her, of having no autonomy; or the aggression and hostility can provoke a fear of the loss of the mother's love, and without her love and protection an excessive fear of annihilation and helplessness" (p. 107).

Melanie Klein (1930) in her analysis of a four year old boy notes, "his defences against his destructive impulses proved to be a fundamental impediment to his development. He was absolutely incapable of any act of aggression, and the basis of this incapacity was clearly indicated at a very early period in his refusal to bite up food" (p. 29). Klein asserts that a child's ability to symbolize, meaning to mentally represent an idea, conflict, person, or wish, is a vital part of development, a process that I will discuss in more detail in a subsequent chapter. Eating disorder patients often express aggression through various modes of eating.

"CHASING MY TAIL"

Shelby, 22, a single woman who sought treatment for bulimia, had a history of anorexia that began in high school, and had recently began bingeing and purging. She worked as a dancer in music videos and stage performances, so her entire professional and personal life centered on her body.

Shelby's earliest recollection was of being alone in her crib, waiting for a seemingly interminable time for someone to come into the room. All her childhood memories suggest this same theme of isolation: spending time alone in her room, watching cartoons alone, playing with her dog in the backyard. Her brother was a few years younger but they had never been close. She recalled going to dinner with her family while she was in elementary school, the only time they all spent time together.

Although Shelby's weight was normal, her mother often criticized the way she looked and was preoccupied with her size. When Shelby was ten years old, she was sent to a weight loss camp for overweight kids. The counselors at this "fat camp" were perplexed as to why she was there, since she was not overweight, and the other campers could not relate to her, ostracizing her because her weight was normal. This was a confusing experience for Shelby, since her mother's constant negative comments had convinced her that there was something unacceptable about her body. To this day, her mother greets her by saying, "Shelby, your body looks good" rather than, "Shelby, you look good," or, "Nice to see you."

Lacking extended family and with few friends, Shelby was isolated throughout childhood. She joined an online community in which players represented themselves through animal avatars. She became part of a pack of online wolves, finding familial connections online that she lacked in reality. This virtual world was her primary refuge.

Shelby's main source of affection throughout childhood was her dog. At age ten she pretended to be a dog and was sent to therapy. Acting like a dog was seen as pathological behavior, rather than understood as representing a wish to be unconditionally loved. She later behaved in an overly pleasing way, like a puppy, to be accepted, and expressed her internal states through identifications with animals. For example, she said in session, "I keep talking about the same things. I keep chasing my tail."

The animal motif permeated many areas of her life: she wanted to play a wolf in a dance interpretation of *Little Red Riding Hood*, planning to symbolically devour others onstage; she described her father as being tricky "like a fox" and referred to vomiting as purging a "hairball" that had to come up. She had fantasies about being locked in a cold meat locker with an axe and attacking the hanging carcasses of cows.

Shelby smiled through anger, pain, fear, and sadness, a fixed joker's grin that made me wonder if her face hurt at the end of the day. As a child, when she had been upset, her parents told her to stop "acting" or "being so dramatic" and to calm down. Her father urged her to "be a warrior" and fight her feelings. After several months of treatment, Shelby finally began to express sadness and anxiety, but never rage. Anger, or anything resembling aggression, was consciously disavowed or unconsciously repressed, yet acted out through bulimia, or displaced onto animals.

Her language often referenced her aggression. She stated, "I've gained weight and I also want to keep eating. I had urges to buy myself a cake or pumpkin pie, and just kill it."

I asked, "Kill it?"

She nodded, seemingly oblivious to the aggressive nature of this fantasy. "Yeah, eat it."

She described her binges as "destructive" and often made references to destroying food. She said, "I have this fantasy lately of wanting to be locked in a cold meat locker with an axe and just going to town on this meat."

I asked her to tell me more about that fantasy. She responded, "Remember I told you I wanted to kill that pumpkin pie? I thought about getting a pie and stabbing it. I feel crazy, telling you this."

Her thoughts then turned to her mother. I speculated, "Perhaps she's the cow you want to attack in that very cold room."

Shelby's mother had never gotten an education or held a job, and lived off a succession of boyfriends and husbands. We discussed how her mother had made both herself, and Shelby, into a proverbial "piece of meat" and caused her to think that her body was the only thing about her that was meaningful. Shelby experienced difficulty tolerating the idea of being angry about this objectification, or about her mother's coldness toward her. Shelby felt guilty of having any aggressive emotions. In her words, "I could be so mad at someone, but as soon as I saw her, I'd be okay and I couldn't feel mad."

Shortly after we began to explore her resistance to experiencing rage, Shelby began to be consistently late to each session. I wondered if her consistent lateness might be a communication of some frustration or anger toward me. When I wondered about this, she initially denied the notion of being upset at me, or anyone, noting, "I'm such a nice little girl. I don't want to ruffle any feathers."

Shelby consistently denied her own human needs and emotions, particularly her aggression, rendering them animalistic. This description of her binges is a good example: "I often don't use utensils. It becomes a violent act and I use my hands. It's like I'm not even human."

Shelby had turned against her humanity. All needs and emotions, whether for food or for connection, were dehumanized, and her aggression was expressed through frenzied eating, subsequent attacks on herself for bingeing, as well as by the violent act of purging.

When we explored this, she said, "I feel so powerless as a human, so vulnerable. Like I'm little me, so helpless—needy, desperate, crying. Animals are powerful. They're powerful and beautiful. Desirable."

Human needs made her vulnerable, weak, and little, and only animals could be powerful, beautiful, and desirable, so there was no room for relationships with others. Shelby viewed all relational dyads as some permutation of the pursuer–distancer paradigm. She either sought out withholding others, as the pursuer, or she made herself an animal onstage, someone—or some thing—to be observed, but not touched, pursued by others, but not reached. Inherent in this outlook was the idea that there is no mutuality in relationships.

Shelby used thoughts about food or binges, as well as attacks on her body ("I'm fat, I'm disgusting") to distract from painful or upsetting states, especially her rage toward others. As she became more aware of her true needs, wishes, and feelings, Shelby began expressing them more directly, rather than through the murky language of disordered eating and dehumanization.

Like Shelby, many of my patients have at least one unresponsive, critical, or abusive parent, as well as a parent who is either unable or unwilling to protect them. I find that despite significant differences in socioeconomic and cultural backgrounds, this particular familial constellation is common for many people with eating disorders. Of course, there is no formula for predicting eating disorders. Many patients with eating disorders come from loving homes, and not everyone with a traumatic history develops an eating disorder. In those instances in which abusive, critical, and unresponsive parents or caregivers have led to internalizations of the abusive attitudes, once those identifications are identified and challenged, people can break free of the past, learning to relate to themselves, and others, in a healthier manner.

Chapter Five

Body Language

S. Freud (1923) writes that, "The ego is first and foremost a body ego" (p. 27), meaning that our earliest sense of self is a bodily self. In describing the genesis of ego development, he posits that, "the ego is ultimately derived from bodily sensations (pp. 26–27). The theory of psychoanalysis thus began with conflicts based on the experience of the body. Many of Freud's patients presented with what was known as hysteria, the conversion of mental conflict into bodily symptoms. Freud's early work was thus concerned with understanding the psychological conflicts that led to these physical symptoms.

Since Freud's time, psychoanalytic thought has shifted away from instinct theory, in which bodily tension was thought to facilitate a drive toward satisfaction, and toward a perspective that privileges relationships with others as a primary factor in human development. Objects relations theorists (Fairbairn, 1941, 1952; Winnicott, 1953, 1965, and others) believe that humans are not driven by bodily tensions but rather by attachment and love and belonging.

Willie Hoffer (1950) notes that an infant's attention is mostly focused upon nursing and avoidance of hunger. As a result, the mouth becomes the first important area of contact with external reality. That external reality is primarily concerned with the relationship to others. As Lewis Aron and Frances Anderson (1998) point out, our first bodily sensations are shaped by the care and quality of holding and handling that we receive from caregivers, and these interactions in turn influence the sense of self. These early experiences impact our expectations about relationships from a biological, relational, and psychological perspective (Cozolino, 2013). Thus, "the internalization of early relationships is a central aspect to the consolidation of self and our ability to cope with challenge, stress and trauma" (Cozolino, 2013, p. 117).

Feldman (2006) suggests that when bodily experiences cannot be reflected and processed, symptoms such as eating disorders can develop. Feldman sees eating disorders as a "second skin" (p. 60) that serves as a psychic layer of protection from the painful emotions associated with trauma, such as help-lessness, betrayal, and neglect. Eating disorder behavior may serve as a form of withdrawal, a way of retreating from the perceived dangers of the external world into an internal world, a type of psychic retreat (Steiner, 1993) that protects from pain but also prevents the pleasure of human connection. By keeping themselves safe from the possibility of being hurt in relationships, eating disorder patients make their bodies into prisons, keeping them safe from pain, at the expense of emotional freedom.

MIND–BODY SPLIT

Eating disorder patients often split themselves into a psychological self and a body self, responding to their bodily needs in a punitive manner, often with undisguised contempt. The body is experienced as something separate, with which a person is at war. Many report looking in the mirror or catching a glimpse of their reflection and feeling a sense of revulsion, along with the sense that the reflected image is not the "real" them. One woman poked at her stomach and declared, "This is not me. I don't know who it is, but it's not me."

Conceptualizing a patient's relationship to his or her own body is a crucial part of therapeutic exploration. Many people conceptualize their bodies as their only self-definition, without any regard for the emotional, relational, creative, intellectual, or spiritual aspects of themselves. I once treated a psy-chotherapy patient who had an extremely harsh internal critic and suffered a great deal because of her self-castigation. When I suggested cultivating a kinder attitude toward herself and practicing a higher degree of self-care, she protested that she took wonderful care of herself. She described herself as the "queen of self care" and pointed out that she treated herself to weekly manicures and hair styling appointments, as well as monthly facials and mas-sages. I acknowledged that she was taking extremely good care of her body, but framed this as grooming, not self-care.

"What do you mean?" she asked, baffled. "What other self is there?"

She had no other concept of her "self" other than her physical form. For her, and for many people with eating disorders and body image disturbances, the body functions as the primary self. Patients who define themselves by their appearance alone believe that they will be good enough only when their bodies are good enough. They think they can get other people to like them, hire them, accept them, and appreciate them by changing their appearance. They unconsciously imagine that by ridding themselves of excess weight they are getting rid of the aspects of themselves they despise. They believe they control their world by controlling their weight.

John Russon (2003) writes of the concept of embodiment, "To be a body is to be a specific identity that is open to involvement with others. Indeed, pleasure and pain are two faces of this involvement, the ways in which that which we are involved either welcomes or hinders our determinacy. Our bodies are the living process by which we establish contact with reality" (p. 21). He goes on to describe how the culture has facilitated a way of thinking about bodies in terms of size and physical attributes, which has created a sense of a body as an object rather than a subject. He notes that this culture has led to a "fundamental separation between body and experience, as if 'to experience' were one thing and 'to be a body' something separate and unrelated" (pp. 22–23).

Our cultural preoccupation with the body has created a zeitgeist in which the body is perceived as the primary self for many people, not just those with eating disorders. Joan Jacobs Brumberg (1997) studied the diaries of teenage girls over the last century and noted major shifts during that time span. A hundred years ago, adolescent girls wrote about their wish to become better people, to embrace certain morals and virtues, which were the keys to self-improvement. Girls in later decades began writing more about their appearance, moving away from embracing values as a means to achieve self-improvement and focusing on their skin, hair, clothes, and weight. By the 1990s, girls were more concerned about improving their bodies than their minds or values.

Simultaneously, there are other societal messages that we are *not* our bodies. After years of publically struggling with her weight, Oprah Winfrey (2008) wrote in an editorial piece, "I am not my body." She was making the point that her body did not define her identity, but in doing so, she appeared to disavow her body as part of her self-concept. These messages and cultural ideals are confusing, since our bodies and our minds are both part of who we are as individuals. The perceived separation between them is problematic for many eating disorder patients, who focus on their bodies over all other aspects of their identities.

Winnicott (1949b) in his seminal article "Mind and Its Relation to the Psyche-Soma" proposes that the mind and body are not separate, but instead are interrelated and influence each other. The psyche refers to the mental structure of a person, and the soma refers to the physical body. When things go well in the early mother–infant relationship, the infant develops a healthy sense of self and feels at one with its body and mind. When things do not go well—especially with respect to erratic, or unpredictable, parenting—an infant does not develop a connection between psyche and soma, leading to a mind–body split.

According to Winnicott (1953), a feeding experience with a "good enough mother" (p. 96) promotes the development of object differentiation and the ability to love and be loved. When things do not go well, development is compromised, leading to maladaptive patterns of relating to self and others. The connection between good maternal feeding and the internalization of a positive maternal object is clear; without it, a person does not develop a consistent "self" in the sense of an entity that exists in both psyche and soma, with an ability to provide self-soothing or comfort. Given such deficits, turning to the body is a strategy to cope, and to find substitutes for unavailable, inconsistent relationships.

Samuel Ritvo (1984) references the use of the body as a way of communicating internal conflict. He stated, "the body, its image, and its functions are the most readily available instrumentality for the representation and actualization of the various aspects of psychic conflict" (p. 467). Similarly Joyce McDougall (1989) proposes that psychosomatic patients have a basic inability to link psyche to soma, and thus cannot symbolize bodily sensations as representations of emotions or conflict.

J. L. Sacksteder (1989) points out that some people experience "estrangement and alienation" between their minds and bodies. Their bodies are often a source of shame, and humiliation, rather than pleasure. They use their minds to control their bodily needs, and experiencing their bodies as being at war with their minds, creating a sadomasochistic relationship between aspects of the self. Sacksteder states that this condition is often exemplified in anorexia nervosa, where the self and the body are seen as separate. He says, "rather than being identified with their body, liking it, enjoying it, caring for it, nurturing and developing it, they hate it, and cruelly, unrelentingly attack it" (p. 38).

In my experience, people with eating disorders turn their bodies into objects rather than experiencing their bodies as subjects. Furthermore, they abuse their bodies, starving, stuffing, hating, despising, and loathing everything about their bodies. Many people who develop eating disorders also utilize their bodies to express what they cannot say in words; often, to articulate through the body what they are unable to consciously allow their minds to think or feel. Christopher Bollas (1987) coined the term "unthought known" to describe the state of knowing something but not allowing oneself to know it, so that it remains unformulated and dissociated from consciousness, not available for discussion or examination. Much like Freud's (1895e) concept of primal repression, the unthought known refers to early ways of understanding and interpreting the world that determine expectations in life but remain out of awareness. Alvin Frank (1969) calls this "the unrememberable and the unforgettable" (p. 48).

These early experiences are stored in the unconscious mind but not consciously remembered. They continue to impact behavior until they are brought to consciousness and processed. The unconscious enactment of the unremembered past is an aspect of what Freud (1914) referred to as "a compulsion to repeat" (p. 151), and which I will discuss in more detail in a subsequent chapter.

For individuals who struggle with eating disorders, their relationship to their bodies serves as a means of reconstructing and repeating past relationships and intrapsychic conflicts. Behavior with food may be understood as a means of expressing psychological conflict through physical action. The body is used as a means of enacting fears and hopes about their relationships and their place in the hearts and minds of others.

Since patients with eating disorders use their bodies to express what their minds cannot, the challenge of treatment is to decode the hidden communication, to bring that which is hidden from awareness into consciousness and make it available for working through, as a means of achieving what Anna O. (S. Freud, 1910) called the "talking cure" (p. 13).

"I FEEL FAT"

When people complain that they "feel fat," I ask them to share what they mean, inviting them to elucidate the associations, fears, disgust, and shame embedded in their use of the word. I remind them that fat is a substance, not a feeling. We must discover the emotions, conflicts, and thoughts that are embedded in their description of themselves as fat. The term "fat" usually functions as an umbrella expression that covers a range of thoughts, emotions, conflicts, and fears. Being fat may express a sense of being too much for others to handle, or of taking up too much in the world, or of having wants, needs, and emotions that are too big and overwhelming. Some people have no language for their internal states, and experience difficulty identifying what's going on in their internal worlds. They use "fat" to describe anything that is too much or too uncomfortable, and often lack the ability to describe any emotion.

In our first meeting, Peter, 59, related a personal history of egregious abuse and neglect by his caretakers in a voice as conversational as if he were discussing the weather. He had survived a schizophrenic mother, an alcoholic father, a verbally abusive stepmother, and he felt tremendous shame at having learning disabilities as a child. Despite these disabilities, he had become an extremely successful businessman. I noted his conversational tone as he described his traumatic history, as well as his generally open and relaxed manner as he spoke. I asked what it was like to tell me about the challenging and painful things that had happened to him. Peter shrugged, and said he was fine with it.

"What are you feeling right now?" I pressed.

He took a moment to reflect. "Well," he said, "It's a little chilly in here."

Peter did not have language for what was going on emotionally and could only speak of his emotions in terms of physical sensations. The inability to symbolize bodily sensations with words is associated with a very early developmental level. Anna Freud (1974) describes this period as one in which, "Every upheaval in the bodily sphere causes mental distress, crying, etc., while every mental upset such as shock, frustration, anxiety causes physical upheaval" (p. 65).

Stanley Greenspan (1997) connects various somatic and mental abilities to different developmental stages. The earliest level, somatic learning, was associated with self-regulation and self-soothing. His concept of a "prerepresentational" level of development, in which there is no "representational elaboration" (ability to symbolize, p. 24) but only a fragmented sense of self and other, can be particularly helpful in terms of understanding a person's internal organization. Greenspan describes how individuals stuck at a prerepresentational level "use acting out of behaviors rather than representing them. Or they use descriptions of behaviors or actions rather than describing their feelings" (p. 403). Lacking the ability to identify and process what is going on in their heads and hearts, they react instead of reflecting.

Rose Edgecumbe (1984) describes how an infant's ability to talk and think is often hindered by a mother's inability to respond appropriately or translate the infant's somatic communications into verbal expressions of needs or feelings. Somatization becomes the only manner of communication available to the child, both relationally and intrapsychically. Jane, who thought she would gain 135 pounds, the weight of her mother, was expressing herself somatically through her weight gain. Developmentally, she had failed to achieve the ability for representational thinking and remained at the level of somatic discharge. My challenge with Jane and with other eating disorder patients is to help them symbolize their internal worlds through words and verbal expression, rather than actions.

Peter Fonagy and Mary Target (1998) propose that "mentalizing" is the result of a process in which children develop the ability to interpret other people's experiences, intentions, and thoughts. This, in turn, helps them achieve the capacity to reflect on their own internal experiences, attitudes, and emotions. Fonagy and Target view mentalizing as "an ability that we suggest underlies affect regulation, impulse control, self-monitoring, and the experience of self-agency" (p. 92). This was the case with Peter, who initially could only register physical sensations such as being chilly. As Peter developed the ability to think about his thoughts, emotions, wishes, and fears, he was able to stop his bulimic behavior and process conflicts, instead of purging them. Recently he wept as he related the news that a friend had passed away unexpectedly, openly grieving and sharing his thoughts and feelings with remarkable eloquence. He recalled his previous inability to identify what he felt, choking out the words through his tears. "This work we do," he said, "it's bringing me alive." My eyes filled as we sat in companionable silence. I thought about how Peter had painstakingly learned to put words to emotions, to hold opposing thoughts about others, and to emerge from inertia into a world of emotional richness. His shift epitomizes the beauty and power of psychoanalysis, and underscores the reality that it's never too late to change.

Other patients report painful events in concrete somatic terms. If someone hurts their feelings, they will often say, "My stomach hurts" instead of something along the lines of, "My feelings were so hurt that I got stomach pain." They do not connect the psyche to the soma, and experience emotional and physical pain as separate and unconnected events. A large part of the therapeutic work with these patients is to help them learn to translate the language of their bodies into verbal communications instead of continuing to express unresolved conflict somatically.

In the absence of a connection between physical pain and mental thoughts or emotions, many patients rely on their bodies as a primary means of expression. As Edgecumbe (1984) puts it, "Body language comprises somatic symptoms and physical actions, verbal language includes the various levels of thought and some levels of fantasy" (p. 153). The body is then the primary means by which a person gives expression to emotions, thoughts, wishes, and conflicts. Hurt feelings are experienced as bodily pain. People who binge the point of physical pain may be converting their emotional pain to physical pain.

The body is the stage on which emotions are acted out, but never truly processed. In a speech on the topic of trauma, Robert Stolorow (October 27, 2011), noted that mis-attunements and traumatic attachments in the mother–child dyad leads to developmental problems, and renders emotional experiences "inchoate, diffuse and largely bodily." This description captures a patient's recent description of her internal struggle after several failed attempts to contact her mother: "I tried to call her maybe three or four times and she didn't pick up. I thought, 'You have to stop. She's not there.' So I thought about that and then my stomach started hurting. I was massaging it. I told myself that I wasn't hungry." In fact, she was hungry, ravenously hungry for the maternal love that eluded her.

Another patient, after a disappointing encounter with a boyfriend, said, "I just realized how ugly it made me feel. I feel like I'm so, so ugly." The only way she was able to express disappointment was by configuring it as physical ugliness.

A man who argued with his wife over her lack of responsiveness to his needs reported, "She's stressing me out. I'm so tired that I'm in pain." In this way, he converted his resentful and hurt feelings about his wife into physical exhaustion and physical pain.

Another man who was dealing with painful memories of his past experienced difficulty expressing that pain in emotional terms. He consistently turned to his physicality to express his emotions. For example, he said, "My skin is so bad. I feel like it has to heal. I can't work with skin this bad. I don't want to cover it up." Unbeknownst to himself, he was expressing that he could no longer deny or cover up many bad feelings, and it was his psyche that needed to heal, although he could only speak of it in somatic terms.

A few years ago I came down with the flu and had to cancel my appointments for a week, causing one analytic patient to miss three days of analysis. Upon my return, she denied having any thoughts or feelings about the three-day break. She said, "What I want to talk about is that I'm dissatisfied with my body. I haven't worked out in three days. I feel so upset with myself."

She could be upset at missing three days of working out at the gym, but could not get in touch with her feelings about missing treatment, or allow herself feelings toward me. She could not entertain the idea of being upset with me, since she knew I had been sick. "That's not fair to you," she later said. "It's not your fault you were sick, so how could I be upset?" Because she could not allow herself to think or articulate her true thoughts, her body became the target for these upset feelings.

Some people report eating until they are so full that they are about to burst. This may be an unconscious way of experiencing limits and boundaries in the physical world. One patient told me that by feeling food pressing out against the limits of her skin, she knew she was there, that she existed as a separate person. She feared losing herself in a merger with another person, and craved reassurance that she was a separate, intact person. Conversely, being separate was also a source of terror, because it meant losing the connection and bond with the other. The physical boundary of skin provided reassurance that her body was whole and separate, and that she had not been engulfed or subsumed by another. She also poignantly stated that when she was full to the point of bursting, "it's like my skin is giving me a hug."

Another way of thinking about being stuffed to the point of bursting is that in the state of fullness, the body is turned into a container. Thomas Ogden (1989) proposes the autistic-contiguous position as a mode of generating experience:

> The autistic-contiguous position is a sensory-dominated, pre-symbolic mode of generating experience which provides a good measure of the boundedness of human experience and the beginnings of a sense of the place where one's

experience occurs. Anxiety in this mode consists of an unspeakable terror of the dissolution of boundedness resulting in feelings of leaking, falling or dissolving into endless, shapeless space. (p. 138)

Ogden's description of the autistic-contiguous position as a "sensory dominated, pre-symbolic mode of generating experience" brought to my mind the possibility that many binge eating disorder patients may use their bodies as containers for overwhelming and anxiety-provoking emotions. They eat to the point of terrible pain; the fullness and pain served as temporary boundaries, but quickly dissolved. Thus, the physical boundary of the body provides an illusion of containment for bad feelings, which are never worked through. The food is metabolized, but not the feelings, and the cycle of eating continues.

"I Can Control Others through Controlling My Body"

Marie, 38, had been morbidly obese since childhood. Both her parents worked long hours in the liquor store they owned. Her mother gave up aspirations to become an actress when she married, and Marie remembered her as angry and depressed most of the time. Marie spent most afternoons after school with her grandmother, who loved to bake strudel, cookies, and cake. If Marie was sad, lonely, or depressed, her grandmother fed her desserts. When Marie was in high school, her grandmother assured her that if she just lost weight, boys would line up around the block to be with her. Throughout college and graduate school, Marie blamed her lack of romantic companionship on her weight. She later discovered in therapy that she was terrified of dating. She equated having a relationship with losing her autonomy and identity, because her mother had given up her dreams to marry. By recognizing and challenging this idea of relationships leading to the erosion of selfhood, she was finally able to lose weight. When she finally started dating, Marie was startled, almost indignant, to discover that finding a partner was a far more complex process than merely changing her size.

"I thought all I had to do was lose weight and somehow the guy would magically appear," she exclaimed, crestfallen that a smaller body would not make a man automatically fall in love with her.

The wish to control others through the control of the body is linked to the concept of omnipotent control, the illusion of influence over all aspects of one's life, the idea that a person has agency over aspects of the self as well as other people. This may be understood as a response to the state of helplessness. Helplessness is one of the most profoundly difficult experiences a human being can have, one that is often met with the wish to "do" something, to turn passive to active. One means by which people deal with the state of helplessness is to take an action. Losing weight or focusing on food can give people a sense of mastery over their circumstances.

Helplessness is a feeling that most people cannot bear to experience, either on its own or because it intensifies other painful or upsetting feelings. Helplessness is defined (*Merriam-Webster*) as the state of being (1) unable to help oneself, (2) weak or dependent, (3) deprived of strength or power, (4) incapacitated. Helplessness is connected to intense feelings of vulnerability and fears about dependency. Anger, productivity, withdrawal, and/or denial are ways of distracting from the intolerable state of helplessness. In his thorough explication of the psychology of addiction, Lance Dodes (1990, 2002, 2011) notes the specific role that the state of helplessness plays in addictive behavior. He posits that patients with addictions are driven to repeat their addictive behaviors in response to feelings of overwhelming helplessness. The addictive act, he says, functions to reverse that helplessness through taking a displaced action. This action, such as taking a drink, turning to food, gambling, working too much, and so forth, becomes what we name the addiction (alcoholism, binge eating, gambling addiction, workaholism).

Hoffer and Buie (2016) maintain that the feeling of helplessness "underlies other intolerable feelings such as incompetence, shame, embarrassment, humiliation, weakness, panic, isolation, rage and hate. It cannot be overemphasized how excruciating and unbearable these feelings can be" (p. 2). As Hoffer and Buie explain, anger is an active emotion, whereas helplessness is a passive emotion. People often get angry with themselves for eating, or for weighing too much, to avoid the passivity of helplessness. Similarly, productivity is another way of turning passive to active. Focusing on achievements is a strategy that distracts from helplessness. Thinking about food, weight, and calories are examples of focusing on "doing" rather than "feeling." Withdrawal is a way of denying helplessness and is often expressed in anorexia, when people withdraw from food, from wants, from needs, and usually from people. This may be helplessness over situations or over biology; anorexia is often triggered by the bodily changes of puberty. Denial, or protestations, that the situation "isn't a big deal" is a way of minimizing the reality of a situation over which a person feels helpless.

In the span of three months, one of my patients lost her father to cancer and her grandmother to heart disease. Shortly afterward, her brother launched a legal battle to take over their father's estate. My patient began to binge and became completely out of control with food. She was helpless in the face of death and powerless to stop her brother from trying to take over the estate. Her solution was to direct her anger toward herself for eating, thereby distracting herself from the intolerable state of helplessness.

Another woman recalled that many years earlier she began treatment with a psychologist to whom she felt a strong connection. She felt a sense of hope that she could overcome the eating disorder she had battled since high school.

When her insurance company made it difficult for her to have access to her benefits, she was unable to continue to see the psychologist. Her subsequent challenges to the insurance company were unsuccessful, leaving her feeling powerless and angry. She began restricting food as a way of both expressing how deprived she felt of the therapist to whom she had bonded, and also a way of taking action, her panacea for helplessness.

Another patient, a survivor of horrific sexual abuse by a trusted family member, a trauma compounded by maternal neglect and indifference, began restricting as an adolescent. She told me that she could not bear "the feeling of food in my body" and felt physically repulsed by eating. Her father's intrusion into her body had become generalized to food. In essence she felt violated by food, raped by food, and keeping food out of her body was a means of having mastery over the abuse and feeling empowered. She poignantly said, "I thought by changing myself, I could change my story." Her anorexia was an attempt to reverse the powerlessness she felt about the abuse, and furthermore to somehow undo the reality of that abuse.

Eating disorders are common among survivors of childhood sexual abuse. It is estimated that over 30 percent of all individuals seeking treatment for eating disorders have a history of sexual abuse (Connors & Morse, 1993) at the hands of parents, family members, teachers, and strangers. In a study of sexually abused children, over 14 percent became obese after the abuse occurred (Dubowitz et al., 1993).

Shame is a common theme in victims of sexual abuse. In his book on shame, Andrew Morrison (1996) explores the connection between the experience of shame and the incidence of childhood sexual abuse. He views eating disorders as a way of trying to control shameful feelings by controlling the body. He sees anorexia or bulimia as a desperate attempt to get rid of intense feelings of emptiness and despair, and as a way to punish the body for the abuse. Anecdotally, I find that the number of my patients who experienced sexual abuse is closer to 50–60 percent. Many identified with the perpetrator in some way, abusing their bodies as a way of reliving and reenacting the trauma. They often feel intense shame and hatred of their bodies.

Childhood emotional abuse has also been found to be a predictor of eating pathology (Groleau et al., 2012). Researchers believe that the experience of abuse impacts self-esteem and the capacity for affect regulation, both of which are factors that impact the severity of eating disorders.

"I'LL BE MORE CONFIDENT WHEN I LOSE WEIGHT"

Delia, 38, a single, professional woman, grew up in a family in which conflict was never expressed. Her parents rarely argued, never raised their voices, and she never saw either of them cry. Her stay-at-home mother and her father, a businessman who worked late hours, drank wine as a way of relaxing and avoiding discomfort. The covert communication was that any modicum of dissention had to be avoided—with alcohol if necessary. Delia never learned how to identify, regulate, and express her emotional reactions. She turned against herself when she was upset with others, attacking her weight or disparaging her food choices as a way of avoiding disappointment in others. Delia also modeled her relationships with others over that of her parents, in which her father's needs and wishes took primacy over those of her mother, who deferred to him. Delia automatically made the wishes of her friends more important than hers and did not allow herself to recognize when she was upset or disappointed in them. Instead, she stuffed those thoughts and emotions down with food and subsequently became upset and disappointed at herself for eating too much.

As Delia learned to identify and tolerate difficult emotions and conflicts, she slowly stopped turning to food to cope and lost a considerable amount of weight. After an incident highlighted a friend's indifference to her feelings, Delia felt extremely disappointed and angry. Instead of turning that anger and disappointment on herself, as she had previously done, she began attacking other aspects of her appearance. She "felt old" and went on to criticize her face, which she thought was "falling down." She said, "My eyes are disappearing, and my smile isn't the same. I look horrible."

We examined her relationship to her friend, whose casual and consistent maltreatment of Delia was "getting old" and causing her to lose her smile. It was hard for her to "face" the "horrible" behavior of this friend. Delia had attempted to convert disappointing emotions into physical characteristics. By identifying the true source of her issues with her body, she accessed her anger, disgust, and disappointment toward her friend.

Another patient was convinced that people were always staring at her and judging her weight. After gastric bypass surgery, she lost over 150 pounds and was overjoyed to finally feel like "a normal person." One day she came to therapy visibly upset and started to cry, again convinced that people were staring at her and judging her appearance. These new fears were centered on her nose, which she feared was now too big for her smaller face. Given this moving target of perceived deficiency, it's crucial to address the underlying sense of defect that is so tormenting. The problem had never been her weight, and certainly was not her nose; the problem was her deep sense that there was something wrong with her.

I previously described Fairbairn's description of "the moral defence" which is tied to the experience of helplessness. Children find it unbearable to feel a sense of helplessness over neglect, abuse, indifference, or even the lack of interest from others, particularly from parents or important caregivers and manage this state by rendering themselves the bad ones; if they can figure out what is wrong with them, they can make themselves good, and in doing so, finally get the good treatment that eludes them. This provides the illusion of control over one's circumstances and of hope, since the notion that changing oneself will lead to a change of environment keeps hope alive. This strategy that is based on hope ultimately becomes a conviction of one's own badness, one that lasts far longer than childhood. Recently a patient revealed that she's always sensed there was something wrong with her. "I feel as if I'm wearing my punishment," she said, articulating how the extra weight kept her from feeling good, believing on some level that she had to suffer for her innate badness.

Embedded in the moral defense is the idea of mastery, that people can control or change their circumstances by changing themselves. For eating disorder patients, the "myself" becomes the physical self. They believe that transforming their physical selves is a means by which they can control their environments, including their relationships to others.

"I Can Lose the Unwanted Parts of Myself by Losing Weight"

Many people hope that when they lose weight or achieve physical perfection, their lives will improve, and they will be more confident, outgoing, and relaxed. They cling to the belief that by controlling the number on the scale, they can manage many aspects of their lives, including their relationships, jobs, and general success. Weight therefore symbolically represents the qualities they want to get rid of—such as shyness, insecurity, anxiety, and so forth—so that losing weight becomes equivalent to losing those unacceptable "parts" of themselves that they despise, concretized as pounds, inches, and flesh. It is far less painful to focus on losing weight than think about shedding disappointments, fears, concerns, worries, and anxieties.

Brittany, 21, had an on-and-off relationship with her college boyfriend, who moved across the country to pursue graduate studies. They continued their relationship on a long-distance basis, until he met someone new and broke things off with Brittany. Her first thought was to speculate whether or not the new girlfriend was thinner than she; her next thought was that she knew exactly how she would get the boyfriend back.

She confidently said, "Once I lose weight, he'll like me again." In this way, Brittany clung to the illusion that she could control her boyfriend's feelings for her by controlling her weight.

Conversely, many people consciously or unconsciously believe that being overweight staves off unwanted attention from the opposite sex. They keep themselves safe by wearing a protective layer of weight. One woman brought in a photo of herself as a chubby, adorable baby, smiling into the camera. She scrutinized the photo and observed, "Look, my body is exactly the same now."

She complained that her weight made her into "a blob" and kept her from being attractive to men. She saw the extra weight as neutralizing her femininity, despite the fact that men often asked her out and showed interest in getting to know her. Underlying her complaints about her size were deep anxieties about relationships. This woman feared that connection meant a loss of self, so her unconscious solution was to avoid relationships by staying a "blob" that was genderless and asexual. Perceiving herself as a "blob" was thus a means of protecting herself from being subsumed in a relationship.

Another patient stated that she preferred being skinny and tiny, like an adolescent girl. Without womanly curves, she maintained the illusion of being a little girl, keeping her stuck in a developmental phase that she had passed decades earlier. She dated older men, hoping to be taken care of in a way that would make up for what she didn't get in adolescence. These stand-in fathers were a source of constant disappointment, as her original father had been.

In all these examples, people used their bodies as a means of reinforcing the an illusion of having omnipotent control over others, protecting themselves from the perceived dangers of connection with others, and furthermore giving themselves the ability to get rid of unwanted aspects of self.

Chapter Six

The Wish–Fear Dilemma

According to Greek mythology, Scylla was a sea nymph who captured the attention of the god Poseidon, whose jealous wife poisoned the waters where Scylla bathed, transforming her into a six-headed beast with rows of sharp teeth. Charybdis also started life as a nymph, but after stealing and eating a god's sheep, she was turned into a whirlpool, doomed to eternally suck in and disgorge water. Thus, both nymphs were punished for transgressions relating to appetite; Scylla for rejecting Poseidon's lust and Charybdis for greed.

Embedded in the myth of Scylla and Charybdis is the notion that hunger—for love, for food—may prove to be dangerous. Similarly, people who struggle with eating disorders often learn in childhood that hungering for love, attention, and kindness is futile. When families covertly or overtly enforce the idea that basic needs for warmth, compassion, safety, and love are wrong, children become hostile to these needs, or embarrassed by them. They grow into adults who struggle with their appetites for love, and for life, and unconsciously use food to enact their conflicts over such longings. They wish for love and connection, yet fear the consequences.

Johnson (1985) describes how this dilemma presents itself in bulimic patients, although the conflict he describes is common to many eating disorder patients. "The wish-fear dilemma revolves around the patient's wish for someone to identify and respond to her needs, which is juxtaposed against her fear that allowing someone to see the needy and dependent side will collapse the self-esteem and self-organization" (p. 33).

The wish–fear dilemma is similar to the "need–fear dilemma" described by Burnham et al. (1969) in relation to schizophrenics, who simultaneously depend upon and fear their objects, but I think restricting this need–fear paradigm to schizophrenics is too narrow a focus. Many people experience conflicts between desire and dread. The hope of a new experience, the wish

83

for a sense of connection, safety, and trust within the context of a relationship may facilitate a concurrent terror of loss, disconnection, abandonment, rejection, and utter loss in all humans, not just those who are schizophrenic. This also plays out in the therapeutic relationship. Patients wish for the analyst to understand and approve of them, but simultaneously harbor fears of discovering a harsh, judgmental critic in their analyst. I prefer the term "wish–fear" to describe this dilemma, as it seems to most accurately describe the quandary of simultaneous hope and dread.

DEPENDENCY VS INDEPENDENCE

Michelle, 47, began a sexual relationship with a married man and soon became upset that she was not a priority in his life. "I want him to choose me," she sighed. "Even though I don't actually want him." Obese since childhood, Michelle had never married, nor had she ever had a romantic relationship with a man, although she had several sexual encounters with married men. She enjoyed the power she felt over men who wanted her as a sexual partner, and asserted that she did not want anything more than sex from these men. Although she rejected the possibility of a deeper level of involvement, she also resented it when these men returned home to their wives. She feared being with someone who was available, yet simultaneously experienced a deep and powerful loneliness that she symbolically filled with food.

Michelle was the oldest of three children. Her mother died when she was five years old and her father quickly remarried a woman who was depressed. Since her father was in the military, he was deployed for months during active service, leaving Michelle and her siblings to the care of his new wife, a virtual stranger who was unable to adequately respond to their needs or emotions. In the absence of a responsive maternal figure, Michelle took on the role of a mother. She recalled leaving elementary school and going to a house where her toddler-age sister was in daycare, picking her up, and walking her home. She then doled out snacks and prepared dinner because her stepmother was too depressed to cook. Michelle became "a little mother" and nurtured her siblings, but had little experience of being mothered by another.

At other times, Michelle's stepmother snooped through her room and read her private diary, or listened in on her telephone conversations with friends. She often walked in on Michelle while she was in the bathroom, oblivious to Michelle's right to privacy. Michelle experienced her stepmother as unpredictably distant or intrusive. All her relationships were marked by withdrawal and loss, because of her mother's death, her father's deployments, and her stepmother's depression, or intrusive, given her stepmother's lack of appropriate boundaries.

Michelle learned that taking care of others was a way of having power in a relationship. As long as other people depended on her for care, she felt a sense of agency and purpose. Michelle's wish–fear dilemma about closeness was expressed in relationship to her body and with people. When she needed maternal care, she turned to food instead of to people. She had no internal maternal figure upon which to draw upon, instead relying on a representation of that maternal function—food. She chose men who were married, as they were safe and "could not leave" her or be too available and thus potentially too close. Despite the safety of these relationships, she felt a constant longing for more connection, one that was satiated by food instead of by relationships. Michelle believed that dependency would lead to pain, loss, or withdrawal, and that only by being fiercely independent could she protect herself.

Inherent in this dilemma is the question of what is meant by the term "self" and how the "self" develops. Margaret Mahler (1963, 1972) developed the separation–individuation theory of child development, positing that an infant first perceives oneness with the mother, and through a series of subphases develops the ability to distinguish himself or herself from his or her mother, and eventually discovers his or her own identity and individuality.

Mahler proposed that an infant initially experiences the mother as part of the self, a unit within the larger environment. The "mother" I refer to may be a biological mother, an adopted parent, or a primary caregiver, regardless of gender. During the first five months of life, the baby experiences herself and the mother as one, and progresses to a phase in which she slowly begins to distinguish herself from her mother, eventually discovering her own individuality. This separation–individuation phase is the period in which the baby begins to explore the environment and starts to recognize she is a separate and different person from the mother. Separation refers to the development of recognizing that the baby and mother are two separate people. Individuation refers to the development of the sense of identity, ego, and having a separate mind.

At around fifteen months, the baby realizes that being physically apart from his or her mother means they are two distinct people. This rapprochement phase is characterized by separation anxiety, which Fred Pine (1979) later defined as the "anxiety over a sense of separateness" (p. 226) rather than of separation. Pine clarifies that true separation anxiety is in regard to an undifferentiated other, so that it is actually a fear of separateness. Pine defines individuation as "the taking on of those characteristics that mark a person in his own right" (p. 226). He also notes the irony that the term "individuation" refers to taking on aspects of others. The child may vacillate between staying merged with the mother and becoming more independent. During the rapprochement phase of this process (around fifteen months of age through two years old), the toddler navigates separation from the mother. I recall each of my children giddily finding their independence and running across a room, then checking back to see that I was there, or returning to the safety of a hug when the distance seemed too far.

Initially, the child starts to explore his or her world on her own and wants to share discoveries with the parents, which leads to a conflict between staying connected to the parents and becoming more independent. Meissner (2009) points out the difficulties that arise at this stage. "At this juncture the child may show increased irritability; an increase of anxiety, particularly in the form of renewed stranger and separation anxiety; sleep disturbances; and a pattern of marked ambivalence and hostility to the mother reflected in alternate clinging and rejecting, as well as in childish attempts at coercing the parent and in negativistic behavior, even to the point of temper tantrums" (p. 263). The risk is that a mother will not be able to discern that underlying the tantrum is a profound wish for comfort and safety, and that she will respond with impatience, anger, or rejection, which can lead to an anxious fear of abandonment in the toddler.

The crisis is resolved through the development of language and communication between child and mother. This process of separation and individuation leads the development of what Hartmann (1952) terms "object constancy," the achievement of a stable internal representation of the mother, when a child can internalize the comfort and support of the mother and draw upon it when the mother is absent.

Babies and children compromised at this early level may turn to food as adults, not only seeking an illusory maternal function in food, but also unconsciously treating their physical and emotional needs with the same hostility, abuse, or indifference that they experienced themselves as being treated by their parents. Individuals internalize mental representations of their caregivers or significant others, so that the dynamics that are at one time relational, between two people, are internalized and reenacted intrapsychically, or internally. In this way, relational conflict becomes an internal conflict between aspects of the self.

If all goes well, the child is eventually able to create a consistent and available mental representation of the mother. Heinz Hartmann (1952) uses the term "object constancy" to refer to the child's growing recognition, between the ages of nine and fifteen months, that when the mother is physically absent, she still exists, and furthermore that she will return, because she values the child. The mother may be physically absent, but she is psychologically present. Furthermore, as the child develops the ability to hold loving feelings toward the mother, as well as disappointment, anger, and hurt, the child can retain an overall positive view of the mother, even during moments of rupture or maternal failure. Ideally, the child is then able to draw upon this internalized representation of the maternal object to soothe and comfort itself in times of stress and anxiety, which allows the child to be less reliant on the actual mother for comfort, nurturing, interest, and security.

Mahler contends that disruptions in the fundamental process of separation–individuation result later in life in a disturbance in the ability to maintain a reliable sense of individual identity. Deficiencies in positive internalization can lead to a sense of insecurity and low self-esteem issues in adulthood. This was the case with Michelle, who lacked self and object constancy, object permanence, and the ability to make use of objects. She avoided the fear of aloneness by using food to fill up her emptiness, staying unconsciously bonded to her absent mother, and never developing the capacity to self-soothe, or to think about herself and the world in any meaningful way. She did not think about what she was doing, or why; she simply experienced an overwhelming compulsion to eat until she could eat no more, at which point she would often go to sleep. This was Michelle's ritual nearly every night of her life, and had been since childhood when she would sneak food from the kitchen to her room, and eat until she was in what she described as a "food coma."

My own association to this behavior was to a hungry infant, who feeds at the breast or bottle until satisfied and then falls into a deep sleep. Michelle lacked the capacity to soothe herself with words, because the only means of soothing she ever experienced had been food. Our challenge in treatment was for her to learn how to experience comfort through talking to herself in words, or hearing words from another, rather than by eating. One occasion she was in the drive-through at a local MacDonald's when she thought, "Wait, what am I doing?" She told me she imagined my voice asking her what was bothering her, and wondering what she needed at that moment.

"I realized I didn't need a bunch of junk food. I needed to talk to someone, but there wasn't anyone I could think of who would make things better."

Michelle went to a local animal shelter instead and brought home a dog, who became her constant companion, a canine friend who was always happy to see her and available to listen. Subsequently, she made new friends at a local dog park and created a new social life for herself. By slowly internalizing my soothing presence, she learned to identify what her true needs were, and find a way to satisfy her loneliness through people, instead of with food.

MERGER VS ISOLATION

The notion of merger refers to being in a state of oneness with another person. For some people, the idea of merger is terrifying because it means being subsumed in a relationship and losing one's sense of self. Frank Lachmann and Beatrice Beebe (1989) state, "Merger experiences may be associated with losing a sense of one's cohesion and experiencing fragmentation and hence are dreaded or avoided. Under these conditions a person may lose the connection to the human milieu through encasing himself in a 'cocoon'" (p. 138). A fat body may be a way of concretizing this idea. By creating a cocoon of fat, a person may be hidden and isolated, but also may feel protected from the outside world.

S. Freud (1930) writes, "Against the suffering which may come upon one from human relationships the readiest safeguard is voluntary isolation, keeping oneself aloof from other people" (p. 77). This concept was amplified by Fairbairn (1952) and Harry Guntrip (1968, 1973) who sought to understand the conflicts of detached, introverted, and self-protected individuals. This is epitomized in a dream reported by one of Guntrip's patients, who "opened a locked steel door and inside was a tiny naked baby with wide open expressionless eyes, staring at nothing" (p. 152). This "baby in a steel drawer" exemplified the dilemma of a person who both wishes for and fears human connection. He or she may withdraw from the dangers of human interaction, but as a result is terribly alone. That resulting loneliness can be experienced as emptiness, and symbolically filled with food, or alternatively a person may restrict and starve as a way of expressing the empty place within.

"I GOT YOU PRETTY GOOD"

Jane, the patient introduced in the prologue who was well on her way to gaining the weight of her mother, learned early in life that people could not be trusted. Her mother was physically and emotionally abusive, alternating periods of showing contempt and hostility with expressions of caring. Her father was a violent alcoholic prone to rages and violence. Jane never had the sense that her parents noticed her or cared about her well-being. She used food for comfort and was overweight until she developed anorexia as a teenager. Those symptoms developed at a time when she was attempting to separate and individuate from her family. She denied her need for food as an expression of her conflict over her need for an alternately unavailable and intrusive mother. To experience object hunger was to feel humiliated and disappointed, so she turned against her need to connect, and by extension, she turned against food.

Jane was in and out of inpatient eating disorders throughout high school. After graduation, Jane moved out of the house and her weight stabilized. She remained slightly underweight until two years before entering treatment with me. The turning point was when she lost a job where—notably—she felt as if she were part of a family. Losing this job facilitated an intense hunger for connection, to fill a void, and this hunger was concretized into physiological hunger. She was ravenous for something relational, but expressed her desire by turning to food.

As noted previously, Jane binged on enormous quantities of food. Notably, much of what she ate was food that she hated and her mother loved. To give up food and the excess weight was unconsciously equivalent to giving up her mother.

For Jane to be independent and individuated she unconsciously felt she must give up her bond with her mother; conversely, to feel connected to her mother, she had to relinquish her autonomy and individuality. Furthermore, through Jane's internalization of her destructive mother, she related to herself and others in destructive ways.

In treatment with me, Jane rapidly gained forty pounds by eating the foods her mother liked, but which she despised. As noted earlier, her idea at the time was that she would continue to gain weight until she had gained the same amount of weight as her mother's weight, until they shared a body born of the food that her mother preferred and Jane hated.

Jane was literally beginning to wear her mother on her body, as a second skin of fat. This was the ultimate merger, a victory over the possibility of separation. If she and her mother were one, there could be no fear of sepa-rateness. As we identified these maternal identifications, Jane was able to distinguish between "me" and "not-me" thoughts. She began to fear separat-ing from her internal mother. She spoke of being "at the end of my rope," possibly relating a terror that the bond between mother and daughter might be severed without the umbilical cord of 135 pounds to keep them together. She often referenced this dilemma about separation, such as in the following examples:

- "I feel like my old self is in me, but physically, I feel like there's another person on top of me, ruining everything."
- "There's this normal, happy Jane underneath, and she's actually better, happier, more confident, and then there's someone else, this layer of fat that's suffocating. I used to scream when I was younger, and my mother would put her hand over my mouth. That's what it feels like."
- "Keeping myself in this state is in some way keeping me to my parents. I don't understand that."

When Jane was growing up, she could rely on her mother to both overfeed her and beat her regularly, often with a belt or a wooden spoon. Jane recalled, "I had bruises all over my body, and I somehow thought it was my fault. Sometimes, my mother would come up and say, 'You okay?' She'd look at my bruise and say, 'I got you pretty good.'

Then she'd rub it. And then she'd say, 'Well, are you ready to come down for dinner?'

It was strange." She paused. "Painful. It hurt."

Jane internalized her mother's relationship to her and repeatedly reenacted that dynamic through food and pain—just as her mother had done. Pain, love, and food were linked to the maternal relationship. Jane stuffed or starved herself until her body hurt, expressing and experiencing emotional pain as physical pain. She used food to seek the experience of being loved by stuffing her body with as much food/love as she could. She also binged to combat loneliness by symbolically filling her emotional void with copious amounts of food.

Jane exhibited a failure to adequately differentiate, as evidenced by her difficulty with self-and-other representation. She often confused herself with her internal mother, as in this recollection: "I remember bringing her my hairbrush to have my mother brush my hair, and she'd take her anger out on my hair. She'd say, 'You have to build a tough head.' She'd just yank my head. That's a good example of how I took her abuse and hatred as love. I bring her my brush. It's like a mother cat hurting her baby instead of being groomed and cleaned." Jane mixed perspective, speaking both as the mother cat and the baby (kitten), and identifying with both, just as she mixed up her mother and herself.

As Jane lost weight, her grip on that internal mother began to loosen. Five months into the analytic treatment, she was able to hold onto an awareness of various internal states. She talked to herself more supportively, sounding less like her critical, disdainful mother and more like a caring other.

This new internal separation from the negative maternal object frightened her, and she began phoning her mother more frequently, hoping for a loving, nurturing, or understanding response—which she never received. When Jane shared her disappointment over a situation at work, her mother said, "You were up so high, I was waiting for you to hit your head."

This comment also relates to Jane conflict about holding onto anything good. She sabotaged many opportunities to succeed as an actress. Similarly, her father had blown many business opportunities and made poor financial decisions. Jane internalized his attachment to deprivation (which was multi-determined) and kept herself from being successful. Thus, she could be like her parents and struggle, which kept her from risking their rejection should she succeed.

In the initial months of treatment, Jane abused her body and gained weight as a way of identifying with her mother, and merging with her, rather than holding onto a differentiated internal image of her mother. By staying deprived and unsatisfied in her job, her relationships, and her career, she identified with her parents and felt like she belonged to "a family of losers."

This was preferable to risking the satisfaction and accomplishment of success, which would underscore her separateness and differentiation from the family. Her wish to be a separate person and her fear that she would lose her connection with her family kept her stuck and unable to individuate, either in terms of her body or her aspirations.

Chapter Seven

An Unlaid Ghost

Sigmund Freud (1909) writes, "A thing which has not been understood invariably reappears; like an unlaid ghost, it cannot rest until the mystery has been solved and the spell broken" (p. 122). Over a decade later, Freud (1920) describes the tendency of some patients to unconsciously repeat their repressed memories instead of remembering them.

Repression relates to internal representations whereas denial usually refers to external reality. Denial is the refusal to accept reality, acting as if a painful event, thought, or feeling does not exist. Many people use denial to avoid facing painful emotions or realities. Denial can range from the pathological to the normal. People who choose to drink and drive are in a state of denial, as are, to some extent, people who choose to live in areas where earthquakes are common, such as the city where I live, Los Angeles. Denial is most commonly seen in anorexic patients, who refuse to believe that there is a problem and believe other people are overreacting or overstating the severity of their condition. They deny the danger to their thin or emaciated bodies, even when their lives are at risk, sometimes until the point of death.

In contrast, repression is a defensive process in which certain mental processes are kept out of awareness. Considered by Freud (1914) to be "the cornerstone on which the whole structure of psychoanalysis rests" (p. 16), it is a defense mechanism that involves the unconscious repudiation of uncomfortable or anxiety-producing thoughts. This motivated forgetting pushes, forbidden memories, thoughts, and ideas out of consciousness. Yet they do not disappear. Instead, these mental conflicts remain hidden from knowledge, while continuing to cause anxiety.

Repression is integral to the phenomenon of repetition compulsion, in which a person acts out the experience of prior relationships, but without consciously realizing that something is being repeated. Freud (1914) states that "the patient does not *remember* anything of what he has forgotten and repressed, but *acts* it out. He reproduces it not as a memory but as an action" (p. 150).

The compulsion to repeat, when it is enacted upon one's own body and psyche, leaves little hope for a different outcome from the original situation. Sharon Farber (2000) writes, "Having been treated as the other and dehumanized, they too, driven by the repetition compulsion, continued to repeat the experience. They became the sadists who treated themselves as the other at the same time that they became the masochists, continually attached to the experience of pain" (p. 115).

Internalization of the abusive other is a defensive strategy that Sandor Ferenczi (1909, 1916) introduced when he originated the term "introjection" (1909) as a mechanism of internalization in which parental attitudes and functions are taken in, not in the service of growth, but as a way of replicating internally what had been experienced externally. Fairbairn (1952) elaborates extensively on this idea, suggesting that infants cope with frustrations in the maternal relationship by internalizing the bad maternal object, with the aim of controlling the object internally. He suggests that an infant tries to control its objects by internalizing them, shifting them "from outer reality, where they elude his control, to the sphere of inner reality" (p. 172) where there is an illusion of control. This strategy internalizes the split view of the good and bad object, then leads to splitting of the self, and often to the "moral defence" in which the child attacks the self, rather than suffer the intolerable reality of having bad parents.

As discussed earlier, this strategy to survive childhood by giving oneself hope for the future often leads to a conviction in adulthood that there is something essentially bad or wrong about their basic personalities. When people think they are intrinsically bad, they believe they deserve punishment, and don't allow themselves to enjoy their lives.

"THERE'S JUST TOO MUCH OF ME"

Morgan, 35, grew up in Ireland and moved to the United States when she was twelve years old. Her eating disorder began shortly thereafter, alternating between anorexia and bulimia. She grew up in a verbally abusive household, listening to her father scream at her mother on a daily basis. Yet when Morgan expressed her own anger, her feelings were labeled as pathological, wrong, and unacceptable.

Morgan recalled that her mother showed little to no response when her father raged. She often shrugged and justified his abuse by saying, "I understand why he was so angry. I provoked him by spending too much money, so I deserve it." In contrast to this high tolerance of her husband's enraged outbursts, she had no tolerance for her daughter's feelings. She compared Morgan to the devil whenever Morgan expressed angry emotions and often threatened to call a priest when Morgan was upset, declaring that she was possessed and in need of an exorcism.

As an adult, Morgan accepted the emotions, needs, and reactions of other people. She tolerated verbally abusive bosses and boyfriends, yet showed a great deal of impatience with her own reactions and perceptions. She reserved her hatred and disgust for herself and her body, expressing self-loathing in vitriolic terms.

"I'm disgusting," she said, poking her stomach and grimacing. "I hate all this gross stuff around my middle. There's just too much of me. I can't get rid of it fast enough."

Morgan had been perceived as "too much" for her parents to handle and unconsciously translated this "too much-ness" into the notion of being bodily and physically too much. She bought into the idea that her angry and upset feelings required priestly intervention. Morgan took on the idea that her emotions represented some evil "other" that resided either within her body or took on the form of extra weight. First through anorexia and then bulimia, Morgan attempted a symbolic exorcism. She tried to rid herself of the devil she perceived to be within her, first starving away the evil that was embedded in her weight, and then attempting to purge it from her body by vomiting.

My thoughts were that Morgan indeed needed an exorcism, albeit one that was psychological in nature. To free herself from the private hell of her eating disorder, she had to banish the internalized representation of her mother, the part of her that reacted with such disdain and hatred to any emotions. She needed to exorcize her mother's thoughts from her own mind.

Morgan responded to her basic biological needs for food and sleep with the same disdain that her mother appeared to have treated her emotional needs as a child. She experienced difficulty regulating sleep and hunger. When she was tired, she could not allow herself to sleep. When she was hungry, she either denied herself food or fed herself too much unpleasant food.

This was a familiar mode of relating, a repetition of her experience with her mother, whose love felt like hate and whose hate felt like love. Morgan hungered for a good maternal function but had none to take in. She rejected therapeutic "food for thought" and filled up on food instead, often food that her mother had prepared, and then purged it all. The binges, therefore, served as a means of both incorporating her maternal object and reenacting her relationship with her mother.

I refer to "incorporation" as defined by Roy Schafer (1968), who describes incorporation as the process of taking "a part or all of another person (or

creature or thing) into one's self corporeally" (p. 20), which leads to privileging the subsequent internal experiences and ideas as one's own. Schafer
discussed oral incorporation as the primary means by which this occurs and
notes that "ideas of incorporation usually express either the wish to continue
one's relations with the other person within oneself (to introject it) or the
wish to assimilate one or more aspects of the person into oneself and thus to
acquire it for oneself (to identify with it)" (p. 20).

Morgan and others who internalize their abusers and then attack themselves do so as an unconscious strategy to gain omnipotent control over those
people who could not be controlled. The dynamics that originally existed
relationally are then taken into the psyche, where they continue to be played
out between aspects of the self. As Eleanor Armstrong-Perlman (1991) puts
it, "Both these stratagems, though they effectively protect the view of the
mother, do not alter the frustrating situation of the unresponsiveness of the
mother. Having successfully protected the object, the only way to cope with
the reality is by attacking the self" (p. 350).

To discard the mother's hostility, indifference, and contempt would be akin
to severing the bond between them. For Morgan, bingeing served to internalize the external relationship with her mother. Food was a symbol of mother
(and mothering) that was always available and could be taken in at any time.
Her mother lived nearby and often cooked food for Morgan and her family,
and these meals were the only thing that Morgan could literally take in from
her mother. Food filled her up, but it hurt, too, another repetition of the original relationship. In her relationship to her body, Morgan was both the hungry
child and the cruel, punitive mother. By inflicting harm on herself through
bingeing, she turned passive to active, transforming herself from the victim
to the aggressor.

Self-harm such as cutting or burning the skin is common in people who
struggle with eating disorders. Patients experience their physical selves as
"the body" and not as an aspect of self, and may even experience a sense of
elation, power, and grandiosity when they hurt upon themselves. Goldblatt
and Maltsberger (2010) suggest, "The self can feel the sadistic thrill of the
torturer and the gratification that such discharge provides" (p. 59). A person
who is bloodletting is trying to solve a psychological problem by cutting, just
as an eating disorder is also an attempt to resolve an internal issue through the
body, but this is akin to trying to buy groceries at a hardware store.

Ritvo (1984) suggests that such attacks on the body are often as hateful
as an attack on someone else. He describes a patient who attacked her body,
which "served as a way of attacking the introjected representations of her
parents" (p. 464). I found that, similarly, Morgan was not merely treating her
body-self as her parents had treated her, she was also punishing those internalized parental objects.

Sharon Farber (2000) writes:

> To be the predator is to be powerful, to be the prey is to be annihilated. Despite the shift from passive to active, by means of internalizing the predator-to-prey object relationship and the attachment to pain and suffering, the predator-to-prey relationship is repeated and attachment to pain and suffering is repeated by means of traumatic reenactments in behavior, and in relationships to others and to one's own body. (p. 193)

Morgan took in her maternal object through the swallowing of her mother's preferred food, and internalized their abusive relationship, treating herself as she was treated. The external relationship was thus internalized.

Anna Freud (1937, 1966) uses the term "identification with the aggressor" to address how children manage anxiety. She writes, "By assuming or imitating this aggression, the child transforms himself from the person threatened to the person who makes the threat" (pp. 121, 113). By identifying with the aggressor and abusing her body-self, Morgan kept the illusion that she was not alone; the sadistic m/other was always with her.

The following examples describe the myriad ways in which identification with the aggressor may manifest in a person's relationship to self and others. Inevitably, these identifications also show up in the transference, where they become available for working through and thus transformation.

IT'S NOT YOU, IT'S ME

Natalia, 36, a financial advisor who struggled with body image issues since high school, experienced her relationship with her father as strained and difficult. She found him distant, critical, and seemingly unreachable. As a child, Natalia sensed she could not measure up to her father's exacting expectations and felt herself to be a disappointment. She was close to her mother but their bond did not mitigate the distance she felt with her father.

Natalia was single, gay, and often found herself extremely attracted to withholding and aloof women, thus repeating the original dynamics with her father. These rejecting women responded to Natalia exactly as she experienced her father; they were detached, indifferent, and critical. Each object of her affection was thus experienced as both an actual object, a real person, and also served as a stand-in for her original rejecting father. Natalia usually blamed her body for the rejection, imagining that if she were thinner or more sculpted, she'd be able to compel withholding women to remain interested in her. In this way, she hoped to change the minds and hearts of others by changing her body.

In Natalia's other relationships, particularly with women who were openly interested in getting to know her, she was the rejecting one, identifying with her father's rejecting attitude toward those who yearned for closeness. When she broke it off with a woman, she said, "It's not you, it's me. I have a problem with intimacy." In all her relationships, someone was the rejecting one and someone was rejected. Natalia oscillated between these two roles, either being attracted to women who treated her with the same disdain she experienced with her father or treating women the same disdainful way her father treated her.

Additionally, she was extremely critical and judgmental toward herself, particularly with respect to her body, which she despised and punished by restricting food and working out at the gym for hours. Thus the conflict that had originally been relational, between herself and her father, and reenacted in her relationships, also manifested as internal conflicts between different parts of her psyche. These identifications can be understood as internal objects that originally represented actual relationships—or Natalia's experience of those relationships—and had been internalized, or taken in, and then become part of her personality structure.

"THIS JUST ISN'T GOING ANYWHERE"

Zach was a likeable, affable man in his thirties who had struggled with his weight since college. At our first meeting, he told me he used food to soothe the pain and loss of broken relationships. He had gained and lost the same twenty pounds on four separate occasions, each one corresponding to the end of each of his four romantic relationships, all of which he ended when he sensed that things "just weren't going anywhere." His relationships with women usually lasted around a year and a half. After each break-up, he would begin bingeing on pasta, pizza, and "everything Italian." Eventually he would decide to lose weight by changing his eating habits. When he reached his goal weight, he then met a new woman and the cycle would repeat.

Zach was the oldest of four children and grew up in an affluent suburban neighborhood. His mother was an Italian immigrant who had come to the country for graduate studies, and his father a successful businessman from a wealthy family. His father played college football and earned an MBA at a prestigious university before joining the family financial services business, building it into an even more successful business entity. His mother abandoned her field of study to raise the children and never completed her graduate degree. Early in childhood, Zach sensed he was not the son his father had envisioned. He said, "My father was a jock, one of those popular guys, totally confident. He was a frat guy, and he probably figured I'd be like him, too." He added, ruefully, "Turned out I'm more of a *fat* guy."

Instead of following his father's footsteps, Zach was a self-described "nerd" who preferred playing video games to participating in sports. He felt socially awkward and remembered feeling nervous and awkward around his father. In contrast, he considered his mother a reliable source of unconditional love, yet also dismissed her unwavering support and affection for him.

"She's my mother," he told me. "Of course she's supposed to love me."

Zach did not give much thought to the fact that all his relationships with women had lasted about a year and a half. He attributed this to coincidence and to the fact that "you don't really know someone until you've known them at least a year." Zach was extremely reliable, almost never cancelled a session, and faithfully came to treatment with an open mind.

As we began to approach the year and a half point in our therapeutic relationship, Zach began cancelling sessions for the first time. When I asked what was going on, he admitted that he had begun to sense that "things aren't really going anywhere" and he was thinking about ending treatment. I pointed out that the duration of our relationship was about a year and a half, the same length of time as his romantic relationships with women. I told him that the way he was talking about our therapeutic connection echoed the way he described the disinterest he described in his romantic relationships, and suggested that we explore this in more depth.

Zach reluctantly agreed. He arrived to the next session in an extremely animated and excited state of mind. The evening before, he had seen a movie *Up in the Air* and had an epiphany: he was going to change everything in his life. He was going to quit therapy and leave his relatively new job, which also "just wasn't going anywhere." He had not realized that both his therapeutic relationship and his job had the same timeline, but he dismissed it as just a coincidence. He reported feeling a familiar, restless anxiety, and a growing conviction that it was time to move on.

I asked him to talk more about that restless anxiety. Zach found it difficult to elaborate. He sensed that he was "just done" and it was time for a change. We explored the pattern of things lasting "about a year and a half" in terms of his thoughts, emotions, fears, and wishes. I also asked him to pinpoint exact dates. It was at this point he realized every relationship and job lasted about seventeen months.

I asked Zach what had happened when he was seventeen months old.

As he thought about it, a startled expression crossed his face. "Now that I think about it, that's how old I was when my sister was born."

Zach was the first-born child and he instantly became the prince of the family. He was the first grandchild and was doted on by his mother and grandparents. When he was seventeen months old, his sister arrived prematurely and the complications of her birth led him to be left with his grandmother while his parents stayed in the hospital for nearly two weeks. When she was finally released from the hospital and allowed to come home, her care required far more than the typical newborn.

We reconstructed what this experience had been like for Zach. Presumably, Zach had felt a sense of being dropped, an experience he did not consciously remember, but it had impacted his expectations of relationships. Zach did not remember the feeling of being cast out of paradise, but his actions later in life served to enact those early memories.

Since his mother was a native born Italian, and it was with whom he had the closes bond, the bingeing on pizza and pasta and "everything Italian" was an attempt to incorporate that lost, perfect, available mother of his childhood and be satiated by her presence.

In contrast to the idea that the compulsion to repeat had its roots in drive theory, subsequent theorists (Segel, 1969; Loewald, 1971; Andresen, 1980) suggest that this repetition compulsion was actually a way of trying to master past trauma. From a mastery perspective, the repetition of self-destructive behavior provides a way of turning passive to active. Zach was unconsciously ensuring that he did not unexpectedly suffer the loss of connection he originally experienced with his mother. By suddenly losing interest in a girlfriend, or a job, he was the rejecting one and thus was actively reassuring himself that he had nothing to fear. Zach was constantly repeating the past in order to have a sense of mastery.

Loewald (1971) notes that transference awakens the ghosts of the past to make them available for working through, ultimately leading to healing and making peace with the past, which he describes as occurring when, "the ghosts of the unconscious are laid and led to rest as ancestors" (p. 29).

Loewald proposes that when the wounds of the past are not truly healed, memories of painful, upsetting, and traumatic events continue to haunt the present. People may recreate past dynamics, unknowingly perpetuating their painful pasts by either seeking out familiar dynamics or perceiving people as if they were the same as the original hurtful or disappointing objects. In this way, the past is continually recreated and experienced in the present, as it was for Zach. Joseph Sandler (1976) refers to the recapitulation of early roles as "role responsiveness" when they are played out between analyst and patient. When the past is mourned, processed, and worked through, those ghosts become akin to ancestors; the past becomes a memory rather than a repeated event.

Contemporary theorists (Schore, 2011) link the compulsion to repeat to implicit memory, the memory system that functions even in utero, the encoding of lived experience. With the right trigger, a past trauma is re-experienced in current time. Intensity, duration, and repetition are factors that affect neuronal pathways. As time goes by and traumatic experience is repeated, less of a trigger is needed to produce the same intensity and duration of what was encoded.

Implicit memory cannot be used for learning, but only for repeating. It must be linked to explicit memory to become available for understanding and working through, and thus for healing. Gwyn Erwin (2005), in her dissertation on identification with unresolved trauma, noted that when an attachment figure is an "inept, dismissing or dangerous source of fright for the child, the child is ensnared in the simultaneous impulse to approach and flee from the same person" (pp. 6–7).

"DANCING TO THE BLUES"

Haley, 23, a fitness instructor, had a history of disordered eating related to unfulfilling relationships. Her single mother was bipolar and often withdrew into her room, literally and figuratively locking Haley out of her life for days. At other times, she was a "fun mom" who spontaneously took her to amusement parks, or she was "crazy mom" who stayed up all night fueled by manic energy.

Haley went on a first date with "Paris" (she referred to him not by name, but by the city where he lived) the night before he returned home to France. The evening struck her as unusual because he did not attempt to have sex with her. She wondered if there was something wrong with him and speculated that he might be gay, since he was "more interested in getting to know me than in getting with me." She thought that perhaps French men were different than the guys she met in Los Angeles. She had little concept of herself as a subject of her own life, and experienced herself as an object for others to use, particularly men. Haley's perception of herself was as that of a body-self that others could use at will.

After Paris departed, the two began an extended email/text/phone relationship. At times, Paris appeared interested in her thoughts and feelings. He was funny and made her laugh. Other times, he was completely unreachable and remote, as unavailable as Haley's mother had been during the periods in which she locked herself into her room on a drunken bender, and Haley could not connect with her in any way.

Thus, Paris's geographic unavailability and emotional inconsistency provided a repetition of the original relationship with her mother. A few months earlier, Haley's mother kicked her out of the house and moved in a new boyfriend. Haley distanced herself from her mother, but acted out the unresolved conflict about the maternal relationship with Paris.

She said, "I fell in love with this international man of mystery, who is ultimately withholding, who wanted to know everything about my life, who seemed so interested. I want to write him and say, are you for real? Are we really not talking? I thought we were close enough to have a spat and still be connected. I don't understand why he doesn't want me in his life."

She paused. "My next thought is about dancing. I dream of dancing to the blues."

As she did consistently throughout our work, Haley used her body to express her feelings, or to distract from them. Thus, she could speak of dancing to the blues, rather than feeling blue. She focused on the "spat" with Paris, and how fragile their bond appeared to be, rather than processing how she felt about her mother prioritizing her new boyfriend over her.

Her attachment was to the unavailable other, to the desire for the other, instead of to a person with whom she could relate and interact. She said, of Paris, "I think about him so much, and I think it's because he's not talking to me."

"LATCHING ON"

Alanna, a thirty-six-year-old actress who entered analytic treatment for bulimia, was also raised by a single mother who was too busy or too tired to play with her. Alanna recalled her mother coming home from work, pouring a drink, and staring at television for the remainder of the night. Meals were take-out or boiled pasta with ketchup, usually consumed in silence in front of the television. Her mother was openly contemptuous of Alanna's wish to cuddle, talk, or be close.

Shortly after Alanna began analysis, she began a tumultuous relationship with a man named Adam. In the beginning phase of their relationship, Alanna experienced herself as the child and Adam as the ideal m/other. After spending the night at his house for the first time, Alanna said wistfully, "I would love it if he could have started the shower, had the sheets pulled back and had breakfast or dinner in bed. I want someone to take care of me."

For Alanna's birthday, Adam presented her with, "Toy things, fun, childish things, like a couple of small stuffed animals." She appeared to settle in and enjoy being "babied" by him, but this period of playful attachment did not last long. Soon, she experienced Adam as a selfish, rejecting maternal figure, and could not tolerate any separation from him. When he did not call her back as quickly as she expected, she was enraged. "He's punishing me. It's okay if I'm not a priority, but don't call me babe. Don't tell me you love me. He doesn't like me."

Alanna could not give up hope that her rejecting mother would become an accepting mother. Conversely, she could not take in any acceptance of her on the part of myself, or Adam. She consciously expected rejection and unconsciously invited it through her behavior toward others.

Alanna expressed fear about her relationship with Adam: "I keep thinking, why am I afraid? Am I afraid he's not going to call? He's going to run away again."

In fact, Alanna ran away from the relationship by severing all contact with Adam for two weeks, in response to a perceived slight. I did not bring this up, but asked why she thought Adam would want to run away from her.

"From me, the fact that I'm *latching on.*"

Alanna's experience of "latching on" to her mother was to equate any need for emotional sustenance with abandonment and rejection. One of her most vivid memories was of hugging her mother, who pushed her away in annoyance, and said, "Get off me, Alanna. You're smothering me."

Adam, too, kept his distance, and their relationship remained platonic. Their lack of sexual intimacy may be explained another way—their relationship was so dynamically similar to that of a parent and child, since his role was to anticipate and take care of her needs, that a sexual relationship may have felt incestuous to both of them.

As the relationship with Adam continued to unfold, Alanna repositioned herself, becoming the rejecting, hostile mother to the scorned child—Adam. In her world, one person had the power, and the other was powerless. One person ate, and the other was eaten. Alanna attacked her body less and turned her rage on Adam, who became the needy one in her mind, and she treated him with the same disdain her mother reserved for her.

She said, contemptuously, "I called and he didn't pick up. I thought, he's a *baby.*"

When Adam told her that he had not eaten anything all day, she thought in disgust, "Grow up and take care of yourself." A few months into their relationship, she reported his concerns and complaints as "whining" and openly disparaged him.

When Alanna tried to "friend" Adam on Facebook, he did not immediately respond to her Facebook friend request. She reported this transgression to me, visibly enraged. She said, "Fuck you. I don't want to be at your show tonight. I hope you get in a car accident. Don't call me baby. Don't tell me you love me. You tell everyone you love them. You call everyone baby. Fuck you."

Alanna actively turned up the heat on hate, unconsciously provoking a repetition of her relationship with her mother. As A. Freud (1937, 1966) writes, "The reversal of roles was complete" (p. 117).

Alanna remained locked in a cycle of retraumatization. She relived original psychic wounds, rather than processing and working through them. Identification with trauma was a hallmark of Alanna's interactions with others. If relating to others may be understood as having reciprocal interactions that are mutually fulfilling, Alanna did not truly relate to other people. Instead, she engaged in power dynamics, unconsciously recreating the familiarity of her original family drama by casting herself in various roles. She was alternately the persecutor or the victim, the abused or the abuser, the deprived child or the selfish mother, the eaten or the eater.

In addition to displacement, Alanna utilized projection to get rid of unwanted aspects of self. Adam most often served as a screen for these projections. Although she initially experienced him as someone with whom she had a strong identification ("He's just like me," and "We're the same person"), she later projected unwanted parts of herself onto him:

She said, "The poor thing needs a lot of therapy. He needs a lot of talking."

When Alanna was facing eviction, with no place to live and no job prospects, she resisted looking for a job. She said, "Adam should be dedicated and focused. He should act like an adult."

She continued to avoid looking for work and often did not pay for her treatment. She said, "He's just really fucked up and I don't want to deal with it."

One day she forgot to pay her fee for therapy and said of Adams, "He's retarded and insensitive and also incapable." One significant aspect of this displacement was its utility as a means of projecting her rage. "Adam is so immature, the way he handles his anger and frustration. He's sharp and bitey." Thus, Adam was viewed the angry, "bitey" one, not her.

Alanna projected her anger and badness onto animals as well as people. She said of her roommate's cat, "It's a bad animal, and it chewed up something of mine. My roommate said she was strapped for cash. I don't care. If you can go out with your friends, you can pay me."

This comment came at the time that she was chewing me up, eating and devouring my therapeutic food and not paying for it, although she did have money for food. The contempt with which she treated me and others, and the helpless rage that I felt, served to indirectly communicate what Alanna had felt like as a child, with an indifferent, contemptuous mother. In the next chapter I explore in depth how these interactions between analyst and patient can be valuable tools for the work.

David Levy (1934) suggests that "affect hunger" arising from early childhood deficits was a cause of relationship difficulties in adulthood. He defines "affect hunger" as "the emotional hunger for maternal love and the other feelings of being cared for in the mother-child relationship" (pp. 643–644). He identifies a number of strategies that individuals deprived of maternal love and affection use to elicit responsiveness from others. These include using helplessness to stimulate responsiveness in the other, being hostile toward others to punish those who withhold love and "excessive demands for food, for money" (p. 651). He describes a common occurrence in children who were adopted in childhood, in which they initially made a good impression on their new families, and appeared eager to please, but soon became insatiably demanding.

Armstrong-Perlman (1991) notes that people often choose significant others who have similar characteristics as their mothers. These new object choices are equally as rejecting and enticing as the original mothers. As Armstrong-Perlman puts it, "The need is related to her alluring, rejecting features" (pp. 351–352).

The goal of dis-identifying with the aggressors of childhood is one of the ways that change takes place. When the psychological wounds of the past are healed, people do not need to unconsciously recreate them in the present, or be drawn toward similar dynamics as to what they had experienced, in an attempt to achieve a different outcome. Often, people who are ambivalent about relationships also express that ambivalence with food, bingeing and purging as a way of managing their conflict about closeness, or restricting as a way of figuratively starving for love.

Part III

TREATMENT

This section covers the specifics of treatment, including the roles of transference, countertransference, and dreams in the psychoanalytic approach to eating disorders. I discuss the use of dream work in the treatment of eating disorders, giving examples of how dreams are a means by which unconscious conflicts can be brought to conscious awareness and made available for working through. I also elucidate the various types of disruptions and impasses that may arise in treatment, such as issues pertaining to the fee and suicidal ideation. Last, I explore love and hate in the analytic setting.

Chapter Eight

On the Couch

The analytic couch creates a kind of time travel, in which the experiences of infancy and childhood can be revisited. The use of the couch in psychoanalysis began because Sigmund Freud wanted to avoid the scrutiny of patients. In his article "On Beginning Treatment" (1913c), he states, "I felt uncomfortable being stared at eight hours a day" (pp. 133–134). When patients recline on the couch, he avoided this discomfort. An unexpected bonus was that the couch facilitated free association, regression, and the development of transference, allowing for unresolved patterns, dynamics, and conflicts from the past to be rediscovered and processed, providing for a new way of being and relating in the present. When patients cannot see the analyst, they expect the analyst to respond to them the same way that figures from the past responded. Rose, whose mother ignored her frantic pleas to talk to her, had little problem with silences when we sat facing each other. On the couch, however, she experienced the smallest silence as unbearably long and felt as if I was being indifferent to her and ignoring her. The couch brought Rose's long dead mother into the room, in the form of a transference onto me, allowing Rose to express and process this "silent treatment" with me, which she could not do as a child with her mother.

Unconscious conflicts are brought into awareness through the use of transference, countertransference, and dreams. Listening for derivatives of the unconscious in speech is another method by which the unconscious can be inferred, such as in slips of the tongue, negation, and sudden solutions to problems. Parapraxis, commonly known as a Freudian slip, refers to an error in speech, action, or memory that reveals an unconscious wish, desire, attitude, or thought (Freud, 1901). These may be a slip of the tongue or the pen, forgetting, misplacing objects, or hearing something incorrectly. I have been struck by how many eating disorder patients say "hate" when they meant to say "ate" in relating behaviors with food. Recently a patient complained of eating a big meal. "I can't believe how much I *hate*," she said, when she meant to say, "how much I *ate*." This parapraxis revealed her disavowed hatred and aggression that was often turned against herself for eating, rather than verbally expressed and emotionally metabolized.

Stella Yardino (2008) recounts that three years into analysis with a patient who habitually showed up late or canceled, she waited for what she thought was a reasonable amount of time before leaving the office (his was her last session of the day). Later she realized she had misremembered the time of the session. The patient's time was at 8:30 p.m. and she thought it was at eight o'clock. Her misremembering was a parapraxis, or motivated forgetting, that ultimately served as a transformative moment in the treatment, since it brought up the patient's memories at being left by his mother. He had been reversing the situation, always leaving instead of being the one who was left. Yardino's error in memory thus allowed for the patient to start processing the painful abandonment, instead of continually enacting it with her.

The term "negation" refers to a mental process in which a wish is expressed in negative form. Negation is the expression of thoughts that are simultaneously denied. A screenwriter married to another writer recently found out his wife had been nominated for an award. He expressed his feelings about his wife's success by saying, "It's not that I want to compete with her," thus revealing a competitive streak that he consciously denied.

"It's not that I'm mad at you," another patient told me, upon learning of an upcoming vacation. "You deserve some time off, too. I'm not upset."

My patient was indeed upset that I was leaving on vacation at a time when she was going through a difficult time, but she felt guilty for this thought and repressed any conscious knowledge of her resentment. However, she expressed her true thought as a negative and eventually "admitted" that perhaps she was upset, even though she did "not think it was fair to be upset" and felt bad for harboring resentment toward me for taking a vacation.

Sudden solutions to a problem are also evidence of the unconscious. The "Eureka, I found it!" moment may reveal that we know something that—until that moment—we do not know that we know it.

Tiffany left home at the age of seventeen and got engaged a few years later. She had no idea how to organize a wedding. Her mother, who lived in a distant city, was more interested in finding a husband of her own than in helping Tiffany plan a wedding. Not knowing what else to do, Tiffany went to a local printer and ordered some inexpensive wedding invitations. The clerk was an older man who dutifully took her order but did not offer suggestions. That night Tiffany dreamed that it was her wedding day and the only person who showed up was her mother, who said, "Of course nobody else will be here. You didn't put the time on the invitation."

Tiffany awoke, her heart pounding. The next day she called the printer and discovered that she had indeed forgotten to put the time on the invitation. Her unconscious mind had registered this fact and found a way to resolve the problem in the form of her mother's dream recrimination. The dream also expressed a wish for her mother to be helpful to her. Dreams are a remarkably helpful window to the unconscious mind, which I will later discuss in greater detail.

TRANSFERENCE

Freud introduced the concept of transference, which is the displacement of patterns of attitudes, emotions, thoughts, fantasies, and behaviors originally experienced in childhood with significant figures of the past, onto people in the present. The original figures are often parents, but can also be siblings, grandparents, teachers, and others. Transference is thus the reexperiencing of childhood or past relationships in the present. Freud (1905a) defines transference as follows:

> What are transferences? They are new editions or facsimiles of the impulses and phantasies which are aroused and made conscious during the progress of the analysis; but they have this peculiarity, which is characteristic for their species, that they replace some earlier person by the person of the physician. To put it another way: a whole series of psychological experiences are revived, not as belonging to the past, but as applying to the person of the physician at the present moment. (p. 116)

Transference is a tool for bringing the past into the present and making it available for understanding and working through. My own experience in psychoanalysis illustrates how powerful transference can be. For years I considered my analyst to be similar in height to me, around five feet six (not coincidentally the height of my mother). One day, when she opened the door to the waiting room, as she had done for years, and I suddenly experienced her as much smaller. I was shocked to realize she is actually petite and nowhere near the height I had imagined her to be. During the period in which we were processing maternal transference, my mind refused the reality of my eyes and recreated my analyst in the image of my mother, including my mother's significantly taller height.

In his 1912 article "The Dynamics of Transference," Freud makes the point that transference exists everywhere, but it is only in the analytic relationship that it is a focus of study and analysis. Many people experience familiar patterns at their jobs, where they may feel an abiding need to please a boss and get praise, or they may be extremely competitive with coworkers. In this way, unbeknownst to them, the work situation replicates their original home dynamics. In the human psyche, bosses become stand-ins for parents and the coworkers represent siblings. Transference causes people to experience others not as they actually are, but as the parents or other familiar figures were, and they never realize the relationship between past and present.

Recently I joined a friend for dinner at a small local restaurant. It was a hot evening, and the air-conditioning was turned off, so we were sweltering. We requested that the waiter turn on the air-conditioning and he was more than happy to accommodate us. During our meal, we noticed the temperature had risen again. When we asked our waiter to check on the air, he told us that the people at a nearby table had complained about being too cold, so he adjusted it.

My friend said, sharply, "That is unacceptable. I'd like to speak to the manager."

When the manager appeared, my friend demanded a different waiter and complained, visibly angry, that that the waiter had "no right to ignore us" and make the other table more important than us.

I asked my friend if she had any thoughts about her strong reaction, she associated to her childhood. "It's how I used to feel when my parents dropped everything to take care of the church kids."

I recalled that my friend was an only child who often felt overlooked by her parents, who were very involved in their church, where her mother taught religious school. My friend experienced herself as constantly in competition with the pupils at the school, who had her parents' attention, whereas she felt herself to be of secondary interest. This dynamic had been reexperienced when the waiter accommodated the people at another table, seemingly privileging their wishes over ours.

Transference thus makes the past available in the present. By recognizing and working through transferences in the analytic relationship, people can come to a resolution about the past.

Whereas classical theorists suggested that a person would create the same transference with any analyst, regardless of the personality and attitude of that analyst, contemporary relational theorists view the transference as co-created between each patient and analyst, given their unique and respective personalities and histories.

Transference allows for the psychological wounds of the past to be healed in the present. For those who have been deprived of the experience of safety and comfort in a dependent relationship, the therapeutic relationship may be their first "taste" of trust in the context of dependency. For some this is a bittersweet experience, for when they finally experience unconditional positive regard and care, they simultaneously get in touch with all that they missed, and makes them painfully aware of that deprivation.

COUNTERTRANSFERENCE

Sigmund Freud (1910b) defines countertransference as the feelings that an analyst has "as a result of the patient's influence on his unconscious feelings, and we are almost inclined to insist that he shall recognize this counter-transference in himself and overcome it" (pp. 144–145). He believed that countertransference was a hindrance to the treatment because it was a manifestation of some unresolved conflicts in the analyst. As psychoanalytic theory evolved, the prevailing views on countertransference began to shift. The term is now defined as the totality of feelings that an analyst had toward a patient. One contemporary view posits that countertransference (as well as transference) is co-created by patient and analyst and thus exists between a specific interpersonal matrix. The phenomenon of countertransference is now considered an invaluable tool for understanding people at the deepest level.

"I DON'T KNOW"

Elle, 28, was the only child of a charming but 'abusive father, and an alternately frustrated, silent, and unresponsive mother. Her parents approved of her intellectual and scholastic achievements but otherwise displayed an utter lack of basic parental aptitude. There was no investigation into her thoughts, emotions, wants, needs, or wishes. She was a talented ballet dancer and hoped to make a career out of her passion for dance. In middle school, Elle developed anorexia, in part a reaction to sexual abuse by her father. Her shrinking body and sad demeanor alarmed her teachers and other adults, particularly her ballet teachers, who contacted her parents to express concern. Elle was informed by her mother that the family could afford either dance lessons or therapy, not both, and left it up to her to make the choice. Neither parent asked what was going on with her, why she had lost weight, or why she was depressed. She was simply given a one-time choice between ballet and therapy. Elle chose to continue her dance lessons, the only place where she felt happy.

Although Elle was dangerously thin, her mother dismissed the anorexia as "just a stage" and did not do anything to get her into treatment. In the years that followed, Elle experienced recurring bouts of depression and anorexia. Her mother occasionally asked, "Are you still doing that not-eating thing?"

As an adult, whenever Elle talked to her mother, their conversations centered on her mother's life and various complaints. Elle longed to connect more deeply with her mother but could not find a way to do so. During a phone conversation, she shared that she was immersed in a riveting book. Her mother asked what she was reading.

"A memoir about a woman who recovered from anorexia," Elle replied.

Her mother said nothing. Elle waited, hoping for some kind of interested reply. At the very least, she hoped for some acknowledgment of what she had just said. Instead, there was no response. As she described the silence that stretched between them in the next moments, I had a sense of the vast, endlessness of space.

Her mother broke the silence by saying, "Did I tell you I had to take my car to the mechanic this week?"

Elle was crushed. She felt "like an idiot" for hoping that she would get a kind, interested response from her mother. Time after time, Elle's emotional pain was met with silence or frustration, instead of recognition and comfort. She resisted acknowledging the pain and rage she felt toward her mother and also felt guilty for these feelings. She assured me that her mother simply didn't know what to say.

At the same time that Elle was so understanding of her mother, she was brutal toward herself. She abused her body, cutting her skin, hitting herself, choking herself, starving herself, and hating herself with a violence and hatred that I found alarming and frightening. I struggled to contain these relentless and sadistic attacks on her body, which were as physiologically painful and damaging as her mother's silence was to her psychological well-being.

At one point, Elle was unable to cope with the horror of her abusive childhood and became suicidal. Her husband notified Elle's mother that she was being hospitalized for suicidal impulsivity. When Elle called her mother from the hospital, her mother started talking about her day as if nothing was going on. Her mother did not visit her in the hospital, an absence that Elle found bewildering and painful. I visited her on two occasions and as Elle later put it, "Your presence highlighted her absence." I believe my visits gave her a new paradigm for what she could expect from others, and this emboldened her to want more from her mother.

Several months later, during another phone conversation, Elle's mother asked if she was upset that she had not known what was going on with her father. Elle, who had been afraid to say anything about this, fearful of making her mother uncomfortable, cautiously admitted that she did have feelings about not being protected.

Her mother was silent. Elle waited for a response, for some acknowledgment of her feelings, but her mother said nothing.

Finally, Elle said she had to go and hung up.

When I heard about this utter lack of responsiveness on the part of Elle's mother, I felt extremely angry at the inhuman and inhumane treatment. I thought, "What kind of mother is this? What is wrong with her?"

I had fantasies of shaking the mother and yelling at her, even slapping her face to wake her up. I was cognizant that my rage and destructive wishes were not something that I normally felt. These thoughts were a "not-me" experience that left me a bit rattled. I also recognized that I was having an intense emotional reaction but Elle was not visibly upset. Was I feeling both my own reaction and also the feelings that Elle had but disavowed? I wondered about this as Elle's hateful, barbaric, vicious attacks on her body continued.

When I suggested that Elle was taking out her rage toward her mother on her own body, she placed a pillow on her lap and crossed her arms. She appeared to sink back into the couch, as if withdrawing as far from possible from my gaze.

I said, "I think we need to understand what just happened. I said you feel anger and hurt toward your mother but you're directing that onto your body. Now we're sitting in silence and I'm the one waiting for you to talk and share your thoughts. I wonder if this is what happened in your childhood. You wanted words, wanted love, wanted something from your mother or from your parents, and you didn't get it."

Elle said nothing.

Shortly thereafter, Elle went on a long vacation. She struggled a great deal with distance between us, fearing that the bond between us would not survive the time apart, and worrying that depending on me would inevitably lead to loss and disappointment. Upon her return, Elle deliberately avoided the couch when she entered my office and instead took a seat in a chair. I asked her why she had chosen to sit there, instead of on the couch, and she lifted her shoulders in a silent shrug. For the rest of the session, my efforts to gain understanding and clarification were met with silence, or with a flat and indifferent, "I don't know."

Over the next few weeks, Elle showed up on time, sat on the chair and looked at me with what felt like utter disdain. Silence filled the space between us. I previously felt warmth and connection between us, but now she appeared cold and unreachable. She fixed a dark gaze upon me, silently emanating a palpable hatred. She ignored my efforts to explore, clarify, and interpret the silence. Occasionally she gave monosyllabic responses or scornfully told me, "This isn't working" or asked, "What exactly are we doing, anyway?"

I felt at once impotent and obliterated. The force of her sudden withdrawal was intensely paralyzing and I was confused. I examined my reactions to this ongoing treatment for clues to what was happening. I realized how completely and utterly insignificant I felt in the shadow of her dark rage.

I finally said, "I think you're letting me know what it felt like when your mother gave you the silent treatment. As if you didn't matter or even exist."

Her eyes met mine.

"You are helping me to understand how shut out you felt, and how confusing and hurtful that was."

Elle's hard gaze began to soften. They slowly filled with tears, pain leaking from her eyes. She did not speak, but in the days that followed she returned to the couch and tentatively started relating to me again.

My countertransference reactions to Elle's withdrawal helped me understand and viscerally resonate with her experience of childhood and beyond. When we began to talk about her relationship with her mother, she knew that I did not merely think about her experience with her mother; I had actually *felt* it myself, through our interaction. Rather than sympathizing with her plight when it came to her relationship with her mother, I had empathy for what she was going through.

Furthermore, I believe I had a visceral sense of what Elle felt when attacked her body with such ferocity; these were the same violent feelings I had toward her mother. Thus her silent communication was extremely powerful and a gift to our work together.

Another common countertransference reaction is what is called projective identification. My use of the term refers to the phenomenon in which a person splits off unwanted aspects of the self, thoughts, or emotions, and attributes them to another person (projection), who then identifies with the projection and experiences the projector's emotions (identification). Recently a patient began his session by telling me, "So, my granddaughter passed away over the weekend."

His tone was utterly conversational as if was telling me about a movie he'd seen over the weekend. I felt my heart constrict, shocked and horrified. I knew his granddaughter was only twenty years old and had been battling a heroin addiction.

My patient went on to tell me that this death, while shocking, was not a surprise, because his granddaughter had been into drugs. As he spoke, I felt a hollowness growing within, a sense of dismal hopelessness, and my eyes filled with tears. I felt devastated at the loss of this young woman. In analyzing my reaction, I questioned why I was having such strong, visceral emotions. It felt more intense than a normal human reaction to loss, and I had not experienced any such losses in my own life. I speculated that I was feeling what my patient could not allow himself to feel.

My reaction was visible because tears were filling my eyes and we were sitting face to face. I said, "It's so interesting to me that I'm feeling such a terrible sense of loss and I notice that your reaction is very different. What are we to make of that?"

He said, "Maybe you're feeling what I can't let myself feel."

At that moment, his eyes began to fill. We sat in silence for many minutes. He whispered, "I just can't go there. Not yet."

He began to cry, tears rolling down his face. And I felt my own grief abate.

Several years ago, I began to notice that one of my obese patients had been gaining weight. She had lost nearly 200 pounds a couple of years earlier, and was still over 100 pounds overweight. She also was grieving the sudden deaths of two family members. She was gaining weight at an alarming speed, growing before my eyes, seemingly bigger with each passing session. I was aware of my countertransference: concern, horror, even irritation. After working so hard to lose weight, how could she regain it so quickly? Why didn't she care? Why wasn't she taking care of herself? I felt a profound helplessness about her ballooning body. I began to think about my helplessness as a communication about her experience.

One day she talked about the two family members who had died suddenly and said, "How could they have left me like that? How could they?"

I recognized the echo of my own thoughts about her weight gain and said, "It sounds as if you're up against an unstoppable force, like a tidal wave, and there's nothing you can do."

She was quiet for a moment, which is unusual for her. She finally said, "It's death. I can't stop it. Everyone is gone."

We had talked a lot about the impact of the deaths in her family, but not of the existential dread and anxiety it evoked. My experience of helplessness regarding her ballooning body gave me a visceral understanding of her sense of helplessness about death.

At other times, countertransference can give the analyst an idea of what it's like for other people to be with the patient outside the consulting room. I once treated a woman who was extremely angry and bitter. Each session she complained of the unfairness of life and recounted the many ways that people had wronged her and rejected her. She also mocked me, responding to my interpretations with exasperated sighs and saying, "I already know that. Can't you say something original?"

She consistently derided my attempts to clarify, understand, and interpret her thoughts, wishes, and emotions. She told me she had "wasted thousands of dollars" on treatment and that nothing had changed, that she felt worse than ever, and was still fat.

One day during her session, when she was being particularly vituperative, I found myself suddenly thinking about earthquakes. My office is located on the twelfth floor and the building sways when there is a seismic tremor. I imagined an earthquake hitting the city, the building rocking, shattering my floor-to-ceiling glass, and pitching my patient out the window.

Naturally this vision was disconcerting. I realized that my fear of the earthquake might actually express a buried wish. In that moment, I had wanted to get rid of this patient. I wanted to pitch her out of my office and be done with her.

I shared that I wanted to help her and believed that I could help her, if she let me, but her scornful remarks and open disdain for my attempts to understand and help were causing me to want to shut down and protect myself. I told her that it was helpful to understand what was happening between us, as what occurred in our therapeutic relationship could shed light on her outside relationships.

She tightened. "I know I'm a bitch. I don't know why."

"Let's find out," I said, "Together." In the ensuing weeks and months, she relaxed her antagonistic stance enough to begin addressing the rejected–rejecter dynamic that permeated all her relationships.

In this way, my countertransference reaction allowed me to open up a dialogue about the original wound to her psyche, the abandonment by her father. She asserted that since she had never actually known her father, his absence from her life had not impacted her. I proposed that the early rejection continued to haunt her, and that she was repeating that dynamic with others. She treated people with such contempt and derision that they, too, rejected her or wanted to reject her.

Transference and countertransference occur together as part of the ongoing analytic matrix. In the following clinical vignettes, I present examples of idealized, erotic, eroticized transferences, as well as transference psychosis and resistance to transference.

IDEALIZED TRANSFERENCE

Rob, 34, came to treatment with two goals: committing to the relationship with his girlfriend and losing weight. He began weekly psychotherapy treatment with enthusiasm. After a year of psychotherapy, he had a much better understanding of himself and the way he related to self and others, but wanted to go deeper. I brought up analysis, and we discussed this for many months before he began analysis as an analytic training case. I noted the enthusiasm with which he committed to analysis and at the time felt hopeful about the work.

Rob's fears about analysis were centered on using the couch instead of facing each other. He imagined I would look at him and think he was fat and lazy, and that I would secretly feel disgusted by him. These were, not coincidentally, the same experience he had with his father, who was openly contemptuous about Rob's weight.

The first time he reclined on the couch, he shared a fear that I was judging his clothes, sizing up his perceived lack of progress, and especially his body. I attempted to explore these anxieties, but Rob hastily reassured me that he knew I "wouldn't really think anything like that" and soon settled in to do the work on the couch. Initially, I was pleased that he felt safe and could embark on the analysis with a feeling of trust. He was always on time, always appreciative of the work we did and often voiced his appreciation, often telling me how lucky he felt to be with such an insightful and perceptive therapist. Now, as I look back, I believe that his compliance prevented the development of a paternal transference. He was deeply afraid of experiencing me as his judgmental father and reexperiencing the most painful aspects of his relationship with his father.

Idealization can serve a defensive purpose. Rob's idealization of me prevented the development of a negative transference and kept things between us harmonious, avoiding hostile, resentful, even hateful feelings. I knew it would be helpful for him to get in touch with those negative feelings so that he could work through them in the service of healing his unresolved relationship with his father.

Rob denied any possible feelings of anger or disappointment with me. He once dreamed that he was watching a porn film in which I was the star, but he was unable to see my naked body due to the positioning of props in the film. He denied any sexual feelings toward me and was horrified at the idea of being attracted to me, although he told me I was "quite beautiful" and "an amazing person." He could only see me in idealized terms lest he feel anger or any other "negative" emotion, which he feared might drive me away, or might cause him to want to leave.

Six months into analysis he began to arrive late for sessions on a regular basis. After months of nearly perfect attendance, he canceled three sessions in two weeks. I wondered if this was a reaction to possible feelings of resentment, disagreement, or something else he thought was negative. He had to keep me at a distance to avoid any anxieties about losing his idealized view of me.

When I brought up the cancellations, he surprised me by asking what I had felt about him canceling. I disclosed that I felt pushed away and unimportant, and wondered if he'd ever felt that way. He was astonished that I would have that reaction. It did not occur to him that I might not be annoyed and/or disappointed in him. In his unconscious relational patterns, he focused on being the disappointing one, which in his mind invariably led to rejection and loss.

He said, "I feel like if I disappoint someone else, like my clients, they'll leave and go to someone else."

This may have expressed both his fear that if he disappointed me that I would get rid of him, and his unconscious fear of being disappointed by me and then wanting to get rid of me to see someone else.

Altman (1995) suggests that for some people, the wish for closeness, nurturance, and bonding push the more aggressive aspects of the transference to the background, because it is too frightening to hold both love and anger. Marilyn Charles (1999) writes that feelings of anger, envy, rivalry, and fear "are often pushed underground, and may be depicted in oral terms, representing fears of starvation, annihilation, or loss of love and nurturance" (p. 270). Although she writes specifically with respect to treating female patients, I find this to be a universal experience. Rob feared that if he got in touch with his erotic, angry, aggressive feelings toward me, the bond would be at risk. His solution was to deny these feelings and bring only his love into the foreground, minimizing the outward risk that he would lose me, but on the other hand never feeling safe that he really had my love, care, and affection.

EROTIC AND EROTICIZED TRANSFERENCE

Karl, a self-described "proud, gay man" in his late fifties, developed a crush on me and began having dreams of romantic and sexual encounters with me. He was quite disconcerted by his sexual attraction to me. Karl had never been attracted to a woman and did not know what to make of these fantasies. We explored his erotic feelings as a means of communicating a wish to be close to me, rather than to be sexually intimate. Erotic transference is a positive transference in which romantic or sexual fantasies often occur. Patients usually understand these transferences to be merely fantasies, and they do not interfere with the ability to do the work of therapy.

In contrast, eroticized transference refers to an intense preoccupation with the analyst in which the patient makes demands for love and/or sex, and sees these wishes as perfectly reasonable. Some patients experience transference reactions that are too intense for them to tolerate. As Sjödin and Conci (2011) put it, "The patient tends to become fixed in a single perspective from which he "sees" the interpretations and the rest of the analysis. The analyst is faced with a patient both who wishes on one level to communicate, but who on quite another level feels petrified by the prospect of doing so" (p. 4). The result is a situation in which reality is denied and patients becomes intent on proving their viewpoints rather than investigating and understanding their internal worlds.

Patients who become overly regressed, meaning that they revert to an earlier stage of development, may develop a psychotic type of transference in which they have little ability to symbolize their experiences in analysis. Rather than think, "my therapist reminds me of my father or mother," they say, "my therapist is exactly like my father or mother." Margaret Little (1960) describes transference psychosis as a state in which, "psychically, nothing is differentiated from anything else; there is apparently awareness of one thing only, distress or pain of an overwhelming intensity, such that all else is annihilated, including any sense of being a person, even that of being a person suffering" (p. 378). Patients in this regressed position often act out violently, view the analytic relationship as a power struggle, and essentially ignore transference interpretations.

The following clinical example of a colleague's experience highlights the potential dangers of this type of regressive transference.

EROTICIZED/PSYCHOTIC TRANSFERENCE

Beryl, 32, sought psychotherapy for binge eating disorder and alcohol abuse. She began weekly sessions with a male therapist who specialized in addiction. She reported a history of incest with her brother and stated that her father "knew but didn't do anything to stop it." Beryl had initially showed a remarkable ability to self-reflect and was interested in understanding herself more deeply. She was intellectually curious and able to connect with the therapist. As time went on, she began to vacillate between loving and hating her therapist, which was part of a borderline personality structure that became more evident as treatment went on.

Borderline personality disorder (BPD) is a personality disorder characterized by a pattern of instability in interpersonal relationships, self-image, and emotions. A personality disorder is a deeply engrained view of self and the world that deviates from the cultural norm and impacts a person's cognition, affect, interpersonal functioning, and/or impulsivity across a spectrum of personal and social situations. Nearly 54 percent of patients with borderline personality disorder have diagnosable eating disorders (Zanarini et al., 2004). People with borderline personality disorder have symptoms of impulsivity, mood swings, inappropriate anger, fear of abandonment, alternately valuing and devaluing others, and an unstable self-image, and some are suicidal. These symptoms may vary in severity in different individuals. Beryl, initially idealized her therapist, but soon began to display anger whenever she perceived him as rejecting her. If he shifted in his seat, she thought that he was bored. When he ended the sessions on time, she was positive that he wanted to get rid of her and imagined that he wanted nothing to do with her. She told him that he was not helping her and he should refer her to someone he knew, someone who "knew what they were doing" and could help her, because he was clearly incapable. Then, terrified that he would actually do this, she tearfully apologized and begged him not to get rid of her.

The therapist interpreted to Beryl that their work was under attack by a *part* of her, the part that equated closeness with vulnerability to being rejected. When she felt close, warm, loving feelings toward him or anyone else, she became frightened and went into attack mode by finding fault with the other person. Her oscillating hate and love was a form of protection from vulnerability.

As the therapy continued, Beryl began to be less reflective and more concrete in her thinking. The extremes between idealization and devaluation began to intensify. One day Beryl left the session and verbally confronted a female patient in the waiting room, accusing her of giving her a dirty look. When the therapist interceded and put a stop to the accusations, she accused him of being "just like" her father by defending the other patient.

She viewed her perceptions as the truth and the only truth. She could not accept that she had acted inappropriately and aggressively, and that the therapist's boundary-setting was a response to her aggression. She then became certain that the therapist was having an affair with this woman in the waiting room. All efforts to interpret this enactment and explore her delusional fantasies were met with denial. She decided to take a break from therapy, ostensibly to save money. When the therapist was out of town at a conference, Beryl requested another session. He responded that he was out of town and Beryl wrote a vituperative email, calling him names and using profane language. This was followed by several more emails in which she apologized and pleaded for forgiveness.

Beryl appeared to be in the grip of psychotic delusions. She was incapable of reality-testing and could not engage in any kind of meaningful therapeutic dialogue or treatment. Upon the therapist's return, she announced that she was leaving treatment. He gave her three referrals and wished her well. Beryl continued to contact him, leaving voicemails begging to see him again, emailing increasingly desperate requests to meet. In these voicemails and emails, her thoughts appeared increasingly disjointed and she vacillating between extremes of rage and seduction. The therapist did not respond and Beryl subsequently wrote bad reviews on multiple social media sites, accusing him of sexual harassment and asserting that he was a terrible therapist. He was forced to bring legal action to remove these bad reviews, a situation that was emotionally and financially costly.

Beryl originally sought therapy because she was bingeing on food and alcohol. During the treatment, Beryl wanted more and more of the therapist, essentially bingeing on him, demanding more of his time through extra sessions and email correspondence. The reality that she could not have him all to herself, as evidenced by the patient in the waiting room, was unbearable and created unbridled rage. This case highlights the potentially explosive and dangerous transferences that may erupt when a patient is in the grip of a transference psychosis, in which reality is denied and delusional fantasies are experienced as real.

PARENTAL TRANSFERENCE

Early in my career I interned with a psychotherapist who had a solo private practice in an upscale part of town. Her office was decorated in the shabby chic style that was popular at that time, with overstuffed couches, white slipcovers, and lots of pillows. The space was neutral and comfortable, with beige tones and soft pink accents. Previously, I'd seen clients at a low-fee clinic, where the décor was shabby and the ambiance decidedly downscale. Several clients from the clinic followed me to the private practice internship. On my first day in the new office space, one of them gave an exclamation of pleasure when she entered the room. "Oh, it's just so beautiful," she said, beaming. "This is such a comfortable, cozy space."

Later, another client from the clinic came for her session. She surveyed the new space with an expression of disdain. "This office is cold and clinical," she said, flatly. "I don't like it at all."

These two women had completely different reactions to the new office, both of which mirrored their experience of me. The first woman viewed me as a warm, safe person with whom she felt comfortable. The second woman feared that I was a cold, indifferent clinician who only feigned interest in her because that was my job and therefore my obligation. Not surprisingly, the first woman had a positive relationship with her mother, experiencing her as a warm, loving person with whom she had a safe bond. She transferred that experience of her mother to the analytic situation and felt safe with me. The second woman grew up with a cold, brusque father and passive mother who showed very little interest in her. She could not imagine that I would be interested in her and experienced me as an indifferent clinician.

The reason that people with negative transferences stay in treatment is twofold. They develop enough of a positive foundation to experience the therapist as a reliable and caring person, so a part of them knows that although they are seeing the therapist as cold, clinical, disinterested, or angry, there is more to their perception than meets the proverbial eye. Also, in treatment they have the opportunity to say things to the therapist that they may never have dared say to the original person on whom the transference is based.

Transferences supersede the realities of gender and age. Patients who are older than I am often experience me as their mothers and fathers. Lenore, 64, grew up with an authoritarian father who flew off the handle at unpredictable moments, becoming enraged when Lenore laughed too loudly, or dropped a plate, and as a result she was terrified to make a mistake. Lenore was a retired professor of geology with an easygoing manner and a quick sense of humor. She sought therapy to stop binge eating, something she had battled since childhood. As treatment progressed, I noticed that Lenore was withdrawing into her shell. One day she was stuck in traffic and arrived ten minutes late to her session. She tearfully apologized, explaining about the traffic situation and clearly very shaken. Lenore was worried that I would be angry with her. I wondered what she imagined the tardiness meant to me.

"I just don't want you to be mad at me," she said. "I can't stand it when people are mad at me."

"I wonder if you are afraid of finding your father in me," I said. "You cannot imagine that being late, or any other kind of human error, is acceptable."

Lenore looked surprised. "You mean you're not mad?"

Lenore could not believe that I would react in a different way than her father had done, or that the slightest mistake was not the end of the world. She felt as if there was something wrong with her when she made any kind of mistake. For most of her life she kept people at a distance, fearing the humiliation that would inevitably occur when something went wrong. She had a relationship with food instead of people, because food was safer but unsatisfying. As we navigated this paternal transference, Lenore became more tolerant of mistakes and strengthened her connections with people, which led to a diminishment in her use of food for comfort and fulfillment.

SIBLING TRANSFERENCE

Eating disorder behavior may be expressed in ways other than only through food. A colleague once consulted with me about a case. Her patient, Joanne, was a professional woman who seemed unable to break a pattern of bingeing by, "eating twice as much as normal" after which she restricted food for several days. My colleague made solid interpretations, relating the behavior with food to her mixed feelings about having needs. Joanne was open to new ways of understanding herself and was outwardly compliant, but her pattern of bingeing, followed by starving, did not change and the therapy felt stalled.

The therapist saw Joanne for double sessions twice a week and noticed a pattern emerging: Joanne complied with treatment for a few weeks, and then abruptly canceled the following week's sessions. She was always apologetic, providing compelling reasons for the cancellations—illness, work issues, and various emergencies—and vowed to "get back on track" upon her return. This pattern had been going on for a period of several months. Despite a great deal of therapeutic insights, interventions, and ideas, the treatment was not progressing. My colleague felt frustrated, lost, and useless.

I was struck by the double sessions, which my colleague explained was a way of being flexible and working within the confines of Joanne's schedule. Although this arrangement appeared reasonable on the surface, it mirrored the problem that had brought Joanne to treatment. I proposed that Joanne was enacting a relational bulimia with my colleague, bingeing on her via the double sessions, getting twice as much time as was customary and normal. This behavior with the therapy was analogous to her periods of bingeing on food, in which she ate "twice as much" as normal. The cancellations were periods of emotional starvation in which she restricted herself from access to the therapeutic feeding. She was, in effect, purging her therapist, leaving my colleague hungry for Joanne's presence, as well as feeling bewildered and stuck. When the therapist explored the experience of feeling stuck, useless, and unimportant, Joanne immediately thought about her older sister, who was sometimes very nice and affectionate and other times, inexplicably, remote and rejecting, leaving Joanne bewildered. She was unconsciously recreating that identical dynamic with her therapist.

When the therapist helped Joanne address the repercussions of these early childhood experiences, the treatment finally began to shift. As this example shows, it is not only parental relationships that leave their mark; sibling and other experiences can leave painful marks on people's psyche, and when they are not resolved, they are often enacted in some behavioral or relational form.

RESISTANCE TO TRANSFERENCE

Some patients resist developing transference, fearing that trust leaves them vulnerable. Often, when these patients begin to experience any kind of dependence on the analyst, they withdraw, leave treatment, or paralyze the treatment because the revival of early dependency experiences seems intolerable. This regression is an important part of the work. As Harold Blum puts it, regression in treatment serves as a way of finding "the child that lived on in the patient" (1984, p. 69), but for some patients, such reversion to an earlier time in their lives is intolerable.

"IT'S NOT MY MOTHER AT ALL"

I previously discussed Alanna, who was raised by a single mother who could not relate to her and often left her to fend for herself. In the first few weeks of treatment, Alanna appeared to experience me as a potentially good maternal object. Reflecting back, I now think that what appeared to be a positive transference was actually an enactment. She started off with three sessions a week, then four, and then finally five. To remain a good object, I had to be a perfect mother with no needs of my own and an endless supply of time and patience with which to meet her needs and wants. At the time, I consciously felt as if she was bingeing on me. She was like a ravenous baby, hungering for more and more of my analytic food, which took the form of time, interest, compassion, and availability.

A few months later, she met her boyfriend, Adam, and began a period of displacement in which she projected her experiences with me onto others. Nine months into the treatment, a negative transference erupted, in which Alanna recreated and reversed her childhood experiences: I was the hungry, angry, bewildered child-analyst to her sadistic mother-patient. This nine-month period seemed at the time to parallel the timeframe of pregnancy, after which Alanna gave psychological birth to a ravenous, angry part of herself.

Initially, there was some indication that Alanna might form a healthy attachment to me. She said she felt comfortable coming to session. "It is not like my mother at all. I thought, 'At least I have her to talk to. It's not my mother at all. It's completely different.'" In this instance, she referred to me as "it" and as "her," talking about me in the third person instead of experiencing me as someone who was actually there in the room with her, listening. Still, I viewed this as a step forward in terms of developing trust in an "other" and in establishing our therapeutic alliance.

Looking back, I was overly optimistic. Alanna's experience of me as a potentially good object began to shift as the maternal transference increased. One morning, a few weeks after we began the analysis, I opened the door to the waiting room, and Alanna held up a large paper bag filled with clothes, which she then left by the waiting room door. In that session, after telling me how she felt like a bad kid for doing bad things, such as eating too much, talking back, and fighting with her brother, she said, "For a good eight years my mother screamed at me for leaving my backpack at the door."

I pointed out that she had left her bag by the waiting room door. She looked surprised and frowned, saying, "Maybe I was testing you to see if it was okay."

Alanna was unable to elaborate on what she meant by this. I now realize the extent to which her inner world was unknown to her. Her development was halted at such an early level, before she had the capacity to symbolize, that her thoughts and emotions were undifferentiated and diffuse, unavailable for identification and processing.

She soon began to experience me as assessing her. She viewed me as an amorphous authority figure with whom she had no relationship. She referred to sessions as "interviews" and gave her full name on phone messages. She referred to treatment as "it" (i.e., "I realize I need it," and "It's okay to lean on it," and "I will be fine without it"). She requested a "phone interview" a few times before I brought the phrase to her attention. She reflected, "The fact that I keep thinking of it that way makes me see how much pressure I put on myself."

I said, "How awful to feel like you're interviewing five times a week for a job you don't know if you're getting."

Alanna was silent for a moment. "Is this a waste? I don't know if I need this, but I don't know if I don't need this."

In fact, she was conflicted about needing anyone, since a need for a connection with another translated into the potential loss of self in the ensuing merger. I recognized Alanna's dilemma, yet I still felt discarded, devalued, and unimportant. I knew this reflected how Alanna experienced her world, since she felt dismissed and unimportant as a child and continued to feel marginalized in all aspects of her life. I found the process of reviewing the clinical material from that time to be challenging, and reflected that the treatment had at times been distasteful. I was then struck by my selection of the word "distasteful," not a word I normally use. The Latin prefix "dis" connotes having a negative or reversing force, and the element "taste," originally referred to exploration by touching. My attempts to reach Alanna, to touch her mind and emotions, felt as difficult as connecting two opposing magnets.

Alanna soon rendered me less of an interviewer and more of a nonentity, possibly a defense against a positive transference and any dependency, which for her was both compelling and frightening. For a period of time, she did not respond directly to any of my interpretations or responses.

Akhtar (2009) defines relational displacement as "changing an instinctual drive's object while retaining its aim" and gave the example that "i.e., hating one person is changed into hating someone else" (p. 82). In Alanna's case, to "hunger" for closeness with me produced too much anxiety, since for her, closeness meant potential loss of self. Her solution was to displace her wishes and fears about me onto others. For example, she said of her roommate, who was rarely at home, and with whom she spent hardly any time, "It was nice to have someone on my side." Of Adam, a few weeks after they started dating, she said, "He really listens to me. I'm very, very happy. He really listens to me. He doesn't push advice. It's nice."

Although she consciously denied the therapeutic relationship, she often made reference to the number of sessions per week (five times per week) and to the fee ($250 per week), which suggested that the work was resonating with her in some way:

- Going "on the internet for five hours"
- Sleeping for five hours on May 5th
- Eating "five days worth of food" at once
- Spending $250 (her weekly fee) on food
- Saying if she were a personal trainer she'd charge $250

Alanna's associations about other people also served as commentaries about me, but they were also displaced. By separating emotion and expectation from its real object and redirecting those emotions and expectations toward someone else, she avoided dealing directly with what was frightening or threatening—in large part, her fear of vulnerability and dependency, which she feared would lead to abandonment and rejection.

Most of the transference material was displaced onto Adam. She often shifted contradictory views of me onto him, as exemplified by these statements: "Adam doesn't judge. He's just observing me. He's concerned about me" and, in the same session, "He (Adam) is good at taking care of me and I wasn't taking it in. I was ignoring it and pushing it away." She appeared to view him/me as both a neutral, nonjudgmental observer and as a concerned other whose care and concern she pushed away, just as she did with my care and concern for her.

Her associations also indicated recognition that she was not making full use of the therapeutic relationship. She said, "He (Adam) is still not taking complete advantage of how good it (their relationship) is." In this statement, Adam appeared as a representation of her, not of me.

While facing financial hardship, she impulsively quit her job and reported, "It was just like my family. Stupid people. Dealing with that for five hours a day, having someone telling you what you need to work on, it's not healthy."

Alanna had difficulty experiencing herself as someone who could be loved. She said, ""Part of me thinks he (Adam) doesn't like me or love me. I'm not a big enough deal to help me, so even if he says 'I love you,' well, he says that to everyone."

These observations may have been an oblique reference to other patients ("everyone"), whose existence weakened my feelings toward her, just as she believed the existence of her brother had weakened her mother's love for her. One of Alanna's most painful memories was asking her mother if she loved Alanna as much as she loved her older brother. Her mother replied that she loved them both, but "you never love anyone like you love your first born."

My attempts to connect these displacements and fears to her experience of our therapeutic relationship were disregarded. Alanna's responses to interpretations or attempts at clarification were either to ignore me or to say, "I thought of that, too." Everything that I had to give her was thus depreciated. In effect, she was telling me that I could not give her any thoughts, interpretations, or alternative explanations that she did not already know. She had no need for my therapeutic food; everything she needed she could produce and give to herself.

My rational understanding of Alanna's conflict over dependency helped me withstand her unrelenting repudiation of my interest, help, and efforts to understand her. I tried to minimize my annoyance, disgust, and even repulsion, believing at the time that those feelings were inappropriate. After reading Winnicott's (1949a) exploration of "hate in the counter-transference" (p. 70), I gave myself permission to hate how Alanna treated me, to hate the choices she made, and even to hate Alanna herself. Winnicott (1949a) suggests that mothers hate their babies for a number of reasons, including that the baby is "ruthless, treats her as scum, an unpaid servant, a slave" (p. 73), which accurately sums up how I felt with Alanna.

Surrendering to hate actually allowed me to open up to more loving feelings toward her. At the time that I was treating Alanna, my youngest daughter was two years old, and had numerous sleep issues, awakening me several times a night for a period of over a year. I certainly did not like being awakened multiple times a night, but I understood my daughter's sleep difficulties and loved her unconditionally. I eventually felt parallel feelings toward Alanna, whose conflicts I understood, and I eventually developed the ability to hold both resentment and warmth toward her.

In time there came a slight shift, perhaps because we both survived our mutual, unspoken hatred. Alanna was sometimes able think about how her actions impacted others and was less locked into a predominantly paranoid-schizoid position, in which people were either good or bad. She had the capacity to be in more of a depressive position, in which others could frustrate or disappoint her but still be held as good objects in some way, as in the following examples:

> My mother gave me $50 to use on gas. I want to use that for bingeing. I felt like it was abusing her, to use it on food.

And:

> Part of me is sad that I can't have him (Adam) completely be there for me, but part of me is okay with what I can get for myself. It's kind of like therapy.

Her tacit acknowledgment that her actions were abusive to others represented a move toward empathy and self-object constancy, as did her ability to hold both sadness and acceptance. I attributed this to our work together, that five days a week, for ten months, she experienced enough consistency and predictability to begin to trust that I was a reliable person who would be there for her. Additionally, there had been enough ruptures and repairs, with Adam, for her to hope that there could be goodness in the relationship, even when she experienced pain.

Despite Alanna's recognition that she was abusing her mother's trust by using gas money for binges, and regardless of her embryonic acceptance that she might have to meet her own needs instead of relying completely on others, she did little to change her circumstances. As Alanna's life unraveled and she faced eviction, she remained jobless and made only sporadic attempts to find work. She continued to defend against any feelings of dependency. She said, "I don't feel the need to call my mother. All I need is a nice place to live and my gym membership." She began to give mixed messages about the importance of our work. When I told her of my upcoming vacation, the first separation in ten months, I asked if she had any reaction to my upcoming absence. She shrugged. "I thought, good for you. It's a lot. I need a break from it."

Later in that session, however, she described a contentious conversation with her mother. She said, "I saw you there as well, sort of in the foreground, kind of on my side, kind of like you would back me up."

She struggled to take me in as a whole object and depend on me, while, at the same time, she purged any representation of me. When I suggested that she see the film *Black Swan*, she saw it a few days later. The film is rife with symbolism about splitting, integration, and the impact of a mother who gives double bind messages, as hers did. Natalie Portman plays the main character whose name is Nina Sayers (similar to Nina Savelle). A number of other patients who saw the film had commented on the fact that the movie character had "my" name. When Alanna and I talked about the movie, I told her I would refer to the main character as "Natalie Portman" because it felt strange for me to call the character Nina by my name.

Alanna shrugged. "Oh, I didn't even notice that."

Although many other patients reported thinking of me when they saw the movie, since the central character shared my name, Alanna had not made that connection. This lack of object constancy was a pervasive feature of her relationships with me and with other people. She could not attach to the person who was available, but turned toward the unavailable other, repeating the desperate yearning of her childhood. If the object of her affection returned her feelings, she spurned him or her, and reversed their roles. In this way, she attempted to turn me into the hungry one, desperate to connect with Alanna, who remained unreachable.

This kept her hungry, unfulfilled, and starving for connection, a state of the heart that was symbolically expressed through her binges on food and subsequent purging.

"NOT ALL OF ME SHALL DIE"

Shelby, the patient who used food to express aggression, grew up in the Los Angeles area. She was an only child and her parents divorced when she was in her early teens, after which she lived primarily with her narcissistic, alcoholic mother. She was an honors student in high school, bright and hardworking, but nobody in her family ever encouraged her to go to college. She developed a passion for dance and aspired to be a professional pole dancer, viewing it as a form of art, rather than a sexually provocative endeavor. Shelby was diligent and smart, but always dismissed those qualities. She privileged her body as her primary self, objectified her body, and expected others to do the same. She felt lovable only when her body was acknowledged and praised.

As a child, Shelby felt miserable at school, where she didn't fit in, and at home, where her mother was either drunk or preoccupied with her brother. She finally felt recognized and accepted when she lost weight in high school and became an object of sexual desire to boys. For the first time, she also won her mother's admiration and love. Shelby feared if she lost her looks, she would lose her mother's love. Her bulimia intensified after an older boyfriend (in forties) rejected her, possibly a retraumatization of the earlier, and ongoing, rejection from her mother.

Although Shelby's sense of self was embryonic at the time she started treatment, there were also glimpses of a wish to relinquish bad introjects. She wanted to get a tattoo that read: *non omnis moriar.*

Translated, "Not all of me shall die."

In our work together, I sought to help Shelby identify and understand the underlying conflicts that contributed to her bulimia, but she only wanted to focus on her body. She did not imagine that her mind, thoughts, emotions, humor, and intelligence could interest me or anyone else. She had internalized her mother's view of the body self as the only self worthy noticing.

She began to notice how pervasive the messages about using the body as a means to influence the world were, as she paid attention to the communications in her family. When she got the highest grade in his college class, their mother attributed this to the teacher wanting to have sex with her, not to her hard work or effort. Shelby now sees her mother's attitude as repugnant but she originally identified with this viewpoint and thought her body was a means of impacting other people's behavior or view of her. This allowed for the illusion of omnipotence: if a guy did not like her, she could lose weight and make him want her. If her mother did not love her, she could win that love by becoming thinner and thus more beautiful.

Shelby recalled that when her mother stayed in bed for days, drunk and depressed, she viewed her mother as a mysterious, romantic figure, not as rejecting and unavailable. Shelby associated battling demons with being interesting. She yearned to be the same tragic, romantic figure, alluring to others. Bulimia was one way to achieve that.

The identification with her mother was most evident in her relationship to her own needs and wants. She treated herself the way she was treated, dismissive of any emotions or needs, and only interested in her body self, a body that she thought was never good enough.

A turning point occurred when her mother was caught shoplifting at Target and her Target credit card was confiscated. The card was under Shelby's name, so her mother demanded that Shelby lie to Target and request a new card under a different name. Shelby was initially conflicted, but ultimately refused, honoring her own moral code. Her mother retaliated by forcing her to move out, ostensibly because her room was too messy. Shelby moved in with her father and finally began to process her rage and disappointment toward her mother.

A month into our analytic work, Shelby commented as she departed the session, "I feel like I'm leaving a lover or something."

A week later, as she prepared to show me a video of a pole-dancing event, she said, "I feel like I need to warn you, it'll be sexy."

When I asked her to tell me more about this warning, she responded, "I guess I'm making you into a judge. I make most people into a judge."

She feared I would judge her emotions as "dramatic" or think that she was "bragging" instead of sharing her accomplishments, all aspects of maternal transference. She also worried that she was not making enough progress. "I keep talking about the same things. I keep chasing my tail."

I noted, "You're a dog again."

She nodded. "I don't want to be human."

Shelby's wish to feel close to me was initially sexualized, as evident in her comment about leaving a lover. She did not want to be human and have needs, because as a child those needs were not met, a lack of responsiveness that was humiliating and unbearable. She could not trust that her mother was interested in her. In the transference, she did not trust that I was interested in her. She had to earn my interest in her through insights and epiphanies. In one session, as she discussed feeling compelled to continually prove herself earn love, she began to crave sugar. Shelby used thoughts about food or binges, as well as attacks on her body ("I'm fat, I'm disgusting") to distract from painful or upsetting states. As she realized this method of protecting herself from difficult feelings, she became more aware of a need inside, not for sugar, but for emotional sweetness.

Other than fears of my judging her, Shelby did not initially relate to me much. She talked and cried and shared, but without interaction. She was not responsive to my attempts to connect with her. I began to point out moments when she fled from my question and attacked her body, a way of avoiding relating with me and feeling uncomfortable.

If I noted something interpersonal between us, she invariable responded with an attack on her body. She referred to me either in the third person or to therapy as "in here" or "this work" or some other vernacular that denied the relational aspect of our work.

Shelby's fears about closeness were enacted in the transference. She often cast me as a teacher, a parent, or an employer, as if I was observing her, rather than someone who was interested in understanding her and also connecting with her. The couch was a stage and I was her audience. She also treated the analysis as an obligation to me, rather than something she was doing for herself. She was aware that the analysis was a part of my doctoral program, and that I benefited from our work together, but she had difficulty imagining there could be a relational aspect to our interaction. She experienced me as a judge who was to be mollified, or a parent who was to be pleased, instead of a person who wanted to talk with her.

Other times she thought of me "like a girlfriend" who she could share her thoughts and dreams. She occasionally elicited a maternal reaction from me, such as when she told me she was driving an unsafe vehicle, and I urged her to make sure the car was safe to drive. She found it touching, and was surprised that I was worried about her. This worry was also an anomalous experience for her, as neither parent ever expressed concern about her safety or well-being.

I recognized that Shelby's fear of closeness derived from her association to closeness as dangerous; if she allowed herself to get close to others, they might destroy her, eat her up, and feast on her, or conversely, she might devour them. If she allowed herself to feel connected with me, would she be the eater or the eaten?

One of her solutions to this dilemma was to focus on her body, and she consistently attempted to make the relationship with her body the primary focus of the work. Each breakthrough we had in terms of understanding her dilemma about connections with others was inevitably followed by a period of intense focus on her physicality—if not her weight, then her sensation of dizziness, her anxiety, and other somatic complaints.

Despite my intellectual understanding that this body-centric focus was a solution to her wish–fear dilemma about relationships, I began to feel increasingly frustrated by her relentless attacks on herself. Her relationship to her physical self was primary, and at times it seemed that I could never hope to break that bond and connect with her.

In considering this further, my countertransference may have given me a visceral understanding of what Shelby felt as a child, standing on the outside of her mother's closed door, feeling frustrated, helpless, and hopeless about ever getting inside or feeling close. Similarly, her mother had privileged the relationship with her brother, and she constantly felt on the outside of their relationship, too. In my attempts to reach Shelby, I constantly felt marginalized by her relationship to her body.

I also had strong reactions to her lack of self-care. She took risks by inviting men she just met to her house. She resisted her needs for food and rest.

When she was hungry, she either starved herself or ate large quantities of unsatisfying faux food, such as protein bars or diet shakes, until she was full and uncomfortable. When she was tired, she rebelled against her need for sleep and stayed up even later. I found it difficult not to react when she shared the harshness with which she treated her basic needs. I did express concern about the safety of her car, but otherwise resisted the impulse to be maternal with her until she told me that she usually fell asleep with gum in her mouth and mixed wine and sleeping pills.

I told her that I was very concerned about the risks she was taking, and explored both the behavior itself and her reaction to my taking a parental stance with her. She told me she liked it when I expressed concern, and it made her feel warm inside. In this way, she was able to make use of me as an auxiliary ego, a new object she could make use of, and internalize. Winnicott (1974) states that the only way for patients to move forward is to utilize the auxiliary ego function of the analyst to deal with that past.

Two years into analysis Shelby said, "I was bingeing and I had this weird feeling and I wanted to write you and tell you I love you. I had food in my mouth. I don't know why I didn't write you, but I wanted to. Then I spit the food out."

In acknowledging the love she felt for me, she was able to fill up in some way. Feeling real love obviated her need for food. She was able to spit out food and retain the good feeling of connection, and allow herself to hold onto the feelings of love.

Chapter Nine

Dreams

Freud (1900) considers dreams the "the royal road to a knowledge of the unconscious activities of the mind" (p. 608) and views dreams as either attempts to resolve conflict or as a means of fulfilling a wish. He theorizes that when dreaming, certain defenses are lowered, so that some areas of mental conflict become available, but in a distorted form. This represents a compromise between the part of the mind that is ready to access repressed material and that part that wants to continue the repression.

Freud believed certain dream images had universal meaning. Dreams about being naked in public are commonly about shame. Authority figures such as bosses or political figures often stand for parents, and objects such as knives, umbrellas, sticks, and swords are considered to be phallic symbols. Despite the universality of certain images, dreams are understood to be the specific production of the dreamer and therefore the meaning of each dream is highly individual. Analysts must explore the patient's own associations, memories, thoughts, and ideas about the dream, rather than relying on external meaning of symbols.

Freud (1900) differentiates between the manifest content of a dream, which is what a dreamer remembers of the dream, and the latent content, which is the symbolic content hidden within the dream imagery. This latent content may be deciphered by exploring the dreams in terms of the following: (1) *displacement*, when the wish something or someone is symbolized by something or someone else; (2) *projection*, when the dreamer puts his or her own wishes into someone else in the dream; symbolization, in which one thing is represented by another; (3) *condensation*, the process by which the dreamer hides feelings and/or urges by amalgamating several thoughts into one symbol, or creating a composite of different people into one; (4) *rationalization*, in which the dreamer reorganizes a threatening or upsetting conflict into one that is logical, reasonable, and safe.

Some dreams are the result of wishes, fears, conflicts, and more rising toward consciousness and simultaneously being prohibited, which leads to those wishes and so forth being disguised through the process of condensation, displacement, symbolism, and secondary revision. Dreams may also serve to resolve problems, or may recreate traumatic situations or express unconscious fears. One patient who underwent a lap band procedure and lost a significant amount of weight began having nightmares about very specific numerical dates: January 3, 1983; August 21, 2009; and so forth. She reported seeing these numbers in her mind's eye, as if on an old-fashioned newsreel, looming toward her, and felt an overwhelming panic. She could not figure out the significance of these particular dates in history. She shuddered, "I don't know why these dates give me the creeps." I recalled that she had recently signed up for an online dating site and was excited to start meeting men, hoping to fulfill her lifelong wish to find a loving relationship and create a family. I wondered if her unconscious mind was expressing fear of dating by converting romantic dates into numerical dates. This interpretation struck a chord with her and as we explored her fears about relationships, the recurring nightmares ceased.

Dreams are often the royal road to connection with the analyst, as well. In exploring the dreams of anorexic and bulimic women in an inpatient program, Brink and Allan (1992) found that patients who resisted talking in session were able to report their dreams. They understand that dreams are "an acceptable avenue for connection, within the framework of a perception of dreams as being outside personal issues. Therefore, producing dreams could be a way to establish a relationship with the therapist and have her full attention, without any threat of personal self-disclosure" (p. 275). They identify four common themes in the dreams of anorexic and bulimic women (p. 283):

1. The presence of a sense of impending doom at the end of the dream.
2. The attitude "whatever I do I won't succeed."
3. Images of the dreamer being attacked by a person, animal, or thing.
4. Images of being watched as if guilty of something, or of being inadequate.

They highlight the prevalence of helplessness in the dreams of these women and concluded that when it comes to treating women with eating disorders, "the therapist is more likely to promote positive transformation through focusing on their dreams than trying to change their behavior" (p 293).

As noted previously, helplessness is an unbearable state. Hoffer and Buie (2016) recall that Freud considered the state of helplessness to be a traumatic situation. For one of my patients, Maryam, 32, her profound terror at the state of helplessness was conveyed through dreams about airplanes. Early in treatment she dreamed, "I was in a house. It was really beautiful on the outside but inside it was dark and dingy and difficult to see. Suddenly I felt as if I was in an airplane with no windows and I couldn't feel where I was. It was as if the house had turned into a plane and it was in a nosedive."

This house/plane represented her sense of self and the world. Like the house, Maryam was a beautiful woman who often had trouble peering into her internal world and complained that she was "in the dark" about who she was, even wondering if analysis would uncover something bad about her. Several months later she had another dream in which she was in an airplane.

"I was on a plane with a guy I knew from the gym and there was no separation between the passengers and the cockpit. There was only one pilot. The plane kept making huge turns and it freaked me out but I tried to trust the pilot. The pilot got up and started talking to the guy from the gym. He told me the plane was on autopilot and not to worry. I began to plead for him to go back to his seat but he wouldn't listen. Then the plane began to come apart. The pilot ran for the controls but I knew it was too late."

In the second dream, Maryam referenced both her wish to trust the pilot, who possibly represented me, and her fear that she could not entrust her emotional safety to anyone else, including me. In our sessions she often wondered if I was following some kind of analytic script, which may be what the "autopilot" meant.

Three years into analysis her dreams about planes began to show a shift in her ability to trust that the analytic experience could be safe.

"I was with a bunch of people in a giant seaplane. The seats were more like twin beds or maybe a couch. Everyone was very, very nice. The plane crashed but we were okay."

We discussed this as signifying a developing trust that the analysis, as represented by the seats that looked like a couch, could "take off" and that no matter what happened she would be okay. More recently she had a dream in which she turned her helplessness into mastery.

"I was on a plane that was more spacious than a plane normally is. The pilot was jovial. As we started taxiing I saw there was a hole in the top of the plane. I said, 'Oh, no,' but nobody else was worried. I went to the pilots and told them. The co-pilot said, 'Oh, the plane is just falling apart.' I said it needed to be fixed and they actually listened to me. They pulled over and started pulling out baggage from overhead so they could get to the hole and fix it."

In this dream, Maryam took action and insisted that the hole in the plane had to be attended to, because she did not want to fall apart. These holes stood for the gaps in her life, her lack of safety and trust. By taking out all the emotional "baggage" the hole could be repaired and she could safely take off into her life.

Dreams may also reveal conflicts about the treatment and can be particularly useful in elucidating unconscious fears about trust, dependency, attachment, and resistance to change, that patients consciously deny. One woman often told me how much she appreciated and enjoyed the experience of psychoanalysis. She also reported two dreams in one night that revealed a different perspective.

"A female serial murderer knew I was onto her. She tried to kill me and I tried to fight back, but she was strong, and it was an even match. I didn't win but either did she. Then the dream shifted and a blonde Valkyrie tried to trick me. She showed me how to go back in time to deliver a message to someone, but really she was going to send me back to be killed."

Franz Alexander (1925) suggests that, "two or more dreams in the same night stand in some sort of relation to one another" (p. 446). He proposes that the second dream is less disguised than the first and serves as a more open expression of the dreamer's conflict. In the first dream, the patient created a disguised version of her conflict; the part of her that wanted to fight me, along with my ability to withstand her resistance, which ended in essentially a draw. This might also be understood as a battle between the part that wanted to change and the part that did not. Interestingly, this patient often binged on cereal, which lends itself to the "serial" killer symbolism. In second dream, I was a blonde Valkyrie who wanted her to go back in time, which we understood as uncovering the past, ostensibly to give a message to someone (her younger self or her unconscious self) but I had destruction in mind, the destruction of a part of her that she did not want to relinquish.

A male patient recalled his dream of the night before:

> I went to a session but your office was completely different and cluttered with all kinds of stuff. I didn't lie on the couch. You didn't seem to know who I was and asked questions that made no sense, which made me realize that you weren't paying attention.

This man's mother was often preoccupied and unable to focus on him, and his dream revealed a transference fear that he would have the same experience with me as he did with his mother.

Many of my patients with eating disorder dream about the dangers of food and aggression. Some examples are as follows:

> I was pregnant with a baby that had an alligator snout. An alien species was wiping out the planet by eating people and I knew this baby would eat me from the

inside out. Then I had the baby and I was hiding her from the others and hoping she would not turn into a meat-eating monster.

This person had been cultivating a new (baby) part of her that could be hungry for life, for love, for connection, and she was simultaneously terrified that getting in touch with her hungry self would be "creating a monster."

"I was on a narrow path. On one side are lots of cute animals. Suddenly lions come out, ready to devour the animals, who run for their lives, and the lions start coming towards me. On the other side is an ocean with shark people, humanoid monsters with fins who are absolutely terrifying."

The dreamer articulated through dream imagery the Scylla and Charybdis dilemma of having two terrible choices, each equally destructive in different ways. Both the choices involve being devoured, and revealed the dreamer's terror of being destroyed by anger, and her wish to express her anger, to "bite the heads off" of people who upset her.

An anorexic woman cringed as she recalled how in childhood her father would comment that she had a "lusty appetite" and therefore imbued food with a tinge of sexuality. That night she dreamed the following:

I was grinding some gross food down the disposal. It turned into snakes and they snaked out of the disposal and the sink, ran around the floor and up my back.

She awakened, shaken and "freaked out" by these horrible dream images. That week she had another dream in which snakes and food figured prominently.

"I was in a hotel pool and a big man was kind of holding me down. There was a giant white snake in the pool, coming towards me. I tried to get away but the big man was pushing me down. My husband helped me get away from the man and then he made sure I got to safety. Later, my husband offered me a snake sandwich, but I refused."

For this patient, snakes represented male sexuality, which was extremely threatening and dangerous to her. The big man holding her down may have been the father who forced his ideas on her, who saw her as "lusty" and the white snake was his dangerous introduction of sexuality into their relationship, through food. Her husband saved her but offered her a snake sandwich, a condensation of food and sexuality. She loved her husband and often was conflicted about sex and felt "like a thing" with him, even when she consciously knew that he was not objectifying her.

A few days later she reported a dream in which, "I was at a restaurant eating meat, raw meat, which I thought was the best meat that I'd ever had, but then the meat made me turn into a vampire."

Her association to vampires was that vampires are driven by their compulsions and are extremely destructive, as well as sexy. She feared her hunger would overwhelm her and take over her life that she would be beholden to the very needs against which she fought daily. She hated being hungry and she resisted sexual feelings, fearing what would happen if she let go. She said, "If I let myself get hungry, I'll eat the world" or, "I don't want to give in to sex. It's so dirty and basic. It makes us like animals." She feared the animal side of herself, and denied the primal, hungry, sexual part of her personality, yet the simultaneous wish to fulfill her hunger and sexuality was evident in her dream.

Shelby, who did not want to be human and had pretended to be a dog as a child, often expressed her fears about closeness and connection in her dreams. In one dream, she reported, "Aliens were feasting on humans and took you by just touching you. They had to get close to you to know if you were human."

In another she dreamed of, "being eaten by huge, faceless leech creatures. A friend of mine, a man who'd been infected by this disease, turned slowly into a leech. This big, black leech with razor sharp teeth, faceless, no eyes, nothing. He was going to kill us all. He was evil. He was so . . . hungry."

These dreams illustrated the perception that hungering for closeness was dangerous and destructive. In addition, these dreams expressed aggression through feasting on, killing, and eating others. Eating and aggression were firmly linked in her mind. For Shelby, relationships were based on playing the role of either the eater or the eaten.

For another patient, Elle, dreams were the key to making contact with me in a meaningful way. When I first met Elle, my first thought was that she could have just walked off the cover of Vogue magazine. Elle sought treatment for anorexia, which she had struggled with on and off since adolescence. I was immediately struck by her guardedness and hopefulness. She initially sat in painful, awkward, tortured silence, unable or unwilling to articulate her thoughts, but I sensed that she truly wanted to connect. She appeared to be locked inside herself yet desperately searching for a way out.

In response to my questions about her current symptoms, history, thoughts, and emotions, she answered either, "I don't know" or said she did not see the point of talking about the past. I later discovered that when she was a child, nobody talked with her; instead, she received orders, commands, and dictums. Her parents did not ask how she was feeling or want she wanted or needed. She therefore had difficulty believing that I wanted to get to know her and was interested in what was going on in her mind and heart.

Elle asked, "What's the point of talking about my feelings? It doesn't change the situation."

I explained that people don't express feelings to change a situation. We do so to change how we feel about that situation. I used the example of mourning a loved one. When someone dies, we don't say, "What's the point of feeling sad or upset? It won't bring the person back to life." We go through the stages of grief, feeling sad, bereft, helpless, and upset because doing helps us come to terms with our loss. By saying goodbye and remembering the person who's gone, we can go on with our lives, missing the dead yet carrying on the memories and the love.

Elle's outlet for expressing herself was as a songwriter, and she also loved singing. One day she volunteered that she had written some new songs, adding, "I'm sure you don't want to hear the dance music. It's not deep."

I said, "I want to hear all of it."

At our next session she related a dream from the night before: she was in a black and white bathroom, had no privacy, and she couldn't go to the bathroom. We explored this in terms of the black and white thinking that dominated her life, the wish for privacy and the feeling of being exposed, which was likely about our therapeutic relationship. She could not let herself "go" in our sessions, could not let out the thoughts, emotions, ideas, wishes, and fears that were inside her.

And yet, she kept trying. After some time together, Elle began talking about her dreams on a regular basis, finding it a safe way for her to communicate her inner world. She did not always have the words to articulate what she was thinking or feeling, but the dreams allowed her to express herself. By interpreting her dreams, I got to know her better and also had a chance to introduce her to herself. I found Elle to be bright, funny, sweet, resilient, and courageous. I liked her very much and hoped that she could eventually begin to see herself through my eyes.

When she brought in one of her songs, I was hopeful that she was beginning to trust me. She could not look at me as I listened to the song, absolutely awestruck. Her singing voice was strong, powerful, and passionate, in contrast to her usually quiet speaking voice. "What a voice," I exclaimed. I wondered aloud what happened to that voice when she walked out of a recording studio and into her life. I knew that I was hearing from a part of Elle that she kept hidden from most people.

Elle brought in more songs to share with me. Her lyrics expressed many of the thoughts, emotions, feelings, and hopes that she struggled to articulate in our sessions. Many of the songs were about conflicts over trust, wanting to be with someone and to trust that person, but fearing that she'd be hurt, betrayed, or lose her identity. This theme also showed up in her dreams. Elle began to have recurring dreams about people breaking into her house and stealing or destroying things. Someone destroyed her artwork and she felt, "betrayed, scared, upset, angry, violated."

She could not associate to any fears about her current situation. I asked if she remembered feeling that way at any point in her life. She could not, yet the dreams of intrusion continued night after night. Her father, who had unexpectedly passed away a year before her anorexia resurfaced, began appearing

nightly in her dreams, bringing uninvited guests into the house of her childhood, cramming furniture into the house, and taking over the space. In the
dreams, Elle could not bring herself to protest at the intrusion and felt she
simply had to submit to her father's wishes.

These thematic dreams continued for weeks. Elle grappled with new feelings of horror that she could not understand. She started to have physical pain
in her stomach. Finally, after several tortured and tormented weeks, Elle haltingly revealed a terrible and horrific secret. When she was seven years old,
her father had sexually abused her. The abuse continued through adolescence,
when he suddenly "dropped" her. She interpreted the abuse as punishment,
believing she must be a terrible person for her father to hurt her in that way.
Restricting food served multiple purposes: although she could not stop the
violation of her body, she could keep food out of her body, creating a sense
of mastery. For many years, her body had functioned as her sole means of
communication, yet nobody had interpreted the language of her body.

Now Elle had a voice and she could speak up. Together, we began to work
through and process the pain and rage of her childhood abuse and neglect.
Her excruciatingly painful memories, awakened in her dreams, ultimately
began the slow, difficult, painful process of healing.

COUNTERTRANSFERENCE DREAMS

Much has been written about the dreams that patients have about the analyst.
Not as much has been written about countertransference dreams, those that
the analyst has about patients. These dreams are an extremely valuable tool
to help analysts recognize and consider features of the treatment that may be
out of consciousness.

During the analysis of Alanna, the patient who resisted the development of
transference, displaced the transference, and rendered me an "it" throughout
our treatment, she was a subject of both my waking thoughts and on one
occasion, a dream. In that dream, Alanna and I were in New York together,
navigating busy streets, and I was unsuccessfully trying to catch up to her.
We were traveling together, but I could not connect with her. As soon as I got
close, she darted off to go somewhere else. At one point, she began hanging
out with someone else, leaving me behind.

This dream paralleled the dynamics of the analytic relationship: Alanna
let herself be with me to a point, but then created distance between us, finding safety either in being alone or with someone else (such as her boyfriend
Adam), until the closeness with that person made her uncomfortable and she
repeated the pattern. For Alanna, connection with others registered as both
compelling and dangerous.

This dream encapsulated my wish to connect with Alanna and my frustration at not being able to do so, at being thwarted at every turn. I wondered what could be done to assuage her fears and trust me. I also experienced a sense of vexation at her elusiveness. My efforts to connect with Alanna are again best described by an idiom, that of trying to capture mercury with bare hands; an impossible and dangerous task to complete.

Another way of understanding this dream is that it communicates Alanna's experience with her mother, to whom she could not relate, and who remained elusive. Favero and Ross (2002) see countertransference dreams as a means of representing aspects of a patient's unconscious communication and may also help the analyst identify his or her own resistances to identifying and processing the transference. As I reflect back now, I see that the dream has multiple layers, including an aspect of wish-fulfillment in my case; in some ways, I did not want to catch up to Alanna, fearing she would deplete me with her ravenous hunger for my time, compassion, and care, along with her simultaneous indifference to me.

Nearly three years into Elle's analysis, I dreamed she was on trial for a serious offense, although the details of her supposed crime were unclear. I knew with absolute certainty that she was innocent of the charges. I sat in a courtroom that looked more like a theater, my youngest daughter beside me. My daughter was seven years old at the time, the same age that Elle had been when the abuse started. Elle's husband kept coming up to check in with me and ask how I thought the trial was going. Eventually Elle was acquitted of the crime for which she had been accused. As onlookers went to congratulate her, Elle made her way straight to me, radiating joy and relief. She hugged me, thanking me for my help, and said, "I love you."

I hugged her back, telling her, "I love you, too."

She looked at me with a hurt expression. "Why aren't you saying anything?" she asked.

"But I did," I quickly said. "I told you I love you."

"Why aren't you saying anything?" she repeated. I realized that she could not hear me. I sensed that she was starting to pull away, withdrawing into herself. I repeated, "But I do love you." She looked as if I'd rejected her instead of professing my loving, caring feelings for her. She turned away, visibly hurt and miserable.

I felt confused, upset, and at a loss. Why couldn't she hear me? Then the dream shifted and I found myself in a hotel that was attached to the courtroom/theater. The hotel was huge, with many levels and countless rooms and suites. I was in a suite trying to put on make-up but I kept misplacing my cosmetics bag. I knew I needed to put on make-up before I could join the victory celebration for Elle. I finally found some lip gloss and had a hard time applying it. When I was finally ready to leave, I could not find my way out of the maze of rooms. I made multiple attempts to get out, without success.

I understood this dream as portraying the experience of our analytic work. My dream cast Elle's husband as someone on the periphery, concerned enough to check in but not be truly present as she faced her "trials" and tribulations. Furthering the theme of the courtroom, I had often told her that she was accusing herself of crimes she had not committed. It is not a criminal offense to be hungry, to eat, to feel, to want, and need, ideas that were thematically articulated in the dream because she was on trial but was innocent of the offense. My daughter's presence in the dream likely represented Elle as an analytic daughter, albeit a daughter who could give but not receive love. She shared her loving feelings for me, as I did for her, but she could not hear me, could not take in my love. Subsequently, I could not "make up" for the past. I could not "make up" with Elle and get her to believe that I loved her. I kept trying to put "on a face" and find my way back to her, and I could not do so. I was stuck, wanting to reach her, yet unable to do so.

I believe that the sense of being stuck also describes Elle's feelings with me during certain stages of the analysis. At the time that I had this dream, Elle wanted to trust me but found it extremely difficult. She believed she had to be perfect to be loved and accepted. She could not "trust the trust" and believe in our connection and our relationship. This dream gave me even more compassion and empathy for her dilemma about trust.

I do not recommend that a therapist ever share a dream with a patient. Sharing a dream means essentially inviting the patient to think about the analyst sleeping, imagining the analyst's bedroom, all of which are too unconsciously seductive. However, the content of these dreams provides extremely valuable information for the analyst about the patient, and about the therapeutic relationship. Therefore, such countertransference dreams must be analyzed alone or through consultation with colleagues.

The patient's dreams, however, are a window into the unconscious mind. Exploring and interpreting dreams allow analyst and patient to access the unwanted, unbidden conflicts that are stored in the unconscious, so that they are available for working through in the service of change.

Chapter Ten

Common Impasses and Disruptions

To become a psychoanalyst, candidates are required to complete a rigorous academic program, to undergo analysis four times a week for a period of no less than four years, and in my institute's program, to complete three analytic "control cases" of a minimum of one year each, plus an additional year of clinical analytic work. Control cases are psychoanalytic cases that are undertaken under supervision and are essential to the completion of the program. My institute requires that patients seen in this capacity are made aware of their status and must agree to a minimum of a year at four times a week. Therefore, from the outset of treatment, my patients who served as control cases knew that I needed them to complete my doctoral requirements. Thus, there was a power differential from the beginning that facilitated disruptions later in the treatment.

Mindy, mid-twenties, was my second control case. She had battled disordered eating for most of her life. Her pattern was to binge for several weeks, and then starve in subsequent weeks, so her weight fluctuated with great frequency. She worked a variety of waitress jobs that paid a meager wage, and relied on a small trust fund that provided a small amount of money each month. She spent more than she received, and her family consistently made up the difference.

Mindy grew up in a family in which money was abundant but thoughts, emotions, ideas, or anything that pertained to the internal world of a human being was devalued, or denied. There was financial abundance but a poverty of expressiveness and relatedness. Mindy believed her parents gauged the validity of her ambitions by how much money she could earn, not whether a particular job or profession might be a good fit for her. Her one sibling, an older brother, became a financial analyst. Mindy was raised by a succession of nannies and recalled feeling invisible to her parents, describing herself as "just an ornament" that they occasionally took out to play with, but soon discarded. She despaired of ever being able to get their attention.

After the stock market crisis in 2008 impacted the family's financial circumstances, Mindy's parents ceased their financial support, forcing her to pay for her own analytic treatment. She could only afford to pay $25 per session, a fraction of my usual and customary fee. At that point, the (eater–eaten) paradigm that was so prevalent in her relationships outside the consulting room finally manifested in the transference between the two of us.

On the first occasion that Mindy was to pay her own fee, which was for a week of treatment, she did not bring any money. She attributed this to ambivalence about giving up her symptoms and worried that "nobody else besides my eating disorder would ever love me or take care of me." She thus anthropomorphized her eating disorder as a loving, compassionate object and simultaneously denied the importance of my care.

She began the following session by sharing how proud she was of herself for ordering a significant amount of sushi the previous night. She spoke at length about the health benefits of sushi and how much sushi she had eaten. At the end of the session, she sat stiffly upright, looking uncomfortable.

"Well, I guess I should pay you now."

I waited. She hesitated. "Should I pay you $25? It's all I have."

I reminded her that her fee was $100 a week, and that she had talked throughout the session about eating sushi, which was expensive. Perhaps she was communicating something about having to pay for treatment?

She nodded. "I get it. It's a lot of guilt I have over spending $100 on food." She ended up paying $30.

The next week she said, "I don't know what to give you. I have $40. I'm going to give you $20." I proposed that again, she was using the fee to express feelings or conflicts instead of talking about those feelings.

She smiled and gave me $40. To keep my growing outrage at bay, I again sought refuge in intellectual understanding. My mind strained to understand Mindy's internal organization, which felt as complex and difficult and fragile as a spider web—and just as sticky. Something about her ensnared, and I had to fight a constant feeling of powerlessness, as well as a feeling of impotent rage. I recognized these reactions, too, were a communication about her feelings in the world.

The next time payment was due, Mindy cancelled her session. Then she lost her debit card and therefore had no means with which to pay her fee. She had not paid rent, either, and had no money coming in. She did find enough money to buy food for binges.

She finally gave me a rumpled $40 check made out to "Nina Seville-Rockland." The message seemed to be that I mattered so little to her that she could not remember how to spell my name (Nina Savelle-Rocklin), a name that she saw on my door five days a week, and to whom she had written checks (with funds provided by her parents) for nearly a year.

This pattern repeated a few times. When again she forgot her wallet and checkbook, I interpreted that part of her wanted to continue to do the work, but another part wanted to deprive me and make me angry.

She nodded. "I already thought of that," she told me, airily.

The following sessions she breezed in, wearing a new outfit. She airily shared that her mother had given her money for gas, and it was "burning a hole" in her pocket. She sighed, "I thought, should I buy gas, or should I buy Christmas presents for some acquaintances?"

I said, "You want to pay for acquaintances but not therapy. It seems you're communicating something about how you feel towards me. What are you telling me?"

She gave it some thought. "There's something about me saying to you, screw you, and it's damaging the relationship and it's damaging the work that we do." She went on, "There's a mix of emotion. There's a mix, because I feel like I can talk about anything, and I'm angry that you're not my mother."

She did not elaborate, nor did she respond to my attempts to clarify this statement. She said only that she felt had taken advantage of whenever she gave anything. She reported, "Everyone I ever leaned on or accepted kindness from has turned around and said, 'You took advantage of me.'"

Apart from the surface communication that she could not trust anyone who was generous to her, I thought at the time that this comment signified her recognition that she was taking advantage of me. Looking back, I did not fully appreciate her extremely early developmental structure and the corresponding deficits in her capacity to relate. I now think she may have been telling me the reverse that she thought I was taking advantage of her. It is possible that, given her confusion of objects and subject, if she gave anything it was experienced as giving too much. To Mindy, the time she spent in therapy may have felt like a gift to me rather than for herself. She gave her time and I took it. She could not bear to give more by paying a fee.

Fairbairn (1952) proposes that for some individuals, giving and taking are perceived as equivalent to parting with "bodily contents" (p. 14). Giving emotional supplies is equivalent to giving up parts of the body. That helped me make more sense of my experience with Mindy. She could not part with money, time, thoughts, or ideas, because the process of giving was tantamount to relinquishing aspects of her body, her primary self.

On the date of the next scheduled payment, Mindy headed toward the door without paying and without mentioning payment. I brought the fee to her attention and interpreted that she operated in a world in which one person was a victim and one was a persecutor. She was both the persecutor who was victimizing me, and at the same time trying to make me persecute her. One person had all the needs and the other had none, and she wanted me to be the latter. I thought she might be letting me feel as deprived as she did. She smiled in a slightly chagrined manner and left without responding.

The following day, she awkwardly took a check from her purse. "I don't know what to give you." She studied the check. "Maybe I should give you the amount I wrote."

She handed me a $30 check with my name spelled correctly.

This exchange took place in the tenth month of the analytic treatment. My fears about Mindy leaving treatment were escalating. I worried both in terms of her emotional health, and because she was a control case. I feared she would abandon treatment and give in to her self-destructive impulses. I felt helpless, powerless, and angry. Although there was a realistic element to my anxiety—failure to complete the control case would put me a year behind in my doctoral progression—the intensity of my anxiety and fear was a distinctly "not-me" experience.

Gerald Adler (1985) suggests that borderline patients use devaluation of the therapist for many purposes, including as a protection against wishes for nurturance and as a transference manifestation in which they become the parent and treat the therapist as they themselves felt treated in childhood. At the time, I agreed with Adler that this patient was attacking the bond, wielding the fee as both threat and punishment. As I consider this now, I find myself focusing on the reasons for this attack on the bond. I think the primary motivation for Mindy's behavior was fear of closeness. She used literal devaluation to defend against her wish–fear dilemma of closeness and dependency on me, since closeness with me equated to loss of self. By keeping me at a distance, she was trying to preserve herself and prevent herself from being subsumed or annihilated. The devaluation was her way of protecting herself from connection and thus loss of self.

Around this time, Mindy was evicted from her apartment for non-payment of rent, and prepared to move in with a friend on a temporary basis. She wondered where she would stay. "Would I sleep on the couch? I'd want to. I would."

She mentioned "staying on the couch" a number of times, an indirect and unconscious confirmation that she was going to stay on the analytic couch.

Mindy did stay on my analytic couch but continued to withhold the fee in a manner designed to goad me into an enactment. She airily and nonchalantly said, "Oh, I had a check written out to you for $10 that I spent on food."

In that moment, and at many other times, I protected myself from losing my temper by fleeing into intellectualism. I feared if I did not seek refuge in my cognitive understanding, I would be overtaken by aggression, by huge, angry feelings of explosive rage and despair at being treated so callously, so indifferently, so inhumanely, and with such casual and purposeful hate. I also thought I understood what Mindy's childhood had been like; how many times had she felt unimportant and powerless to get the attention and recognition she craved?

Although Mindy ostensibly had no money, she visited her dermatologist for skincare. When I inquired about that, she said the doctor charged "only $25" and gave her free samples.

I observed, "That $25 is the same as your weekly fee right now. You gave him $25 but it is hard for you to pay me anything. Perhaps you're giving me a sense of what it's like to be you, to feel so deprived."

At our next session, she brought a $10 check dated two weeks earlier and asked when she should pay me again. I told her she needed to pay every week and at minimum pay what she paid the dermatologist. When she protested that she had no money, I said, "You're telling me you had money for binges and for the dermatologist, but not for analysis."

The following week, she paid $25 and said, "I felt angry, like I was writing an unnecessary check."

At the end of the session she stopped awkwardly at the door and said, holding out the check, "So here's this."

As I reached for it, she pulled it away. I commented, "You have a hard time giving me that check."

She looked surprised, asking, "Is it that obvious?"

Our session, in part, had been about her ambivalence over giving to and taking from her various friends. I recognized that she was expressing her ambivalence about giving to and taking from me. I decided it was imperative to implement boundaries and set limits, thus demonstrating my unwillingness to participate in the role Mindy had assigned to me, that of deprived analyst–child to her withholding and sadistic patient–mother. By setting limits, I hoped to open psychic space for an alternative paradigm. I told Mindy that she would be required to pay her weekly fee of $25 before the last session of the week. She agreed, without reaction or comment. I invited her response but she gave none.

The following two weeks, she paid cash before the session, without comment. On the third week, she said, "I just realized I forgot my money."

"Oh. What are we to do?" I said in a neutral voice.

She said, "I want to go back to the car."

I nodded. "Okay."

She looked like a tentative child. "Can I go now?"

I nodded again. "Absolutely."

"Okay, thanks."

Upon her return from the car, she brought a check for the correct amount. I asked how she understood the "forgetting" the check in the car. She sighed. "This is hard."

I asked her to tell me more about that. She said she still felt like a bad person, intimating that the treatment had been of no value to her. Again, my attempts to draw out more information through clarification were met with silence. Then she changed the subject.

The following week, she started the session by saying, "So I'm really mad at myself, but I didn't bring cash."

I told her that I could not see her unless she paid, but that she was free to go to the bank and come back. She thanked me and left, returning fifteen minutes later with a check.

She said, "I'm glad you did that. It's significant." She could not elaborate on the "glad" feelings or what felt significant. She then spoke of a recent nightmare in which her mother was angry at Mindy because she could not reach her on the phone. This was, in fact, what had actually happened the day earlier. Her nightmare reflected the experience of one person not being able to connect with another and becoming enraged.

Mindy was bringing me vivid material about her internal world, but did not have the willingness, or perhaps the capacity, to make sense of it. She could not translate her wish–fear dilemma about interpersonal relationships into words. Unable to mentalize or verbalize her conflicts, she expressed them by recreating various forms of the abuser–abused model, acting out what could not be thought, spoken, or processed.

Mindy utilized both food and money to convey her internal conflicts, a means of unconscious expression that is not uncommon. I have treated bulimic patients who go on shopping binges and then return everything, just as they binge and vomit food, or use compensatory measures such as exercise to get rid of what they have consumed. I have several anorexic patients who cannot bear to part with money, and others who deny themselves food but spend a lot of money on their wardrobe. Many patients with binge eating disorder also binge on shopping, stuffing their closets and homes with things that take up space, just as food takes up space in their bodies.

Mindy, for example, never felt "fulfilled" in a relationship with other people, whether in her personal life, at work, or in treatment with me. She was always hungry for more, yet could not fill up on what she really wanted. She "had a problem with sugar" and regularly consumed a gallon of ice cream at night. She also "had a problem with money" and spent more than she made. This inevitably led to a crisis about paying the rent, or making her car payment, and she counted on her parents to bail her out financially.

Mindy remained financially in need and dependent on her parents as a way of managing her conflict about separation. Money linked her to her parents, and was the primary bond that connected them. As long as she kept herself financially hungry, they fed her money. To behave in a financially responsible manner and to be an adult who made her own money were threatening to that bond. She unconsciously feared that if she did not need their money, she would lose her connection with her parents. She also attempted to convert me into a parent who would bail her out, instead of asking for money.

Mindy binged, yet reported no purging behavior. She remained preoccupied with her weight and only felt adequate when she felt thin and was able to fit into smaller clothes. Obsessed with her weight, she predicated her sense of self on her appearance and therefore fit the profile of bulimia nervosa more than that of binge eating disorder. I often puzzled over this discrepancy, since Mindy's symptoms did not fit either diagnosis. My experience with Mindy was that she was bingeing on me, as if she was ravenously and aggressively trying to suck me dry and deplete me of my time and my compassion. I considered my simultaneous experience feeling purged by her, of feeling dismissed, rejected, and dehumanized, as I detailed earlier. I then began to consider the possibility that there was a displacement element to the purging element of bulimia.

I wondered if Mindy's behavior—bingeing on food and purging her financial resources—were in fact a form of bulimia, using two different symbols of love, that is, food and money, to express her conflicts about connection. She filled herself up with food for reasons that were multi-determined—to soothe, to distract herself from internal emptiness, filling the symbolic inner space where a maternal representation should have been, and depleting herself of money to remain dependent, symbolically ridding herself of a toxic, unusable m/other.

She managed this conflict by what I conceived of a type of bulimic equivalency, bingeing on food (which was a representation of maternal nurturance and love) and purging money (which represented paternal love). Both food and money were used as symbolic representations of lost, missing, or inadequate maternal and paternal functions such as love, comfort, and care.

"A $150 WHORE"

Luke initially paid $25 per session when we first began working together, which was all he could afford at the time. At the time I was a trainee at a low-fee clinic and this was an acceptable and normal fee. Our initial focus was his thirty pound weight gain and his depression, both of which were the result of the downward momentum of his business. Luke thought he was a huge disappointment to his mother, who often made disparaging remarks about his weight and lack of success. Luke found himself unable to make his weight decrease or his bank account increase. Interestingly, his father had a history of earning and losing millions of dollars in his tenure in business. He seemed to enjoy taking risks and was currently very wealthy, although Luke feared, "it could all be gone tomorrow." He referred to himself as a "guy" and reported mixed feelings about becoming what he considered a "man." He always wore shorts and tee-shirts, and once made the observation that he dressed like a kid, not a grown man. He equated being a man is with being a "suit" like his father, someone who had a big corporate job and "balls of steel."

Luke wished to succeed and also grappled with a concurrent fear of success, connecting success with loss and not wanting to compete with his father. In the following years, he made a great deal of progress. He began applying himself and started his own business, working hard and applying himself. He left therapy, feeling good about his prospects.

When Luke returned to treatment, I was licensed with a private practice, and I was in the middle of doctoral training. He became one of my analytic training cases, attending sessions four times a week and paying $75 per session, which was half my usual and customary rate at the time. He was uncertain if he could continue to pay this fee, since he worried that his business would decline, and we agreed to revisit the fee after three months. The week before we were to discuss the fee, he brought up the subject and proposed an increase to $90, which I accepted without discussion. At the time, I found it difficult to delve deeper into the meanings and associations around the fee because it triggered my own feelings of guilt and greed, since I felt grateful to Luke for entering analysis at a time that I needed a training case.

Although the fee arrangement went largely unanalyzed due by me until later in treatment, Luke's conflict about the fee was evident in his clinical material from the beginning. In one session he described one of his earlier attempts at a screenplay and described that time of his life as, "I had so much stuff going on under the surface, clearly not just in the script but in me. That experience *bankrupted* me."

At other times, the fee issue was displaced onto other women with whom he had fiduciary arrangements. He left his male accountant who was "too aggressive" and returned to his previous female accountant, with whom he had arranged a trade in services as payment to her. He said, "She's giving me more than I'm giving her." He initially had gone to this accountant the same year he first came to me, and she helped him sort out his taxes, which were by his own admission "a mess." He was embarrassed to return, worrying that she would judge him for not keeping up with the tax plan she had arranged for him, concerned about what she might think of him. I wondered if he might have some similar concerns with me, that I might view him as a mess. He acknowledged the parallels but resisted further exploration.

His next association was to a female friend for whom he did some consultation work. He gave her a profession discount, but she thought he charged too much. She was angry that he raised his fee and he felt cheated out of money he should be making. In his mind, the paradigm was either that someone is being cheated or someone is not paying enough. When I explored whether he thought he was not paying enough or feared that I felt cheated by him, he dismissed the possibility. In retrospect, I unconsciously colluded with his wish to avoid deeper discussion out of my own conflicts about the fee. I was grateful for the opportunity to do analytic training and felt in some sense as if he was doing me a favor. I did not follow up on communications I might otherwise have examined. For example, Luke excitedly shared that his company had earned one million dollars in gross profits the previous year but quickly added that "it all went back to the business" and his salary was relatively miniscule. I am embarrassed to say that I did not explore this with him, probably out of a fear of feeling, or appearing, greedy.

Finally, we experienced a therapeutic rupture with regard to the fee that forced deeper exploration. Luke mentioned that his fiancée would start seeing her therapist (a referral that I had made) twice a week and he had to figure out how to come up with an extra $400 a week to cover the expense, since this therapist charged $200 per session. Luke's fiancée worked for him and her salary came directly from his company. Given that Luke paid $90 a session, I immediately felt devalued and dismissed. I could not contain my feelings and sat him up from the couch by saying, "I think we need to talk face to face."

I told Luke that I wanted to discuss what he was communicating with respect to the fee, and he was initially confused as to why I was upset. He said, "My fiancée only pays forty dollars more than I do." I had to point out that I saw him at a reduced rate for four sessions per week. His fiancée saw her therapist twice a week for $400. I saw him four times a week for $360. I'd given him a greatly reduced rate based on his reported inability to pay my usual and customary fee. Luke therefore had the money for his fiancée to see a therapist at a high fee, but couldn't pay me more than a nominal fee.

Luke thought about this and reflected, "I haven't thought about the fee. I just come in, plop down a piece of paper and that's it. I forget that this is your job, this is what you do for a living."

This ultimately provided an opportunity for us to analyze the meaning of the fee. We came to understand that Luke experienced the low fee as meaningful, as it made him feel as if I had a special place in my heart for him. If he paid a nominal fee and viewed the check as "just a piece of paper" and therefore did not hold much value, he maintained a sense of specialness. The less he paid, the more he was convinced that I was truly interested in him. The special low fee therefore made him feel special and worthy of special treatment. If he paid more, he might have a different experience.

The fee also reinforced the defense of transference—if he saw me as a good person who gave him a greatly reduced fee, he felt enormous gratitude and therefore could not hold any angry, hostile, aggressive, or sexual feelings toward me. Until that point in the treatment, I had unconsciously colluded with him in keeping the fee artificially low, thereby keeping a negative transference at bay.

As a result of this discussion, Luke quickly suggested that he would double his fee to $150. His next thought was an association to his future brother-in-law's inappropriate dinner conversation over the holidays, in which the brother-in-law told the family about "talking a $150 an hour whore down to $5 a session." Luke then wondered whether or not he was a good man or a bad man, at heart.

When I tracked these associations, exploring his fears of being a bad man because he had convinced me to lower my fee, and examining his thoughts about me as a symbolic whore, he quickly said, "I was honestly just telling a story." I noticed that whenever I explored possible unconscious thoughts or associations, he became defensive, as if I had caught him doing something bad. It was difficult for him to think about the meaning of paying for my time and expertise.

He was eventually able to elucidate his conflict over the fee. Part of him was grateful that I had given him a "special" low fee, but another part of him felt humiliated by his wish to take a lower fee. He wanted to pay a fee commensurate with the earnings of a successful man, rather than maintain a low boyish fee. He said, "When I started therapy all those years ago and I could barely scrape together $25, I could never have imagined that one day I'd be able to pay you $150." He spoke with pride, indicating that he felt good about his ability to be a successful man.

Impasses and disruptions such as the ones I described in this chapter are a common part of treatment. They are emotionally difficult to survive, both for patient and analyst, yet offer opportunities for greater understanding and elucidation of unconscious motives. The goal of psychoanalytically informed treatment is to decode behavior; such clinical ruptures bring unconscious material to the surface through reenactments in the analytic relationship. When the conflict is in the consulting room, it can be more readily identified and worked through.

SUICIDAL IDEATION

Suicide has been found to be the major cause of death among people with anorexia (Farber et al., 2007). Killing oneself is often conceived as a way of punishing the self and others, escaping from untenable emotional pain, and reuniting with the dead. Patients say, "I have to pay the ultimate price" or, "I cannot live with this pain." They imagine being united with lost parents, grandparents, siblings, and friends, denying the finality of death. Suicide may be understood as an outcome of the splitting that often occurs in anorexia, in which the body and self are felt to be separate. This is consistent with the body–mind split evident in so many patients with eating disorder, in which they conceive of their bodies and selves as separate. There is intense and violent hatred of the body self, which is experienced as a separate entity.

When I asked one suicidal anorexic patient what she imagined would happen after death, she responded, "I'd be free of my body and I'd float around, being with everyone I love but not feeling this pain anymore." She imagined that she would still exist without her body, and that the source of pain was localized within her body. Others imagine death as a permanent sleep, but they do not truly conceive of their nonexistence.

People in the grip of suicidal wishes usually begin to lack psychological mindedness.

They often need supportive therapy to manage their symptoms until they are able to regulate themselves and their impulsivity (Farber, 2000; Farber et al., 2007). Safety plans and hospitalization may be necessary. In addition to taking steps to ensure the patient's safety, the therapist must consult with colleagues and get supervision to stay legally and ethically safe. In California, where my practice is located, psychotherapists have the option to break confidentiality when a patient has suicidal thoughts. I have chosen to err on the side of caution and inform family members at those times (thankfully rare) when a patient has suicidal thoughts.

When it comes to actively suicidal patients, it is important to recognize and accept the range of reactions and responses one has to such a situation. It is common (and human) to occasionally feel exasperation toward patients who facilitate such terror and anxiety, and it is natural to sometimes even wish they would get on with it already (Maltsberger & Buie, 1974). Simultaneously, the analyst must always keep in mind those qualities in the patient that are likeable or lovable.

I find it crucial to explore the patient's hopelessness and utter despair, as well as talking about the psychological dimension of the wish to die. Understandably, there is a wish to provide a sense of hope to someone in the grip of suicidal despair, but in my experience that falls on proverbial deaf ears. Only when patients sense the therapist knows the extent of their horror, pain, and despair, do they feel understood.

"PRECIOUS"

Chrissy, 22, sought psychotherapy for what she referred to as being "totally and completely and absolutely out of control" with food. A student at a local university, she was raised in a small Midwestern town where she lived all her life. She found the Los Angeles area to be overwhelming, but acknowledged her courage in leaving a familiar childhood town for a big city where she did not know anyone. She often experienced intense periods of anxiety, fearing that people hated her for some unknown reason and imagining they wanted nothing to do with her. During these anxious times, she holed up in her small apartment and binged for days until she felt safe enough to emerge. She could not articulate what made her feel safe; she only knew that she no longer felt under scrutiny.

Chrissy's goal for treatment was to stop bingeing. She had gained more than twenty pounds over the past few months by consuming a gallon of ice cream nearly every night. She was emotionally ravenous for connection, yet could only fill up on copious amounts of food—specifically ice cream.

In our weekly therapy sessions, we explored the underlying conflicts that led to these binges. Chrissy emailed almost daily, sometimes only an hour before our session, sharing details of her binges and detailing the painful loneliness of her childhood. She had trouble making friends. Both her parents worked and were often exhausted at night, unable to do more than eat a quick meal and watch television. When she was a teenager she began to drink at parties, usually to excess, and once got alcohol poisoning. She was rushed to the hospital, where the doctors summoned her parents. She recalled her mother looking frightened and saying, "You could have *died.*"

Chrissy left messages each weekend, usually on Sundays. "I don't want to live," she sobbed. "I don't want to be here anymore."

I returned the calls immediately, interrupting family functions, meals with friends, and even a child's birthday party to make sure she was not actively suicidal. Each time, she reassured me that she was perfectly fine, but had simply "lost it" before she called. She often sounded cheerful while giving these assurances, and my initial concern began shifting toward annoyance. Soon, I dreaded checking messages. My experience was that of being binged upon, as if she were metaphorically gobbling up my time, energy, and compassion.

I was able to hold onto my compassion for her by recognizing the underpinnings to her behavior—I thought she was trying to connect the only way she could. Despite my understanding of her actions, I continued to feel intruded upon, invaded by the force of her needs.

I also knew that as a child, Chrissy only received attention when she was suicidal. She unconsciously believed she needed to threaten her own life, or be in constant crisis, to capture and keep my interest. When I brought this to her attention, the frequency of the Sunday calls began to diminish. At the time, I attributed this to Chrissy's making use of my interpretation. I thought we were building a therapeutic alliance, and she was feeling safer with me. I did not realize, however, that concurrent with her hope of feeling connected was a simultaneous terror of being subsumed in the relationship. This manifested in a retreat from therapy, when Chrissy decided to visit her parents.

Chrissy's mother accompanied her when she returned to Los Angeles and joined one of our therapy sessions. Chrissy shared what she was going through and how painful and difficult it was for her to feel safe in the world. By the end of the hour, Chrissy was weeping, shoulders bowed, tears rolling down her cheeks. Her mother appeared impervious to her daughter's pain. This maternal detachment struck me as both inhuman and inhumane, and I was stunned by her indifference. I asked Chrissy's mother what it was like to see her daughter crying.

Her mother sighed, openly exasperated. "I feel like Chrissy needs to see the movie 'Precious' so she'll know she doesn't have it so bad."

Chrissy cried harder, wracked by intense sobbing. My heart went out to her. She desperately wished to be precious to her mother, yet her attempts to connect appeared to activate her mother's indifference and, at times, her sadism. Deprived of caring, loving, concerned, and nurturing parents, she symbolically filled the emptiness within with food, which served as a representation of mothering. She experienced this emptiness as an internal black hole, a void that could not be filled. The only thing that helped, albeit temporarily, was food.

For infants and babies to experience physical hunger without gratification causes them to experience a painful awareness of that which is missing, or what may be thought of as the presence of the absence. For Chrissy, this painful absence was something she experienced emotionally, and also relationally. Her mother could not nourish her mind, body, or psyche, and because of that deficit, Chrissy failed to learn how to relate to herself in a nurturing manner and used food instead. As I discussed earlier, food is unconsciously experienced as a symbolic representation of a bond with another.

Chrissy clung to the hope of a satisfying relationship with her mother, yet internalized the toxic connection between them. In our work together, the goal of treatment was for her to take me in and incorporate me as a new object, identifying with my compassion, interest, and care, thus creating a paradigm of psychological fulfillment that differed from everything she had known previously. To accomplish this, Chrissy had to confront the loss of her idealized mother, and relinquish her hope of unconditional love from her parents. She eventually learned to express her rage, instead of directing it at herself.

"IF I DIE, THEN NOBODY WILL DIE ON ME"

When Elle, the patient who started communicating with me via her dreams, confronted the memories of being sexually abused by her father, she initially could not bear to live with what had happened. She began fantasizing about suicide. She wanted to die rather than live with the horror of the abuse. She cut her skin with razors, converting emotional pain to physical, wearing her emotional wounds on her body. She flirted with death, cutting deeper and deeper, in part because having her life in her own hands gave her a sense of control and empowerment that she lacked as an abused and helpless child. I felt an increasing fear and escalating powerlessness, reactions I intellectually recognized as communications about what Elle felt as a child, mirroring the utter helplessness and hopelessness she endured during her abuse. By threatening to kill herself, she also created in me the same fear and dread. In addition to my concern and worry, I felt helpless to stop her relentless assaults on her body.

One day, Elle asked if she were too much and wondered if I wanted to get rid of her. I said, "Elle, I know you are suffering. I also know that you're a kind, smart, warm person. I'm impressed with your good heart, your intelligence, and with how hard you're working. I do not want to get rid of you. Yes, it can be a lot to deal with some of this, but I can handle it."

Elle looked uncomfortable and told me that I was being "too nice."

She wrote poignant, profound emails about why she wanted to die. She felt herself to be contaminated and disgusting, turning against her body with stunning vitriol. She told me that she could not bear to die, "like this" and waved a hand over her slim body, contemptuously saying that she would have killed herself already but could not stand to leave "a gross and disgusting corpse."

I noted that her emails were impressive and beautifully written. On the other hand, despite this capacity to express her thoughts, it seemed difficult for her to realize that her suicidal wishes were not about her body, but about the turmoil that was stuck inside her. Instead of being disgusted by what had happened to her, she was disgusted by her body. Instead of finding her father's behavior to be gross, she thought her body was gross. I told her that the temptation to play out the emotions in the bodily form would not change until we worked through the pain, anguish, horror, and rage of the abuse. I noted that suicide was certainly one option to end her misery, but there were other ways to deal with that pain. I suggested that she could turn to a person for comfort, and that she could turn to me instead of to a razor.

There was another dimension to Elle's suicidal ideation. She had lost many important relationships in her life by betrayal or death. Her father betrayed their bond and she was deprived of the experience of having a safe, loving father. Her mother refused to face reality and did not protect her or investigate her emotional life. The safe people in her life were the babysitter who cared for her from the time she was a newborn, her grandmother, and her aunt. Sadly, by the time she graduated college, Elle had lost all of these beloved figures to illness.

The closer she felt to me, the more she feared that I would suddenly be gone. She worried that I would die suddenly, give up my practice, or decide that she was too much for me. We explored this fear of reexperiencing loss, and how unbearable it was to lose people. As she put it, "Everyone I love dies on me. If I die, nobody will die on me."

She did not speculate on what other people would feel if she died, but her suicidal thoughts might have represented the ultimate in mastery and retaliation. By killing herself, her mother would be left with the same crushing hopelessness, fear, and despair that Elle had felt throughout her childhood, and which her mother refused to recognize.

Elle worked through her suicidal crisis by recognizing that her wish to die expressed a wish to be rid of the pain. She slowly and painfully grieved for what had happened to her, and mourned for what had not happened—the birthright of a safe and protected childhood—allowing herself to express anger and hurt toward her parents, who both abused and ignored her, instead of enacting that pain and rage on her body. She was eventually able to take in my loving view of her, and to begin giving herself the care that had been denied her.

Chapter Eleven

A Consideration of Hate and Love

HATE

In his seminal paper on the subject of hate in the analytic setting, Donald Winnicott (1947) writes of the analyst's experience, "However much he loves his patients he cannot avoid hating them and fearing them, and the better he knows this the less will hate and fear be the motives determining what he does to his patients" (p. 195).

Mindy, who withheld payment for therapy while paying for sushi, dermatologists, and other expenditures, was the patient who stirred up the most countertransference within me. At the time that Mindy was mounting her most vicious attacks on the treatment, she made a comment that added a new element to my perspective. At the end of one session, she sat up from the couch and looked at me with a shy smile. This was a departure from her usual haughty demeanor and her usual hurried and silent exit from the office. She said, "I know I'm my parents' favorite, because of all the abuse. All that . . . pain."

She said it in a pleased way, as if sharing a wonderful secret. I suddenly had the same feeling I have only experienced during a creepy scene in a movie or television show, a sense of gradual horror and dread. I felt a frisson of unease.

"All that pain," she repeated, and smiled.

Realizing that I was holding my breath, I slowly exhaled. I said, "The more pain, the more love?"

She nodded with a knowing, Mona Lisa smile. I then understood that her hateful attacks on me were also attempts to experience love, as well as to destroy love. For Mindy, love felt like hate, and hate felt like love. The only way she could feel connected in a dyad was to create as much hate as possible. In her vacillating experience of relationships, she was either actively hating the other or she was the object of the other's hate.

Thomas Ogden (2002) writes that, "sadism is a form of object tie in which hate . . . becomes inextricably intertwined with erotic love, and in this combined state can be an even more powerful binding force (in a suffocating, subjugating, tyrannizing way) than the ties of love alone" (p. 776). Mindy's attachment to sadism did not seem to be erotically charged (although I did not explore this idea with her, so it might have been there and I missed it), yet it served to give her hope for a different type of relating, for the connection she both longed and feared. The hate between us certainly felt like the "powerful, binding force" that Ogden describes. As discussed earlier, I often experienced anxiety about my own hate toward Mindy, and found refuge in supervision and in Winnicott's (1949b) description of the type of child who, "can believe in being loved only after reaching being hated" (p. 72).

At the point in treatment at which Mindy made the connection between hate and love, I was experiencing enormous frustration and anger toward her, as well as a sense of impotence. I felt hostage to her demands and machinations, emotionally and because I needed her to complete the control case, which was a necessary part of my doctoral matriculation process. As I look back now, I feel more compassion for her conflict. Through the enactment between us, she was communicating what it was like to grow up in a severely depriving, abusive environment and wish for something that she was not given, something she could not provide for herself. As a result of what developed in the therapeutic relationship, I experienced a visceral sense of how intensely powerless, angry, and emotionally ravenous she felt inside.

Winnicott (1969, 1971) proposes that the capacity for object usage is a necessary part of healthy development, and that the shift from object-relating to object-usage is accomplished through unconscious destruction, an aspect of primary aggression. Winnicott writes, "This change (from relating to usage) means that the subject destroys the object" (p. 89) in fantasy. When the object survives, without retaliation or punishment, the infant is able to view the object as whole, separate, and external, which leads to healthy object usage.

Expanding on these concepts, Martin James (1979) differentiates between "conscious hate" (p. 415), which is connected to the ability to verbalize, and thus symbolize, and "unconscious aggression" (p. 415), which is associated with the early, preverbal period of development, and can only be expressed through action. He states that the capacity for conscious hate "marks the passage from mere *relation* to objects to the ability to *use* objects" (p. 416, italics by James) and is associated with viewing people realistically, instead of through the lens of projection and introjection. C. G. Schulz (1989) describes what he termed "warmth by friction" (p. 542), in which hostility is actually a way of attaching to a love object. Schulz writes, "When self representations are not clearly established as differentiated from object-representations there is vulnerability toward fusion and confusion of self and object" (p. 542).

I vacillate between thinking that Mindy's hate was a form of love, and also wondering if she was capable of experiencing me as anything other than a part object, for whom she both yearned and hated. She was internally so young that she never developed the capacity to view me as a whole object, and to experience connection or any loving feelings. Mindy was unable to access her feelings toward me, whether positive or negative, and was only able to express them through the transference. As with her conflicts in other areas of her life, she could not use words, only actions.

Throughout my work with Mindy I struggled to hold onto my compassion and affection for her during various stages of the transference. I initially experienced her as bingeing on me, voraciously depleting my time, energy, and emotional resources. I later shifted into feeling being attacked, deprived, obliterated, and erased. My final challenge was to survive her attacks on the analytic frame, specifically with regard to the fee, and also to survive my own rage toward her. I did this by holding in my mind an image of Mindy as a hungry little girl, ravenous for love and affection, yet deprived of these basic human supplies. The transference enactments between us left me with a visceral sense of what it was like to feel abused and helpless, simultaneously longing for connection and fighting annihilation.

When she left, I was left with a sense of loss and disappointment. She moved out of the state shortly after leaving therapy and disappeared from my consulting room, but not my thoughts. In the years that followed, she sent cards and occasional emails, thanking me for the work we did together and letting me know that that she was doing well.

The type of unending sadistic attack on the analyst such as the one Mindy launched can be addictive to some people. They enjoy the discharge of aggression that isn't available anywhere else in their lives. Analysts seek to understand, not retaliate, and therefore they become safe targets for scorn, hatred, disdain, and mockery. One colleague reported that one of her male patients disparaged her on almost a daily basis, attacking her thoughts, interpretations, clarifications, silences, and appearance with vituperative glee. He contemptuously told her that analysis was a waste of time and money, that she was worthless and that nothing was ever going to change.

After one particularly vicious attack, my colleague finally shared her thoughts. "I felt attacked and hurt by you, and so tormented by you," she said, "that yesterday for the first time I thought about giving up."

The patient looked at her in astonishment and fear. My colleague continued, "Let me be clear about this. You're human and I'm human. You have feelings and I have feelings. Your feelings and thoughts are much more important to us, and that's why we're here, but there has to be a limit to how much you can distort what I say, and to what you are saying to me. I felt that I was reaching my end point, because I like you and I'm trying to help you."

She explained that the past trauma caused him to feel tremendous rage, and also he felt guilt over that rage. However, attacking the person who was trying to pull him from the abyss would cause that person to eventually give up. She also pointed out that although he was convinced that nothing would ever change, he continued to come to analysis. Clearly, his words were communicating a lack of hope but his presence showed some hope.

When patients are actively hostile, it is sometimes helpful to put them in contact with their hatred, while at the same time explaining their hostility. Sometimes, the experience of feeling understood and cared for creates hurt and anger because for the first time they realize what they did not get in childhood. As one patient put it, "I know you care about me, and that feels good. But at the same time, I hate it because now I know what I didn't get."

LOVE

The relationship between analyst and patient is one of the primary means by which change occurs. In a letter to Carl Jung (McGuire, 1974), Freud writes, "Psychoanalysis is in essence a cure through love" (pp. 12–13). Regarding the nature of love, Rollo May (1969) elucidates the different types of love in ancient Greek culture, including the concept of *agape*, a type of love that is characterized by the dedication of one person to the welfare of another. This is the type of love that flows back and forth in the analytic dyad and ultimately it is the foundation of love that allows both patient and analyst to survive the hate, and to forge ahead on their journey, which like that of Odysseus is marked by both calmness and chaos.

Winnicott (1947) notes, "the couch and warmth and comfort can be *symbolical* of the mother's love" (p. 72, italic in the original). A patient's experience is that of being heard, feeling understood, accepted, and having the undivided and interested attention of the analyst, which can be understood as an idealized version of parental love. Modell (1976) describes the analytic situation as "an idealized maternal holding environment" (p. 291) in which patients experience a consistent, reliable, nonretaliatory, and safe space.

Richard Fox (1998), in his assessment of love in the analytic setting, writes, "I have come to regard as a critical dimension of the therapeutic process—the analyst's 'loving' feelings for the patient" (p. 1080). The bond between analyst and patient may be the first experience of feeling known at a core level, and accepted for oneself—the parts one likes and those one does not like, such as the aspects of self that have been actively disavowed. These are the aggressive, sad, murderous, angry, helpless parts that they hide from themselves and from others, fearing that the existence of such wishes or emotions makes them unlovable. By having an analytic experience of regressing and surrendering to the possibility that they can be loved, they must accept those aspects of their personality that they find objectionable.

Jekels (1941) states, "the reason that our patients woo the analyst's love so persistently; that there is nothing they crave so much as this love" (p. 237). He believed the deepest anxiety is not that people think they are unlovable, but that they fear the loss of that love. Many people resist a regression into the comfortable safety of feeling lovable and symbolically held in the analytic relationship precisely for this reason. As one male patient told me, "I know you like me. Sometimes I even feel like you love me. But one of these days I'm going to say something and you're going to change your mind. I just couldn't handle that."

I have heard this type of fear from many people, caught in a dilemma between yearning for the unconditional love that eludes them and fearing that having it will mean they are setting themselves up for rejection and the loss of love. Winnicott (1974) suggests that just a mother must be able to tolerate her hatred of a child, an analyst must tolerate his or her hatred of a patient. Only by allowing the hate can the love be accepted. Winnicott suggests that an analysis is incomplete without the interpretation of the analyst's hate to the patient.

Frank (1987) points out, analysis is not simply concerned with interpretation and insight, but also with the continued development of one's personality, which is done in a loving and caring manner. He states,

One way of thinking about psychoanalytic treatment is that in working through transference one helps the patient work through that which keeps the person from feeling loved and/or lovable. In the end, the patient should be able to feel like a worthwhile (i.e., lovable) and loved (that is, cared for by the analyst) individual. (p. 93)

The question about whether or not analytic love is "real" comes up a lot. I believe there is a danger in viewing the love a patient has for the analyst, and the love the analyst feels for the patient, as an illusion of love, as merely a manifestation of transference and countertransference. For a patient, it is humiliating to feel loving feelings and be told by the object of those feelings, one's analyst, that they are not "real" feelings. The situation is not that simple, for the loving feelings that flow between patient and analyst are certainly real, although they also may hide, deflect, or avoid other kinds of feelings or conflicts. In all our relationships, we must learn to hold love and hate, love and disappointment, love and resentment. This is not limited to the consulting room, as evidenced by a friend recently relating the story of being awakened night after night by her toddler. "It's a good thing he's cute," she said, "because sometimes I want to kill him." By highlighting how cute her son is, how lovable, she mitigated the angry, hostile, and resentful feelings.

Axel Hoffer (1993) proposes that, "love in an analytic relationship—whether or not we call it transference and countertransference—is the same and as real as ordinary love outside of therapy. The difference is not to be found in its reality but in its unique one-sidedness" (p. 349). He suggests that the uniqueness of the analytic relationship lies in its "purpose and unilateral focus" of providing understanding, growth, and development in the patient. Love in the analytic setting is not an imitation of a feeling, but a very real experience between patient and analyst. The analyst must resist the pull to create mutuality and thus undermine its specialness, with all its inherent difficulties and opportunities, the working through of which promotes transformation. Thus, the matter of a patient feeling loved by an analyst is something on which many theorists and writers agree.

Yet what of the analyst's real and loving feelings toward the patient? The analytic relationship is comprised of a patient and an analyst, and both are changed by the experience. Weinstein (1986) notes that the intensity of his feelings toward his patients is correlated with a better outcome of the treatment. He differentiates between the inner awareness of his feelings, rather than an overt expression of them.

During the difficult time that Elle was at the nadir of her life, feeling hopeless, angry, and powerless, she frequently needed contact outside the analytic hour, sometimes derided the treatment ("this is pointless") and regularly threatened suicide. This went on for a period of months and I did my best to be responsive and available, to walk the tightrope of keeping her safe and making analytically sound choices. I wanted to protect the analytic relationship, recognizing that what was happening was a symptom of something that needed understanding, albeit a scary symptom.

One night she exploded in rage, accusing me over text of not caring, of being indifferent and rejecting. This was the first time she had directly stated her displeasure with me. The nontherapist part of me felt somewhat affronted, given my level of commitment over several months. From a therapeutic perspective, however, I saw this as a positive development. Elle had given expression to her rage by turning on me, instead of against herself. She also transferred the resentment she felt toward her indifferent mother onto me, instead of onto her body. In considering this, I felt hopeful.

The next session she came in looking sheepish, worried that her rage had frustrated and upset me. She was afraid that I was angry and was going to dismiss her from my practice.

I said, "It's been difficult for you to tell me how you feel, especially when you're upset at me. But I notice that you can allow yourself to express those feelings in the text messages. I think that's a good start."

She looked surprised. I then compared her expressions of rage and hatred to that of a child who's mad at her mother and says, "I hate you, Mommy." I explained that a mother knows her child is angry and hates her in that moment, but also recognizes that her child still loves her. I said, "When you tell me you hate me, I know you still love me."

Her eyes widened and she remained silent the rest of the session.

The following day she told me she had not been able to stop thinking about our previous session. I asked what it was that she had been thinking about so much.

"Well . . ." she cautiously began. "The word love was mentioned."

Elle said she could not believe that she was "allowed" to feel such feelings, much less talk about those feelings. I responded that we could—and must—talk about everything. She then asked me when my birthday was, the first personal question she had ever asked. I thought it took tremendous courage for her to ask me this question so I answered directly, before inquiring why she had asked.

She responded that the people who are most important to her were born in February, and she figured I was also born in February. I interpreted that she was indirectly telling me that I was very important to her.

She nodded, and her expression softened. She shared that she was starting to trust that everyone did not see her as disgusting, since I could see her as lovable even when she was difficult. She felt a responsibility knowing that love has a place in therapy, "as if there is something that needs tending to."

Months later she summoned the courage to ask a simple but complicated question. "Do you love me?" I gave the only answer that I could give, which was the truth. I said, "Of course I love you. That is not in question. *We* cannot do this work without love. What else could have sustained us through this challenging time? My love for you is not in question. The question is, what does that love mean to you?"

Children who do not feel loved do not experience themselves as lovable. For this reason, Elle struggled to feel worthy of love, which is why it was so difficult for her to take in my love. It was also hard for her trust that she could hold onto love without losing it, or losing me. And yet she prevailed, allowing hope to conquer fear, steadily and consistently facing the horrors of her childhood and started to view herself as a person worthy of love.

I believe that Elle could finally take in my love because she knew I had survived her hate, along with her nearly indescribable pain, fear, and despair. Because we had both withstood that intense hate, the love was something that she could trust.

In the years that I've been privileged to do this work, I have come to appreciate the tremendous courage of the patients on the couch. They delve into the most traumatic memories of their past, confront their unexplored and unresolved wishes, and explore the pain and hope of being human. They embark a journey that is as challenging as that of Odysseus, navigating the journey from darkness to light, from the depths to the surface.

Psychoanalysis is reparative on the deepest level, helping individuals identify how the past is alive in the present and creating a new relationship to themselves and to others. I am deeply privileged to do work in which patients entrust me with their fears, secrets, terrors, and deepest anxieties, along with their hopes, wishes, and dreams. Patients seek to make peace with food and discover a path to a new way of being and relating. They face what they cannot see, fight what they do not know, hope in the face of hopelessness, and trust when past experience has given them no reason to do so. They come to psychoanalysis seeking help and find transformation. In learning to assuage their hunger for connection and authenticity, they claim the birthright of their humanity.

References

Abbate-Daga, G., Amianto, F., Delsedime, N., De-Bacco, C., & Fassino, S. (2013). Resistance to treatment and change in anorexia nervosa: a clinical overview. *BMC Psychiatry*, 13 (1) DOI: 10.1186/1471-244X-13-294.

Abraham, K. (1923). Contributions to the theory of anal character. *International Journal of Psychoanalysis*, 4, 400–418.

Adler, G. (1985). *Borderline psychopathology and its treatment.* Northvale, NJ: Jason Aronson.

Ainsworth, M.D.S., & Bell, S.M. (1970). Attachment, exploration, and separation: Illustrated by the behavior of one-year-olds in a strange situation. *Child Development*, 41 (1), 49–67.

Akhtar, S. (2009). *Comprehensive dictionary of psychoanalysis.* London: Karnac Books.

Alexander, F. (1925). Dreams in pairs and series. *International Journal of Psycho-Analysis*, 6, 446–452.

Altman, M.L. (1995). Vicissitudes of the erotized transference: The impact of aggression. *Psychoanalytic Review*, 82, 65–79.

American Psychological Association. (2013a). *Diagnostic and statistical manual of mental disorders* (5th ed.). Washington, DC: Author.

American Psychological Association. (2013b). Recognition of psychotherapy effectiveness. *Psychotherapy*, 50, 102–109.

Anderson, R., & Dartington, A. (eds.) (1999). *Facing it out: Clinical perspectives on adolescent disturbance.* London: Karnac Books.

Andreasen, N.C. (2001). *Brave new brain: Conquering mental illness in the era of the genome.* New York: Oxford University Press.

Andresen, J. (1980). Conflict and the origins of identification. *Psychoanalytic Review*, 67, 25–43.

Arcelus, J., Michell, A.J., Wales, J., & Nielsen, S. (2011). Mortality rates in patients with anorexia nervosa and other eating disorders. A meta-analysis of 36 studies. *Archives of General Psychiatry*, July; 68 (7) 724–31.

Armstrong, J.G., & Roth, D.M. (1989). Attachment and separation difficulties in eating disorders: A preliminary investigation. *International Journal of Eating Disorders*, 8 (2), 141–155.

Armstrong-Perlman, E., (1991). The allure of the bad object. *Free Associations*, 2, 343–356.

Aron, L., & Anderson, F.S. (1998). *Relational perspectives on the body*. London: Routledge.

Becker, A.E. (1995). *Body, self and society: The view from Fiji*. Philadelphia: University of Philadelphia Press.

Becker, A.E., Burwell, R.A., Gilman, S.E., Herzog, D.B., & Hamburg, P. (June 2002). Eating behaviours and attitudes following prolonged exposure to television among ethnic Fijian adolescent girls. *British Journal of Psychiatry*, 180, 509–514.

Bell, R. (1985). *Holy anorexia*. Chicago: University of Chicago Press.

Blackman, J.S. (2004). *101 Defenses: How the mind shields itself*. New York: Brunner-Routledge.

Blinder, B.J., Chaitin, B.F., & Goldstein, R.S. (1988). *The eating disorders*. New York: PMA Publishing.

Blos, P. (1967). The second individuation process of adolescence. *Psychoanalytic Study of the Child*, 22, 162–186.

Blos, P. (1974). The genealogy of the ego ideal. *Psychoanalytic Study of the Child*, 29, 43–88.

Blos, P. (1983). The contribution of psychoanalysis to the psychotherapy of adolescence. *Psychoanalytic Study of the Child*, 38, 577–600.

Blum, H.P. (1994). The conceptual development of regression. *Psychoanalytic Study of the Child*, 49, 60–79.

Bollas, C. (1987). *The shadow of the object: Psychoanalysis of the unthought known*. New York: Columbia University Press.

Bollas, C. (1987). *The evocative object world*. New York: Routledge.

Bowlby J. (1965) *Attachment*. New York: Basic Books.

Bratman, S. (1997). Health food junkie. *Yoga Journal*, 1997, 42–50.

Brink, S.G., & Allan, J.A. (1992). Dreams of anorexic and bulimic women: A research study. *Journal of Analytic Psychology*, 37, 275–297.

British Journal of Psychiatry (2000), 176, 132.

Bruch, H. (1963–1964). Psychotherapeutic problems in eating disorders. *Psychoanalytic Review*, 50D, 43–57.

Bruch, H. (1973). *Eating disorders: Obesity, anorexia nervosa, and the person within*. New York: Basic Books.

Bruch, H. (1978). *The golden cage: The enigma of anorexia nervosa*. Cambridge, MA: Harvard University Press.

Bychowski, G. (1950). On neurotic obesity. *Psychoanalytic Review*, 37, 301–319.

Brumberg, J.J. (1997). *The body project: An intimate history of American girls*. New York: Random House.

Brytek-Matera, A. (2012). Orthorexia nervosa—an eating disorder, obsessive-compulsive disorder or disturbed eating habit? *Archives of Psychiatry and Psychotherapy*, 1, 55–60.

Burnham, D., Gladstone, A., & Gibson, R. (1969). *Schizophrenia and the need-fear dilemma.* New York: International Universities Press.

Cain, A., & Cain, B. (1964). On replacing a child. *Journal of the American Academy of Child Psychiatry*, 3, 443–456.

Campeau, P.M., Foulkes, W.D., & Tischkowitz, M.D. (2008). Hereditary breast cancer: New genetic developments, new therapeutic avenues. *Human Genetics*, 124 (1), 31–42.

Candland, D. (1993). *Feral children and clever animals: Reflections on human nature.* New York: Oxford University Press.

Caparrotta, L., & Ghaffari, K. (2006). A historical overview of the psychodynamic contributions to the understanding of eating disorders. *Psychoanalytic Psychotherapy*, 20, 175–196.

Cassin, S.E., & von Ranson, K.M. (2005). Personality and eating disorders: A decade in review. *Clinical Psychology Review*, 25 (7), 895–916.

Castelnuovo-Tedesco, P., & Reiser, L. (1988). Compulsive eating: Obesity and related phenomena. *Journal of the American Psychoanalytic Association*, 36, 163–171.

Castonguay, A. L., Sabiston, C. M., Crocker, P. R., & Mack, D. E. (2014). Development and validation of the Body and Appearance Self-Conscious Emotions Scale (BASES). *Body Image*, 11(2), 126–136.

Chabris, C.F., Hebert, B.M., Benjamin, D.J., Beauchamp, J., Cesarini, D., van der Loos, M., et al. (2012). Most reported genetic associations with general intelligence are probably false positives. *Psychological Sciences*, 23 (11), 1314–1323.

Charles, M. (1999). The promise of love: A view among women. *Psychoanalytic Psychotherapy*, 16, 254–273.

Charney, E. (2013). Still chasing ghosts: A new genetic methodology will not find the "missing heritability." *Independent Science News.* Retrieved from https://www.independentsciencenews.org/health/still-chasing-ghosts-a-new-genetic-methodology-will-not-find-the-missing-heritability.

Chessick, R.D. (1984). Clinical notes toward the understanding and intensive psychotherapy of adult eating disorders. *Annual of Psychoanalysis*, 12, 301–322.

Connors, M.E., & Morse, W. (January 1993). Sexual abuse and eating disorders: A review. *International Journal of Eating Disorders*, 13 (1), 1–11.

Cozolino, L. (2006/2014). *The neuroscience of human relationships: Attachment and the developing brain.* New York: W.W. Norton.

Cui, H., Moore, J., Ashimi, S.S., Mason, B.L., Drawbridge, J.N., Han, S., et al. (2013). Eating disorder predisposition is associated with ESRRA and HDAC4 mutations. *Journal of Clinical Investigation*, Nov;123(11):4706–13.

Davis, C., Loxton, N.J., Levitan, R.D., Kaplan, A.S., Carder, J.C., & Kennedy, J.L. (2013). Food addiction and its association with a dopaminergic multilocus genetic profile. *Physiology and Behavior, Impact Factor*, Jun 13;118:63–9.

DelPriore, D., & Hill, S. (2013). The effects of paternal disengagement on women's sexual decision making: An experimental approach. *Journal of Personality and Social Psychology*, 105 (2), 234–246.

Dodes, LM. (1990). Addiction, helplessness, and narcissistic rage. *Psychoanalytic Quarterly*, 59, 398–419.

Dodes, LM. (2002). *The heart of addiction.* New York: HarperCollins.

Dodes, LM. (2011). *Breaking addiction: A 7-step handbook for ending any addiction.* New York: HarperCollins.

Dubowitz, H., Black, M., Harrington, D., & Verschoore, A. (1993). A follow-up study of behavioral problems associated with child sexual abuse. *Child Abuse and Neglect,* 17, 743–754.

Eating Disorder Hope. Retrieved from www.eatingdisorderhope.com.

Edgecumbe, R. (1984). Modes of communication—the differentiation of somatic and verbal expression. *Psychoanalytic Study of the Child,* 39, 137–154.

Ellis, B.J., Schlomer, G.L., Tilley, E.H., & Butler, E.A. (2012). Impact of fathers on risky sexual behavior in daughters: A genetically and environmentally controlled sibling study. *Development and Psychopathology,* 24, 317–332.

Erwin, G. (2005). *The cherished wound: Theoretical and treatment implications for identification with unresolved trauma* (doctoral dissertation). Tustin, CA: Newport Psychoanalytic Institute.

Fairbairn, W.R. (1941). A revised psychopathology of the psychoses and psychoneuroses. *International Journal of Psychoanalysis,* 22, 250.

Fairbairn, W.R. (1952). *Psychoanalytic studies of the personality.* London: Tavistock.

Farber, S. (2000). *When the body is the target: Self-harm, pain, and traumatic attachments.* Northvale, NJ: Jason Aronson.

Farber, S.K., Jackson, C.C., Tabin, J.K., & Bachar, E. (2007). Death and annihilation anxieties in anorexia nervosa, bulimia, and self-mutilation. *Psychoanalytic Psychology,* 24, 289–305.

Favero, M., & Ross, D. (2002). Complementary dreams: A window to the subconscious processes of countertransference and subjectivity. *American Journal of Psychotherapy,* 56, 211–224.

Feldman, B. (2006). A skin for the imaginal. *Fort Da,* 12, 50–78.

Fenichel, O. (1945/1996). *The psychoanalytic theory of neurosis* (50th anniversary edn). New York: W.W. Norton.

Ferenczi, S. (1916). *Contributions to psychoanalysis* (E. Jones, Trans.). Boston, MA: Richard G. Badger (original work published 1909).

Ferenzi, S. Introjection and transference. In *First Contributions to Psychoanalysis, E. Mosbacher* (Trans.) London: Karnac, 1980, pp. 35–93.

Fonagy, P. (1991). Thinking About Thinking: Some Clinical and Theoretical Considerations in the Treatment of a Borderline Patient. *International Journal of Psychoanalysis.* 72:639–656.

Fonagy, P., & Target, M. (1998). Mentalization and the changing aims of child psychoanalysis. *Psychoanalytic Dialogues,* 8, 87–114.

Fox, R.P. (1998). The "unobjectionable" positive countertransference. *Journal of the American Psychoanalytic Association,* 46, 1067–1087.

Frank, A. (1969). The unrememberable and the unforgettable—passive primal repression. *Psychoanalytic Study of the Child,* 24, 48–77.

Frank, G. (1987). Weinstein revisited: Should analysts love their patients? *Modern Psychoanalysis,* 12, 89–95.

Freud, A. (1937/1966). *The ego and the mechanisms of defense* (revised edn). New York: International Universities Press.

Freud, A. (1974). *The writings of Anna Freud volume VIII: Psychoanalytic psychology of normal development 1970–1980.* New York: International Universities Press.

Freud, S. (1894a). The neuro-psychoses of defence. *The standard edition of the complete psychological works of Sigmund Freud*, Vol. III (1893–1899). Early Psycho-Analytic Publications, 41–61.

Freud, S. (1896). Further Remarks on the Neuro-Psychoses of Defence. *The Standard Edition of the Complete Psychological Works of Sigmund Freud*, Volume III (1893-1899): Early Psycho-Analytic Publications, 3: 157–185 London: Hogarth.

Freud, S. (1900). The interpretation of dreams. In J. Strachey (Ed. and Trans.), *The standard edition of the complete psychological works of Sigmund Freud*, Vol. IV. London: Hogarth Press.

Freud, S. (1901). The psychopathology of everyday life: Forgetting, slips of the tongue, bungled actions, superstitions and errors. *The standard edition of the complete psychological works of Sigmund Freud*, Vol. VI (1901), vii–296. London: Hogarth Press.

Freud, S. (1905a). Fragment of an analysis of a case of hysteria. In J. Strachey (Ed. and Trans.), *The standard edition of the complete psychological works of Sigmund Freud*, Vol. VII. London: Hogarth Press.

Freud, S. (1905b). On psychotherapy (1905 [1904]). In J. Strachey (Ed. and Trans.), *The standard edition of the complete psychological works of Sigmund Freud*, Vol. VII (1901–1905). London: Hogarth Press.

Freud, S. (1908). Character and anal eroticism. In J. Strachey (Ed. and Trans.), *The standard edition of the complete psychological works of Sigmund Freud*, Vol. IX (1906–1908). London: Hogarth Press.

Freud, S. (1909). Analysis of a phobia in a five year old boy. In J. Strachey (Ed. and Trans.), *The standard edition of the complete psychological works of Sigmund Freud*, Vol. X (1909). London: Hogarth Press.

Freud, S. (1910a). Five lectures on psycho-analysis. *The standard edition of the complete psychological works of Sigmund Freud*, Vol. XI (1910). Five Lectures on Psycho-Analysis, Leonardo da Vinci and Other Works, 1–56. London: Hogarth Press.

Freud, S. (1910b). The future prospects of psycho-analytic therapy. *The standard edition of the complete psychological works of Sigmund Freud*, Vol. XI (1910). London: Hogarth Press.

Freud, S. (1912). Types of onset of neurosis. *The standard edition of the complete psychological works of Sigmund Freud*, Vol. XII (1911–1913). The Case of Schreber, Papers on Technique and Other Works, 227–238. London: Hogarth Press.

Freud, S. (1913c). On beginning the treatment. *The Standard Edition of the Complete Psychological Works of Sigmund Freud*, Volume XII: 123–144. London: Hogarth.

Freud, S. (1914). Remembering, repeating and working-through (further recommendations on the technique of psycho-analysis II). *The standard edition of the complete psychological works of Sigmund Freud*, Vol. XII (1911–1913). The Case of Schreber, Papers on Technique and Other Works, 145–156. London: Hogarth Press.

Freud, S. (1915e). The Unconscious. *The Standard Edition of the Complete Psychological Works of Sigmund Freud*, Volume XIV (1914-1916). 14: 159–216 London: Hogarth.

Freud, S. (1920). Beyond the pleasure principle. In J. Strachey (Ed. and Trans.), *The standard edition of the complete psychological works of Sigmund Freud*, Vol. XVIII (1920–1922). London: Hogarth Press.

Freud, S., (1923). The ego and the id. In J. Strachey (Ed. and Trans.), *The standard edition of the complete psychological works of Sigmund Freud*, Vol. XIX (1923–1925). London: Hogarth Press.

Freud, S. (1926). The question of lay analysis. *The standard edition of the complete psychological works of Sigmund Freud*, Vol. XX (1925–1926). An Autobiographical Study, Inhibitions, Symptoms and Anxiety, the Question of Lay Analysis and Other Works, 177–258. London: Hogarth Press.

Freud, S. (1930). Civilization and its discontents. In J. Strachey (Ed. and Trans.), *The standard edition of the complete psychological works of Sigmund Freud*, Vol. XXI (1927–1931). London: Hogarth Press.

Freud, S. (1938). An outline of psychoanalysis. In J. Strachey (Ed. and Trans.), *The standard edition of the complete psychological works of Sigmund Freud*, Vol. XXIII (1937–1939). London: Hogarth Press.

Garner DM. (1997) The 1997 body image survey results. *Psychology Today*. Jan-Feb:31–44. 75–84.

Gearhardt, A.N., Corbin, W.R., & Brownell, K.D. (2009a). Food addiction: An examination of the diagnostic criteria for dependence. *Journal of Addiction Medicine*, 3, 1–7.

Gearhardt, A.N., Corbin, W.R., & Brownell K.D. (2000b). Preliminary validation of the Yale Food Addiction Scale. *Appetite*, 52, 430–436 [PubMed].

Gearhardt, A.N., Grilo, C.M., DiLeone, R.J., Brownell, K.D., & Potenza, M.N. (2011). Can food be addictive? Public health and policy implications. *Addiction*, 106 (7), 1208–1212.

Glucksman, M. (1989). Obesity: Psychoanalytic challenge. *Journal of the American Academy of Psychoanalysis and Dynamic Psychiatry*, 17, 151–171.

Glucksman, M., Rand, C., & Stunkard, A. (1978). Psychodynamics of obesity. *Journal of the American Academy of Psychoanalysis and Dynamic Psychiatry*, 6, 103–115.

Goldblatt, M.J., & Maltsberger, J.T. (2010). Self-attack as a means of self-preservation. *International Journal of Applied Psychoanalytic Studies*, 7, 58–72.

Goldfield, G.S., Blouin, A.G., & Woodside, D.B. (2006). Body image, binge eating, and bulimia nervosa in male bodybuilders. *Canada Journal of Psychiatry*, 51 (3), 160–168.

Goldner, E.M., Cockell, S.J., Srikameswaran, S., Flett, G.L., Hewitt, P.L. (Eds). (2002). *Perfectionism: Theory, research, and treatment*, 319–340. Washington, DC: American Psychological Association.

Goodsitt, A. (1983). Self-regulatory disturbances in eating disorders. *International Journal of Eating Disorders*, 2, 51–60.

Goodsitt, A. (1997). *Handbook of treatment for eating disorders* (D. Garner & P. Garfinkel, Eds). New York: Guilford Press.

Grawe, K. (2007). *Neuropsychotherapy: How the neurosciences inform effective psychotherapy*. New York: Psychology Press.

Greenspan, S. (1997). *Developmentally based psychotherapy*. New York: International Universities Press.

Groleau, P., Steiger, H., Bruce, K., Israel, M., Sycz, L., Ouellette, A., et al. (2012). Childhood emotional abuse and eating symptoms in bulimic disorders: An examination of possible mediating variables. *International Journal of Eating Disorders*, Apr;45(3):326-32. Epub 2011 Jun 7.

Guinjoan, R., Ross, D., Perinot, L., Maritato, V., Jorda-Fahrer, M., & Fahrer, R. (2001). The use of transitional objects in self-directed aggression by patients with borderline personality disorder, anorexia nervosa, or bulimia nervosa. *Journal of the American Academy of Psychoanalysis and Dynamic Psychiatry*, 29, 457–467.

Guntrip, H. (1968). *Schizoid phenomena, object relations, and the self*. London: Hogarth Press.

Guntrip, H. (1973). *Psychoanalytic theory, therapy, and the self*. London: Basic Books.

Hartmann, H. (1952). The mutual influences in the development of ego and id. *Psychoanalytic Study of the Child*, 7, 9–30.

Herzog, D.B., Franko, D.L., & Brotman, A.W. (1989). Integrating treatments for bulimia nervosa. *Journal of the American Academy of Psychoanalysis*, 17, 141–150.

Hoffer, A. (1993). Is love in the analytic relationship "real"? *Psychoanalytic Inquiry*, 13, 343–356.

Hoffer, A., Buie, D.H. (2016). Helplessness and the Analyst's War against Feeling it. *American Journal of Psychoanalysis.*, 76:1–17.

Hoffer, W. (1950). Development of the body ego. *Psychoanalytic Study of the Child*, 5, 18–23.

Huffington Post UK. Retrieved from http://www.huffingtonpost.co.uk/2012/03/20/average-woman-61-diets-age-45_n_1366665.html.

Hunsley, J., Elliott, K., & Therrien, E.Z. (2013). *The efficacy and effectiveness of psychological treatments*. Ontario, Ottawa: Canadian Psychological Association.

Irving, L.M. (2001). Media exposure and disordered eating: Introduction to the special section. *Journal of Social and Clinical Psychology*, 20 (3), 259–269.

Jackson, M. (1993). Manic-depressive psychosis: Psychopathology and individual psychotherapy within a psychodynamic milieu. *Psychoanalytic Psychotherapy*, 7, 103–133.

James, M. (1979). The non-symbolic nature of psychosomatic disorder: A test case of both Klein and classical theory. *International Review of Psycho-Analysis*, 6, 413–422.

Jekels, L. (1941). Psycho-analysis and dialectic. *Psychoanalytic Review*, 28, 228–253.

Johnson, C. (1985). Initial consultation for patients with bulimia and anorexia nervosa. In D.M. Garner & P.E. Garfinkel (Eds), *Handbook of psychotherapy for anorexia nervosa and bulimia*. New York: Guilford Press.

Jones, E. (1916). The theory of symbolism. In *Papers on psycho-analysis*. Boston: Beacon Press, 1961, pp. 87–144

Joseph, J. (2015). *The trouble with twin studies: A reassessment of twin research in the social and behavioral sciences*. New York: Routledge.

Joseph, J. (2006). *The missing gene: Psychiatry, heredity, and the fruitless search for genes.* New York: Algora.

Joseph, J., & Ratner, C. (2010). The fruitless search for genes in psychiatry and psychology: Time to re-examine a paradigm? *Council for Responsible Genetics.* Retrieved from http://www.councilforresponsiblegenetics.org/pageDocuments/1NX6VC0254.pdf.

Joseph, J. (2010). Genetic Research in Psychiatry and Psychology: A Critical Overview. In K. Hood, C. Tucker Halpern, G. Greenberg, & R. Lerner (Eds.), *Handbook of Developmental Science, Behavior, and Genetics* (pp. 557-625). Malden, MA: Wiley-Blackwell.

Klein, M. (1930). The importance of symbol-formation in the development of the ego. *International Journal of Psychoanalysis*, 11, 24–39.

Klein, M. (1935). A contribution to the psychogenesis of manic-depressive states. *International Journal of Psychoanalysis*, 16, 145–174.

Klein, M. (1940). Mourning and its relation to manic-depressive states. *International Journal of Psychoanalysis*, 21, 125–153.

Kohut, H. (1968). The psychoanalytic treatment of narcissistic personality disorders outline of a systemic approach. *Psychoanalytic Study of the Child*, 23, 86–113.

Krueger, D. (1989). *Body self and psychological self: A developmental and clinical integration of disorders of the self.* New York: Brunner/Mazel.

Krueger, D. (1997). Food as self-object in eating disorder patients. *Psychoanalytic Review*, 84, 617–630.

Kristeller, J.L., & Wolever, R.Q. (January 2011). Mindfulness-based eating awareness training for treating binge eating disorder: The conceptual foundation. *Eating Disorders*, 19 (1), 49–61.

Kullman, A. (2007). The "perseverant" personality: A preattachment perspective on the etiology and evolution of binge/purge eating disorders. *Psychoanalytic Dialogues*, 17, 705–732.

Lachmann, F., & Beebe, B. (1989). Oneness fantasies revisited. *Psychoanalytic Psychology*, 6, 137–149.

Latham, J., & Wilson, A. (2010). The great DNA data deficit: Are genes for disease a mirage? *Bioscience Research Project.* Retrieved December 18, 2010, from http://www.bioscienceresource.org/commentaries/article.php?id=46.

Latzer, Y., & Gerzi, S. (2000). Autistic patterns: Managing the "Black Hole" in eating disorders. *Psychoanalytic Social Work*, 7, 29–55.

Lee, S., Ng, K., & Kwok, K. (2010). The changing profile of eating disorders at a tertiary psychiatric clinic in Hong Kong. *International Journal of Eating Disorders*, 43, 307–314.

Levy, D. (1934). Primary affect hunger. *American Journal of Psychiatry*, 94, 643–652.

Lewontin, R. (2011a). It's even less in your genes. Review of *The mirage of a space between nature and nurture* by Evelyn Fox Keller. Duke University Press. *The New York Review of Books*, May 26, 2011. Retrieved from http://www.nybooks.com/articles/2011/05/26/its-even-less-your-genes/.

Lewontin, R. (2011b). What genes can't tell us. Retrieved from http://www.nybooks.com/articles/2011/10/13/what-genes-cant-tell-us-exchange/.

Lidz, T., & Lidz, R.W. (1976). An anaclitic syndrome in adolescent amphetamine addicts. *Psychoanalytic Study of the Child*, 31, 317–348.

Lief, H.I. (1962). Silence as intervention in psychotherapy. *American Journal of Psychoanalysis*, 22, 80–83.

Little, M. (1960). On basic unity. *International Journal of Psychoanalysis*, 41, 377–384.

Loewald, H. (1971). Some considerations on repetition and repetition compulsion. *International Journal of Psychoanalysis*, 52, 59–66.

Lomas, P. (1961). Family role and identity formation. *International Journal of Psychoanalysis*, 42, 371–380.

Lunn, S., & Poulsen, S. (2012). Psychoanalytic psychotherapy for bulimia nervosa: A manualized approach. *Psychoanalytic Psychotherapy*, 26, 48–64.

Mahler, M. (1963). Thoughts about development and individuation. *Psychoanalytic Study of the Child*, 18, 307–324.

Mahler, M. (1972). On the first three subphases of the separation-individuation process. *International Journal of Psycho-Analysis*, 53, 333–338.

Maine, M. (2004). *Father hunger: Fathers, daughters, and the pursuit of thinness* (revised edn). Carlsbad, CA: Gurze Books.

Maltsberger, J.J., & Buie, D.H. (1974). Counter-transference hate in the treatment of suicidal patients. *Archives of General Psychiatry*, 30, 625–633.

Marketdata. Retrieved from http://www.prweb.com/releases/2012/12/prweb10278281.htm.

Masson, J.M. (Ed. and Trans.). (1985). *The complete letters of Sigmund Freud to Wilhelm Fliess, 1887–1904*. Cambridge, MA: Belknap Press of Harvard University Press.

May, R. (1969) *Love and will.* New York: W.W. Norton.

Mazzeo, S.E., & Bulik, C.M. (2009). Environmental and genetic risk factors for eating disorders: What the clinician needs to know. *Child and Adolescent Psychiatric Clinics of North America*, 18 (1), 67–82. Retrieved from http://www.ncbi.nlm.nih.gov/pmc/articles/PMC2719561/pdf/nihms83877.pdf.

McDougall, J. (1989). *Theaters of the body: A psychoanalytic approach to psychosomatic illness.* New York: W.W. Norton.

McGuire, W. (Ed.) (1974). *The Freud/Jung letters*. Princeton, NJ: Princeton University Press. pp. 12–13.

Meissner, W.W. (2009). The genesis of the self: III. The progression from rapprochement to adolescence. *Psychoanalytic Review*, 96, 261–295.

Merriam-Webster Dictionary. Retrieved from http://www.merriam-webster.com/.

Minami, T., Wampold, B.E., Serlin, R.C., Hamilton, E.G., Brown, G.S., & Kircher, J.C. (2008). Benchmarking the effectiveness of psychotherapy treatment for adult depression in a managed care environment: A preliminary study. *Journal of Consulting and Clinical Psychology*, 76, 116–124.

Minuchin, S., Rosman, B., & Baker, L. (1978). *Psychosomatic families: Anorexia nervosa in context.* Boston, MA: Harvard College Press.

Modell, A. (1976), The holding environment and the therapeutic action of psychoanalysis. *Journal of the American Psychoanalytic Association*, 24, 285–308.

Moriceau, S., & Sullivan, R. (2005). Neurobiology of infant attachment. *Developmental Psychobiology*, 47 (3), 230–242.

Morrison, A. (1996). *The culture of shame*. Northvale, NJ: Jason Aaronson.

Morton, R. (1694). *Phthysiologia, or, a treatise of consumptions*. London: Smith & Walford.

Newsweek. Fighting anorexia: No one to blame (December 4, 2005). Retrieved from http://www.newsweek.com/fighting-anorexia-no-one-to-blame-113855.

Newton, M. (2002). *Savage girls and wild boys: A history of feral children*. London: Faber & Faber.

Noordenbox, G. (2002). Characteristics and treatment of patients with chronic eating disorders. *International Journal of Eating Disorders*, 10, 15–29.

Ogden, T.H. (1989). On the concept of an autistic-contiguous position. *International Journal of Psychoanalysis*, 70, 127–140.

Ogden, T.H. (2002). A new reading of the origins of object-relations theory. *International Journal of Psychoanalysis*, 83, 767–782.

Pal, T., Permuth-Wey, J., Betts, J.A., Krischer, J.P., Florica, J., Arago, H., et al. (2005). BRCA1 and BRCA2 mutations account for a large proportion of ovarian carcinoma cases. *Cancer*, 104 (12), 2807–2816.

Pies, R. (2015). Why doctors don't have clients. *Psychiatric Times*. Retrieved from http://www.psychiatrictimes.com/clinical-scales/why-doctors-dont-have-clients.

Pine, F. (1979). On the pathology of the separation-individuation process as manifested in later clinical work: An attempt at delineation. *International Journal of Psychoanalysis*, 60, 225–241.

Pollock, G.H. (1970). Anniversary reactions, trauma, and mourning. *Psychoanalytic Quarterly*, 39, 347–371.

Rado, S. (1928). The problem of melancholia. *International Journal of Psycho Analysis*, 9, 420–438.

Raeburn, P. (2014). *Do fathers matter? What science is telling us about the parent we've overlooked*. New York: Scientific American/Farrar, Straus & Giroux.

Rand, C.S., & Stunkard, A.J. (1977). Psychoanalysis and obesity. *Journal of the American Academy of Psychoanalysis*, 5, 459–497.

Reich, G., & Cierpka, M. (1998). Identity conflicts in bulimia nervosa: Psychodynamic patterns and psychoanalytic treatment. *Psychoanalytic Inquiry*, 18:383-402.

Ritvo, S. (1984). The images and uses of the body in psychic conflict—with special reference to eating disorders in adolescence. *Psychoanalytic Study of the Child*, 39, 449–469.

Ritvo, S. (1985). First day. *Bulletin of the Anna Freud Centre*, 8, 84–110.

Russek, L.G., & Schwartz, G.E. (1997). Feeling of parental caring predict health status in midlife: A 35-year follow-up of the Harvard Mastery of Stress Study. *Journal of Behavioral Medicine*, 20 (1), 1–13.

Russon, J. (2003). *Human experience: Philosophy, neurosis and the elements of everyday life*. Albany: State University of New York Press.

Sacksteder, J.L. (1989). *Sadomasochistic relatedness to the body in anorexia nervosa*. Madison, CT: International Universities Press.

Salimpoor, V.N. (2011). Anatomically distinct dopamine release during anticipation and experience of peak emotion to music. *Nature Neuroscience*, 14 (2), 257–262.

Sandler, J. (1976). Countertransference and role-responsiveness. *International Review of Psycho-Analysis*, 3, 43–47.

Sands, S. (1991). Bulimia, dissociation and empathy: A self-psychological view. In C. Johnson (Ed.), *Psychodynamic treatment of anorexia and bulimia*, 34–50. New York: Guilford Press.

Sato, Y., Saito, N., Utsumi, A., Aizawa, E., Shoji, T., et al. (2013). Neural basis of impaired cognitive flexibility in patients with anorexia nervosa. *PLoS ONE*, 8 (5), e61108.

Savelle-Rocklin, N. (2015). The origins and fundamentals of psychoanalysis. In A. Hoffer (Ed.), *Freud and the Buddha: The couch and the cushion*. London: Karnac Books.

Schafer, R. (1968). *Aspects of internalization*. New York: International Universities Press.

Schilder, P. (1950). *The image and appearance of the human body*. New York: International Universities Press.

Schooler, D., & Ward, M. (2006). Average Joes: Men's relationships with media, real bodies, and sexuality. *Psychology of Men and Masculinity*, 7 (1), 27–41.

Schore, A. (2000). The self-organization of the right brain and the neurobiology of emotional development. In *Emotion, Development, and Self-organization, Dynamic Systems Approaches to Emotional Development*, M. Lewis & I.Granic (eds.), Cambridge University Press, 2000, pp. 155–185.

Schore, A. (2001). Interview. Retrieved from http://www.thinkbody.co.uk/papers/interview-with-allan-s.htm.

Schore, A. (2002). Disregulation of the right brain: A fundamental mechanism of traumatic attachment and the psychopathogenesis of posttraumatic stress disorder. *Australian and New Zealand Journal of Psychiatry*, 36, 9–30.

Schore AN. (2010). Attachment and the regulation of the right brain. *Attachment and Human Development*, 2, 23–47.

Schore, A.N. (2011). The right brain implicit self lies at the core of psychoanalysis. *Psychoanalytic Dialogues*, 21, 75–100.

Schore, J.R. & Schore, A.N. (2008). Modern Attachment Theory: The Central Role of Affect Regulation in Development and Treatment. *Clinical Social Work Journal*. 36:1, pp 9–20.

Schulz, C.G. (1989). Discussion from an object relations view: A resilient fist in a velvet glove. *Psychoanalytic Inquiry*, 9, 539–553.

Schwab, G. (2009). Replacement children: The transgenerational transmission of traumatic loss. *American Imago*, 66, 277–310.

Schwartz, H.J. (1986). Bulimia: Psychoanalytic perspectives. *Journal of the American Psychoanalytic Association*, 34, 439–462.

Schore, A. (2010a). Relational trauma and the developing right brain: The neurobiology of broken attachment bonds. Chapter in T. Baradon (Ed.) *Relational trauma in infancy* (pp. 19–47). London: Routledge, 2010.

Schore, A.N. (2011). The Right Brain Implicit Self Lies at the Core of Psychoanalysis. *Psychoanalytic Dialogues*. 21:75–100.

Scott-Van Zeeland, A.A., Bloss, C.S., Tewhey, R., Bansal, V., Torkamani, A., Libiger, O., et al. (2013). Evidence for the role of EPHX2 gene variants in anorexia nervosa. *Molecular Psychiatry*, 19 (6), 724–732.

Segal, H. (1957). Notes on symbol formation. *International Journal of Psychoanalysis*, 38, 391–397.

Segel, N.P. (1969). Repetition compulsion, acting out, and identification with the doer. *Journal of the American Psychoanalytic Association*, 17, 474–488.

Shakespeare, W. (1623/1964). *The tempest*. R. Langbaum & S. Barnet (Eds). New York: Signet.

Shedler, J. (2010). The efficacy of psychodynamic psychotherapy. *American Psychologist Magazine*, 98–109.

Shedler, J. (2013). Bamboozled by bad science. *Psychology Today* website. Retrieved from https://www.psychologytoday.com/blog/psychologically-minded/201310/bamboozled-bad-science.

Shedler, J. (2015). Where is the evidence for "evidence-based" therapy? *Journal of Psychological Therapies in Primary Care*, 4, 47–59.

Shengold, L. (1988). Halo in the sky: Observations on anality and defense. New York, NY: The Guilford Press.

Shipton, G. (2004). *Working with eating disorders: A psychoanalytic approach*. New York: Palgrave Macmillan.

Shulman, D. (1991). A multi-tiered view of bulimia. *International Journal of Eating Disorders*, 10, (3), 333–343.

Sjödin, C., & Conci, M. (2011). Twenty productive years with the International Forum of Psychoanalysis. *International Forum of Psychoanalysis*, 20, 1–5.

Slatkin, M. (2009). Epigenetic inheritance and the missing heritability problem. *Genetics*, 182 (3), 845–850.

Sloate, P.L. (2008). From fetish object to transitional object: The analysis of a chronically self-mutilating bulimic patient. *Journal of the American Academy of Psychoanalysis and Dynamic Psychiatry*, 36, 69–88.

Smitham, L. (November 26, 2008). *Evaluating an intuitive eating program for binge eating disorder: A benchmarking study*. South Bend, IN: University of Notre Dame.

Steiner, J. (1993) *Psychic retreats: Pathological organizations in psychotic, neurotic, and borderline patients*. London: Routledge.

Sterba, R. (1934). The fate of the ego in analytic therapy. *International Journal of Psychoanalysis*, 15, 117–126.

Stern, D. (1977). *The first relationship*. Cambridge, MA: Harvard University Press.

Stolorow, R. (2011). World, Affectivity, and Trauma. Rose City Center, Pasadena, CA. 27 Oct. Speech.

Sugarman, A. (1991). Bulimia: A displacement from psychological self to body self. In C. Johnson (Ed.), *Psychodynamic treatment of anorexia and bulimia*, 3–33. New York, NY: Guilford Press.

Sugarman, A., & Kurash, C. (1982). The body as a transitional object in bulimia. *International Journal of Eating Disorders*, 1 (4), 57–67.

Sullivan, P. (1995). Mortality in anorexia nervosa. *American Journal of Psychiatry*, 152 (7), 1073–1074 .

Swift, W.J., & Letven, R. (1984). Bulimia and the basic fault: A psychoanalytic interpretation of the binging-vomiting syndrome. *Journal of the American Academy of Child and Adolescent Psychiatry*, 23 (4), 489–497.

Szymanski, M., & Cash, T.F. (1995). Body-image disturbances and self-discrepancy theory: Expansion of the body-image ideals questionnaire. *Journal of Social and Clinical Psychology*, 14 (2), 134–146.

Thomä, H. (1967). *Anorexia nervosa*. New York: International Universities Press.

Tribole, E. (2011). Can you really be addicted to food? Retrieved from www. IntuitiveEating.org.

Tuttman, S. (1986). The father's role in the child's development of the capacity to cope with separation and loss. *Journal of the American Academy of Psychoanalysis*, 14, 309–322.

Volkan, V. (1981). *Linking objects and linking phenomena*. New York: International Universities Press.

Volkow, N.D., Wang, G.J., Fowler, J.S., & Telang, F. (2008). Overlapping neuronal circuits in addiction and obesity: Evidence of systems pathology. *Philosophical Transactions of the Royal Society B: Biological Sciences*, 363 (1507), 3191–3200.

Volkow, N.D., Wang, G.J., Tomasi, D., & Baler, R.D. (2013). Obesity and addiction: Neurobiological overlaps. *Obesity Review*, 14(1), 2–18.

Wadden, T.A., Foster, G.D., Sarwer, D.B., Anderson, D.A., Gladis, M., Sanderson, R.S., et al. (2004). Dieting and the development of eating disorders in obese women: Results of a randomized controlled trial. *American Journal of Clinical Nutrition*, 80 (3), 560–580.

Wade, T.D., Keski-Rahkonen A., & Hudson J. (2011). Epidemiology of eating disorders. In M. Tsuang & M. Tohen (Eds), *Textbook in psychiatric epidemiology* (3rd ed.), 343–360. New York: Wiley.

Waller, G., Stringer, H., & Meyer, C. (2012). What cognitive behavioral techniques do therapists report using when delivering cognitive behavioral therapy for the eating disorders? *Journal of Consulting and Clinical Psychology*, 80, 171–175.

Weinstein, R.S. (1986). Should analysts love their patients? *Modern Psychoanalysis*, 11, 103–110.

Williams, G. (1997). Reflections on some dynamics of eating disorders: "No entry" defences and foreign bodies. *International Journal of Psychoanalysis*, 78, 927–941.

Winfrey, O. (2008). On body image: What I know for sure. June 2008 Issue of *O, The Oprah Magazine*. Retrieved from http://www.oprah.com/omagazine/ Oprah-Winfrey-on-Body-Image-What-I-Know-for-Sure-by-Oprah.

Winnicott, D.W. (1949b). Hate in the counter-transference. *International Journal of Psychoanalysis*, 30, 69–74.

Winnicott, D.W. (1949b). Mind and its relation to the psyche-soma. *British Journal of Medical Psychology*, 27 (4), 201–209.

Winnicott, D.W. (1953). Transitional objects and transitional phenomena—a study of the first not-me possession. *International Journal of Psychoanalysis*, 34, 89–97.

Winnicott, D.W. (1958). The capacity to be alone. *International Journal of Psychoanalysis*, 39, 416–420.

Winnicott, D.W. (1969). The use of an object. *International Journal of Psychoanalysis*, 50, 711–716.

Winnicott, D.W. (1965). *The Maturational Processes and the Facilitating Environment: Studies in the Theory of Emotional Development*. The International

Psycho-Analytical Library, 64:1-276. London: The Hogarth Press and the Institute of Psycho-Analysis.

Winnicott, D.W. (1971). *Playing and reality.* London: Tavistock.

Winnicott, D.W. (1974). Fear of breakdown. *International Review of Psycho-Analysis*, 1, 103–107.

World Health Organization. (2015). Retrieved from http://www.who.int/mediacentre/factsheets/fs311/en/.

Yardino, S.M. (2008). "Break point": A significant moment in the transference. *International Journal of Psycho-Analysis*, 89, 241–247.

Yarock, S.R. (1993). Understanding chronic bulimia: A four psychologies approach. *American Journal of Psychoanalysis*, 53, 3–17.

Zanarini, M.C., Frankenburg, F.R., Hennen, J., Reich, D.B., & Silk, K.R. (2004). Axis I comorbidity in patients with borderline personality disorder: 6-Year follow-up and prediction of time to remission. *American Journal of Psychiatry*, 161, 2108–2114.

Zerbe, K.J. (1993). *The body betrayed: A deeper understanding of women, eating disorders and treatment.* Gurzee Publishers, Carlsbad, CA.

Ziauddeen, H., Farooqi, I.S., & Fletcher, P.C. (2012). Obesity and the brain: How convincing is the addiction model? *Nature Reviews Neuroscience*, 13 (4), 279–286.

Ziauddeen, H., & Fletcher, P.C. (2013). Is food addiction a valid and useful concept? *Obesity Reviews*, 14 (1), 19–28.

Zuk, O., Hechter, E., Sunyaev, S.R., & Lander, E.S. (2012). The mystery of missing heritability: Genetic interactions create phantom heritability. *Proceedings of the National Academy of Sciences*, 109 (4), 1193–1198.

Index

Abraham, Karl, 44

addiction. *See* food addiction

Adler, Gerald, 148

adolescent girls: bodies of, 82; in Fiji, 10; in France, 11; outpatient, 12–13; risky sexual behavior in, 57

affect hunger, 104–5

aggression: feelings of, 30; food patterns from, 64–67; identification with, 97–98; unconscious, 162–63

Ainsworth, Margaret, 8

Akhtar, Salman, 49, 55, 127

Alexander, Franz, 138

Allan, J. A., 136

all-or-nothing thinking, 13

altruistic surrender, 34

analyst: child-, 126; countertransference in, 113, 116, 118, 144; dreams of, 144; hatred towards, 163–66; as interviewer, 127; love of, 166–67; semantics of, xvi; training of, 145

analytic couch, symbolic, 109–10, 148, 164

analytic food, 125–26

analytic relationship: BPD in, 121–22; countertransference in, 113–18; dream work in, 136–37, 140–41; erotic transference in, 120–21; expectations in, 20; fear of, 128; hate in, 161–64; idealized transference in, 118–20; love in, 164–68; parental transference in, 122–23; sibling transference in, 124–25; transference in, 111–12; in treatment, 154

Anderson, F. S., 69

Anderson, R., 41

Andreasen, Nancy, 9

Andresen, J., 100

anger: in bulimia, 30, 35, 66; eating out of, xi, 18, 44, 55; as rage, 44; towards mother, 86, 115, 159; towards self, 28

animal motif, 65

Anna Freud Centre, 64

anorexia: appetite in, 36; case studies of, 38–41; denial in, 93; in DSM-5, 36; family patterns in, 11–12; incidence of, 3; manorexia, 39; mind-body split in, 72, 155; mortality rates in, 3; needs in, 36–37; OCD with, 42; overprotective parenting in, 37–38, 40; reverse, 10; suicidal ideation with, 114, 154–55; weight restoration in, 13

appetite: in anorexia, 36; in family, 18–19; transgressions related to, 83

Armstrong-Perlman, Eleanor, 96, 105
Aron, Lewis, 69
attachment patterns: in brain, 8;
    early, 37
attention, eating disorders for, 45–46
autistic-contiguous position, 76–77

babies, 129
"bad milk," 61–64
Bauer, William, xvi, 60
Becker, Ann, 9
Beebe, Beatrice, 87–88
behavior: addiction to, 28; in adolescent
    girls, 57; in eating disorders,
    14–15; genetic components of, 5–6;
    repetition of, 73, 93
beliefs: under eating disorders,
    18–19; about weight loss, 81–82
Bell, Rudolph, 35, 41
bigorexia, 10
binge eating disorder: classification of,
    21–22; control in, 24–25; emotions
    in, 22–23; food addiction in, 7;
    incidence of, 3; mortality rates in, 3;
    overeating vs., 23; from overwhelm,
    156; "resistance is futile" in, 23–26;
    self-esteem in, 22
Blackman, Jerome, 21
Black Swan, 130
Blos, P., 49
Blum, Harold, 125
BMI. *See* body mass index
body centric focus, 131, 133
body dissatisfaction: boundaries in,
    76–77; conflicts in, 69; image
    in, 10
body image: broad view of, 10; in men,
    10; in object hunger, 69; splitting of,
    70–73, 155
body mass index (BMI), 4
Bollas, Christopher, 72
borderline personality disorder (BPD):
    devaluation in, 148; examples
    of, 121–22
boundaries, 76–77

Bowlby, John, 8
BPD. *See* borderline personality
    disorder
brain: -based explanations, 4–9;
    mapping, 8; sugar changing,
    8, 26
Bratman, Steven, 41
BRCA genes, 5
Brink, S. G., 136
British Journal of Psychiatry, 38
Bruch, Hilda, 36, 50
Buie, D. H., 78, 136, 155
Bulik, Cynthia, 5
bulimia: anger in, 30, 35, 66; case study
    of, 32–35; disassociation in, 63; in
    DSM-5, 30; incidence of, 3; mortality
    rates in, 3; needs in, 34; relational,
    124–25; self-regulation in, 31–32
Burnham, D., 83

Cain, A., 27–28
Cain, B., 27–28
Caparrotta, L., 35
Carpenter, Karen, 36
Cash , T. F., 10
Castelnuovo-Tedesco, Pietro, 22
CBT. *See* cognitive behavioral therapy
Chabris, C. F., 6
Character and Anal Eroticism,
    (Freud), 44
Charles, Marilyn, 120
Charybdis, 83
Chessick, R. D., 32
child-analyst, 126
childhood: aggressors in, 105; ego in,
    53–54; emotional abuse in, 32–33,
    79; helplessness in, 80–81; revisiting
    of, 109; sexual abuse in, 53–54, 59;
    split view in, 94
children: development of, 85–86; as
    egocentric, 53–54; feeling lovable,
    167; independence in, 56; with single
    parents, 56–57; somatization in,
    74; symbolization in, 64; view, of
    parents, 55–56

Cierpka, M., 30–32
clients: semantics of, xv–xvi; therapist relationship with, xv, 20. *See also* analytic relationship
cognitive behavioral therapy (CBT), 14
cognitive disorders: blame on, 12–13; therapy for, 13–14
compulsive eating. *See* binge eating disorder
Conci, M., 120
control: in binge eating, 24–25; of others, 77–79
countertransference: in analyst, 113, 116, 118, 144; in analytic relationship, 113–18; in dream work, 142–44; hate in, 128–29; meaning of, xvii, 113; role of, 107; in treatment, 117–18, 133
courage: for asking questions, 167; for leaving home, 156; of patients, 168
Cozolino, L., 9, 69
crack, sugar as, 28–30

Dartington, A., 41
defense mechanism, 21
DelPriore, D., 57
denial, 93
dependency: conflicts in, 18–19; independence vs., 84–87
developmental age, 12
Diagnostic and Statistical Manual of Mental Disorders, Fifth Edition (DSM-5): anorexia defined in, 36; bulimia defined in, 30; eating disorders in, 44–45
diets, 11
disordered eating. *See* eating disorders
divorce, 45–46
Dodes, Lance, 78
dopamine, 7, 26
dream work: in analytic relationship, 136–37, 140–41; countertransference in, 142–44; eating disorders in,

138–39; hunger in, 140; meaning in, 135–36; purpose of, 135; role of, 107; sexuality in, 139–40, 142; sharing of, 144; treatment conflicts in, 138–39; unconscious mind working in, 110–11; view of, xvii, 135
DSM-5. *See* Diagnostic and Statistical Manual of Mental Disorders, Fifth Edition

eating disorders: for attention, 45–46; behavior in, 14–15; beliefs under, 18–19; BPD with, 121; brain-based explanation for, 4–9; CBT for, 14; combined, 45–46; in dream work, 138–39; in DSM-5, 44–45; family explanations for, 11–12; genetic components in, 5–6; "giving and taking" concept in, 147–48; incidence of, 3; media blamed in, 9–11; medical complications of, 4; mind-body split in, 70–73, 155; misconceptions about, 12–15; mortality rates for, 3; origins of, 47–51; outpatient facility for, 12–13; parental relationships contributing to, 51–58; as second skin, 69–70; after sexual abuse, 79; subclinical, 41–46; as symptom, 14–15, 18–20; understanding of, 49–51; in unique individuals, xv. *See also specific eating disorders*
Edgecumbe, Rose, 74–75
ego: as body ego, 69; in childhood, 53–54; observing of, 54–55
Ellis, Bruce, 57
emotional abuse, 32–33, 79
emotional hunger, 55
emotions: ability to manage, 8–9; in binge eating, 22–23; defense mechanisms from, 21; denial of, 119–20; expression of, 73–77; in family, 18–19; purging of, 34–35; regulation of, 37
environmental factors, 7

epigenetics, 6
eroticized/psychotic
    transference, 121–22
erotic transference, 120–21
exorcism, 95

Fairbairn, W. R., 54, 69, 80, 88,
    94, 147
family: appetite in, 18–19; bonds to,
    51–52; eating disorders blamed
    on, 11–12; emotions in, 18–19;
    individuation from, 88–91;
    outsider in, 24–26, 99–100;
    rigidity in, 38
Farber, Sharon, 94, 97
fashion industry, 10–11
fat camp, 65
fathers: absence of, 57–58; early
    relationships with, 9; hunger for,
    55–58; mothers role vs., 55–56;
    relationships with, 98–99;
    self-esteem from, 57; sexual abuse by,
    79, 113, 158
Favero, M., 143
fear: of analytic relationship, 128; of
    love, 165; of mothers, 64; need-,
    dilemma of, 83; wish-, dilemma
    of, 83–84
Feldman, B., 69
Fenichel, Otto, 50
Ferenczi, Sandor, 94
Fiji, 9–10
financial decisions: advisor for,
    97–98, 145; poor, 90; support for, 34,
    146, 150–51. *See also* money
Fletcher, P. C., 26
Fliess, Wilhelm, 49
Fonagy, Peter, 74
food addiction: in binge eating disorder,
    7; dopamine in, 7, 26; filling void,
    20; helplessness in, 78; love/hate
    relationship in, 29; neurobiology in,
    26–27; pleasure in, 29; preoccupation
    with, 26; as "reunion with objects,"
    50; studies of, 26

foods: aggression and, 64–67;
    ambivalence about, 105; analytic,
    125–26; love/hate relationship with,
    61–62; money conflicts with, 150–51;
    symbols of, 60–61; as transitional
    objects, 62
Fox, Richard, 164
France, 11
Frank, Alvin, 72, 165
Freud, Anna, xvi, 21, 34, 64, 74, 97
Freud, Sigmund: on character traits,
    44; countertransference concept of,
    113; on defense mechanisms, 21;
    on dream work, 135; on ego, 69; as
    "father of psychoanalysis," 17; on
    love, 49–51, 60, 164; on repeating
    behavior, 73, 93; on symptoms, 12;
    on training, xv–xvi; transference
    concept of, 111
Freudian slip, 109

gay relationships, 97–98
genetic components: of behavior,
    5–6; in eating disorders, 5–6; in
    personality traits, 5
Ghaffari, K., 35
The Gilded Cage (Bruch), 36
"giving and taking" concept, 147–48
Glucksman, M., 62
Goldblatt, M. J., 96
Goldner, E. M., 8
Goodsitt, A., 63
Grawe, Klaus, 9
Greenspan, Stanley, 74
Grogan, Sarah, 10
Guntrip, Harry, 88

Hartmann, Heinz, 86
hate: in analytic setting, xviii,
    161–64; conscious, 162–63; in
    countertransference, 128–29; towards
    analyst, 163–66
helplessness: in childhood, 80–81;
    in food addiction, 78; in moral
    defense, 80

Hill, S., 57
Hoffer, A., 78, 136, 166
Hoffer, Willie, 69
Holy Anorexia (Bell), 35, 41
hunger: affect, 104–5; for closeness, 127, 157; in dream work, 140; early life learning about, 50; emotional, 55; for father, 55–58; for mothers, 125–26, 157; object, 49–51, 69; in psychoanalysis, 168; psychology of, 23
"hysterical vomiting", 49–50

idealized transference, 118–20
independence: in children, 56; dependency vs., 84–87; from family, 88–91
introjection, 94

Jackson, Murray, 51
James, Martin, 162
Jekels, L., 165
Johnson, C., 83
Jones, Ernest, 60
Joseph, Jay, 6–7
Jung, Carl, 164

"kitchen spirituality", 42
Klein, Melanie, xvi, 60, 64
Kohut, Heinz, 49–50
Krueger, David, 62
Kullman, Alitta, 63
Kurash, C., 32, 62

Lachmann, Frank, 87–88
Letven, R., 32
Levy, D., 104
Lidz, R. W., 32
Lidz, T., 32
Little, Margaret, 120
Loewald, H., 100
Lomas, P., 36
love: of analyst, 166–67; in analytic setting, 164–68; children feeling of, 167; fear of, 165; Freud's view of, 49–51, 60, 164; from mothers, strategies for, 104–5; nature of, 164; "real," 165–66
love/hate dynamic: in analytic setting, xviii, 161; in food addiction, 29; with foods, 61–62; hate, 161–64; love, 164–68

Mahler, Margaret, 85–86
Maine, Margo, 55
Maltsberger, J. T., 96, 155
manorexia, 39
Masson, J. M., 50
maternal transference, 132
May, Rollo, 164
McDougall, Joyce, 72
McGuire, W., 164
media: fashion in, 10–11; in Fiji, 9–10
medical complications, 4
medical doctors, xv–xvi
Meissner, W. W., 86
memory, 100–101
men: body image in, 10; manorexia, 39
mentalization, 63–64, 74
merger: case study of, 89; isolation vs., 87–88
mind: in suicidal ideation, 155; unconscious part of, 19–20, 110–11
"Mind and Its Relation to the Psyche-Soma", 71
mind-body split: in anorexia, 72, 155; components of, 70–73
Minuchin, Salvador, 12, 37
money: feeling cheated with, 152–53; food conflicts with, 150–51; giving and taking of, 147–48; mismanagement of, 149–50; risks with, 151–52; as symbolic, 153–54; for treatments, 145–46, 152–54. *See also* financial decisions
moral defense: helplessness in, 80; learning of, 54; mastery in, 81; splitting self in, 94

mortality rates: in anorexia, 3; in binge
    eating, 3; in bulimia, 3
Morton, Sir Richard, 35
mother-patient, 126
mothers: absence of, 63; abusive,
    88–90; anger towards, 86, 115, 159;
    criticism from, 65; deprived love
    from, strategies for, 104–5;
    early relationships with, 9; fathers
    role vs., 55–56; fear of, 64; first
    experience of, 49; hating babies,
    129; hunger for, 125–26, 157;
    identification with, 131–32;
    internalization of, 51–52, 95;
    lacking connection with, 52–54,
    114–15; learning hunger from, 50;
    nurturing of, 60; rejection of, 102–3;
    separation from, 85–86; symbolic,
    164; unavailable, 101–2
muscle dysmorphia, 10

need-fear dilemma, 83
needs: in anorexia, 36–37; in bulimia,
    34; denial of, 66; feeling needy by
    having, 46
"negation," 110
neurobiology, 26–27
numbing out, 63

obesity, 22
object constancy, 86
object hunger: body image in,
    69; development of, 50–51;
    terms of, 49
object-usage, 162–63
observing ego, 54–55
obsessive-compulsive disorder
    (OCD), 42
Ogden, Thomas, 76, 162
oral fixation, 40–50
oral incorporation, 95–96
orthorexia: case study of, 42–43;
    diagnosis of, 41; motivation of,
    41–42; new developments in, xvi; as
    subclinical, 3, 17

outpatient facility, 12–13
overeating: being stuffed in, 76; binge
    eating vs., 23

parapraxis, 109–10
parental transference, 123–24
parents: child view of, 55–56; critical,
    66–67; divorce of, 45–46; financial
    support from, 146; overprotective,
    37, 40; role, in eating disorder
    development, 51–58; single, 56–57.
    See also fathers; mothers
patients: courage of, 168; hatred in,
    163–65; love in, 165; mother-,
    126; out-, 12–13; semantics of,
    xv–xvi; sharing dreams with, 144;
    understanding of, 14–15; utter despair
    of, 155
payment. *See* money
"perseverant personality", 63
personality traits: development of, 44;
    genetic components in, 5; in OCD,
    42; "perseverant," 63
physical abuse, 89–90
Pies, Ronald, xvi
Pine, Fred, 85
Pollock, George, 27
Portman, Natalie, 130
Poseidon, 83
predator-to-prey, 97
prefrontal cortex, 7–8
pregnancy, psychological, 126, 138–39
primal repression, 72
psyche, 71–72
psychiatric disorders: environmental
    factors in, 7; genes in, 6; personality
    traits in, 5
psychoanalysis: as biological, 9;
    cautions of, 4; father of, 17; goals
    of, 18–19; hunger in, 168; as
    journey, xviii; love/hate dynamic
    in, xviii, 161; psychology vs., 12;
    relationships in, xvi, 20; theory
    of, 17–18
psychoanalyst. *See* analyst

psychological intrusion, 41
psychology: of hunger, 23; psychoanalysis vs., 12
psychotic transference, 121–22

Rado, Sandor, 23
Raeburn, P., 57
rage, 44
regressive transference, 120–21
Reich , G., 30–32
Reiser, Lynn Whisnant, 22
relational bulimia, 124–25
relational displacement, 127
relationship. *See* analytic relationship
repetition compulsion: in relationships, 100–101, 103–4; theories of, 93–94
replacement child, 28
repression: denial compared to, 93; in repetition compulsion, 93–94
reverse anorexia, 10
Ritvo, S., 64, 72, 96
Ross, D., 143
Russon, John, 71

Sacksteder, J. L., 72
Sandler, J., 100
Sands, S., 63
Schafer, Roy, 96
Schilder, Paul, 10
Schore, A., 100
Schulz, C. G., 162–63
Schwab, G., 28
Schwartz, G. E., 32
Scylla, 83
"second skin," 70
"security blanket," 61
Segal, Hanna, 60
Segel, N. P., 100
self, development of, 85
self-denial, 41
self-esteem: in binge eating disorder, 22; after emotional abuse, 79; from fathers, 57
self-mutilation, 61, 96, 158

self-regulation: being alone for, 61; in bulimia, 31–32; after emotional abuse, 79
separation-individuation theory, 85, 90–91
sexual abuse: in childhood, 53–54, 59; eating disorders after, 79; by father, 79, 113, 158; shame in, 79; suicidal ideation after, 157–58
sexuality: of adolescent girls, 57; in dream work, 139–40, 142
shame, 79
Shedler, Jonathan, 14
Shipton, Geraldine, 63
Shulman, Diane, 63
sibling transference, 124–25
Sjödin, C., 120
Sloate, Phyllis, 63
soma, 71
somatization, 74
spirituality: through food, 42; kitchen, 42; lack of, 70
Star Trek (film), 24–25
Sterba, R., 49
Stern, Daniel, 37
Stolorow, Robert, 75
stomach ache, 43
stress: biological, 12; respite from, 21; from trauma, 69
subclinical eating disorders: case studies of, 43, 45–46; disordered eating, 44–45; orthorexia, 41–42
"substitutive gratification", 22
sugar: biological response to, 29; brain chemistry changed by, 8, 26; as crack, 28–30
Sugarman, A., 32, 62
suicidal ideation: with anorexia, 114, 154–55; attention from, 156–57; examples of, 114, 121; mind in, 155; in relationships, 157–59; after sexual abuse, 157–58
survivor guilt, 28
Swift, W. J., 32
"symbolic equation," 60

symbolic whore, 154
Szymanski , M., 10

Target, Mary, 74
television, 9–10
therapist-client relationship:
    expectations in, 20; semantics in, xv.
    See also analytic relationship
Thomä, Helmut, 11
transference: resistance to, 125–34;
    role of, 107; in treatment, 111–12.
    See also specific type
transitional object: food as, 62; purpose
    of, 63; understanding
    of, 60
trauma: history of, 21; impact of, 7, 18,
    20; protection from, 69–70; stress
    from, 69
treatment: analytic couch in,
    109; analytic relationship in,
    154; components of, 107;
    countertransference in, 113–18,
    133; dream work conflicts in,
    138–39; eroticized/psychotic
    transference in, 121–22; erotic
    transference in, 120–21; goals
    of, 21; idealized transference in,
    118–20; as "it," 126; money for,
    145–46, 152–54; outpatient, 12–13;
    parental transference in, 123–24;
    regressive transference in, 120–21;
    sibling transference in, 124–25;
    transference in, 111–12

Tribole, E., 26
trust, 18–19
Tuttman, S., 55

unconscious: aggression in,
    162–63; compulsions, 47; conflicts in,
    109–10; in dreams, 110–11; in
    mind, 19–20, 110–11; in past,
    72–73; psychotherapy focus on, 18;
    understanding of, 19
United Kingdom, 11
"unthought known", 72

Veran, Olivier, 11
verbal abuse, 94–95

weight loss, 81–82
weight restoration, 13
Weinstein, R. S., 166
Williams, Gianna, 41
willpower, 26
Winfrey, Oprah, 71
Winnicott, Donald, 60, 71–72, 129, 134,
    161–62, 164
wish-fear dilemma, 83–84
wish-fulfillment, 49–50
"working through" process, 19

Yardino, Stella, 110
Yarock, Sandra, 55

Ziauddeen , H., 26
zoning out, 63

About the Author

Nina Savelle-Rocklin, PsyD, is a Los Angeles–based psychoanalyst who specializes in weight, food, and body image issues. A recognized expert on eating disorders, she is a frequent guest expert on online summits, podcasts, radio and other events. She also writes an award-winning blog, *Make Peace With Food*; hosts a popular podcast, "Win the Diet War with Dr. Nina"; and offers "food for thought" on her video series, *The Dr. Nina Show*. She has written chapters in *Freud and the Buddha: The Couch and the Cushion* (edited by Axel Hoffer, 2014) and *Mistrust: Developmental, Cultural, and Clinical Realms* (edited by Salman Akhtar, 2016).